OCD:

A LIFE AMONG SECRETS

By

Steven Diamond

© Copyright 2003 – Diamond Omni Media LLC.

All Rights Reserved. No part of this work may be reproduced, stored in a retrieval system, or transmitted in any form or by any means, electronic, mechanical, photocopying, recording or otherwise, or adapted to any other medium now known or to be invented, without the prior express written permission of Steven Diamond and the publisher. Brief quotations in articles or reviews are permitted and publisher requests a copy of article or review. For more information, please contact the publisher at: info@attackanxiety.com

ISBN 978-0-6151-4049-0

TABLE OF CONTENTS

PREFACE	I
CHAPTER ONE The Calm Before the Storm	1
CHAPTER TWO The Not-So-Perfect Storm	23
CHAPTER THREE School Daze	45
CHAPTER FOUR The Time of My Life	57
CHAPTER FIVE How You Gonna Keep Me Down on the Farm	69
CHAPTER SIX Him Again	89
CHAPTER SEVEN Viva Las Vegas	107
CHAPTER EIGHT Lost Vegas	133
CHAPTER NINE Leaving Lost Vegas	177
CHAPTER TEN Mission Impossible	195
CHAPTER ELEVEN Viva Las Vengeance	207
CHAPTER TWELVE Bienvenidos a Lima	223
CHAPTER THIRTEEN Seventeen Days	245
CHAPTER FOURTEEN The End's Beginning	265
CHAPTER FIFTEEN Branson, Missouri	291
CHAPTER SIXTEEN The Greekarican	301
CHAPTER SEVENTEEN The Answers	319

PREFACE

Aloha. My name is Steven Diamond, and I have OCD, Obsessive Compulsive Disorder. I'm not crazy. OCD is something you can live with, something you can control through therapy, learning the right skills and sometimes medication, but don't let this scare you. I also suffer with acute stress, manic depression and anxiety as well. Life is good.

I want to personally thank you for buying my book because I'm using the proceeds of every book that's sold to fund a foundation to help young people with OCD. Treatment can be pretty expensive. My medication alone at this writing costs me well over three hundred dollars a month, plus the additional cost of therapy. So now that I know what's wrong with me, now that I have it under control, I wanted to do more than put my money where my mouth is. I want to put money where your problem is or, the problem of someone with OCD that you care about. That's why I wrote this book and developed my audio course. I wanted to help those suffering like me find the peace they deserve. Suffering is something I know a little about.

So what is OCD, how do you get it and how do you cure it? Well, grasshopper, in due time all will be revealed. Medical science still doesn't know that much about OCD, and it's often confused with other illnesses. We do know that it's a brain disorder, sometimes called a chemical imbalance, that makes you do things that you realize are irrational, but you can't help doing them, and the fact that you do them only makes you feel more anxious about doing them in the first place. Because if you don't do them, and you know you should have done them, although it's a complete waste of your time -- unless of course, what if you didn't do them and something terrible did happen because you didn't do them and... See what I mean? On, and on, and on. Endlessly, in some cases. A chemical imbalance is to blame here, not you. But you don't know that yet.

OCD affects everyone differently and has as many ways of manifesting itself as a dog has hairs. Sometimes its effects can be completely absurd. Take this, for example: Let's say you've misplaced your car keys. You know you left them on the top of the dresser, but they're not there. So you check your pockets. They're not there. So you go back and check the top of the dresser again. Still not there. Check your pockets again. Still, not there either. Pesky car keys, they ought to have the common courtesy to re-materialize on the dresser any time now!

When George Carlin does a routine like that, people get a great laugh because it's something silly we've all probably experienced at one time or another. Normal people will catch themselves looking in the same place twice, laugh and curse at the absurdity of it, and then check someplace new until they find their keys. "Well, whaddaya know? Here they are on the kitchen table!" Life goes on. Right? Not when you have OCD.

You check the top of the dresser and your pockets a hundred times. You do it all day long. Your heart begins to race. You might begin to panic. Those keys become the only impor-

Preface

tant focus in life at that moment and remain that way until you find them, regardless of where they are.

Any pointless repetitive behavior taking over huge chunks of your time although the rational part of your mind is screaming, "Why the heck am I doing this?" is OCD. It's not like a drug addiction. No, it's not something you do over and over again because it gives you some form of pleasure or "pay-off." That is a logical process.

It's something you do over and over while you hate doing it. You derive no pleasure at all from it, but you must do it. There is no logic here. It eats away your life. It is OCD. I've had it since I was seven years old. It controlled me until I was thirty.

Thanks to the heavens above, newfound knowledge, therapy, and medication, I've learned how to control it. Now, I have my life back. The real me is alive once again. In many ways for the very first time. I haven't seen him since I was seven years old.

It's been more than twenty-five years since I began to feel that something was different about me, that something was wrong. I had no idea why so much of my internal life was so painful. Neither did the seven different doctors I went to see over those years. In my case, eight was the charm. It was the eighth doctor who correctly diagnosed me and convinced me that no, I was not and I am not crazy. I have OCD. Now, I don't expect the story of my life so far to be exactly like that of any other human being, since we are all unique individuals. I do believe that many of you who read this will see similarities in your behavioral patterns to mine if you have OCD or if you suspect that you may have. As for those of you who don't, I will assume that you're reading this because you know someone who does. I've tried hard to write this book in chronological order, but since I have OCD, I tend to skip around a bit. I am a non-linear thinker and my mind jumps now and then. Sometimes it's a smooth story, sometimes it's a little choppy, but it does highlight what I've experienced so far, and what I think is most important to share with you as each event relates to my OCD experience. I tried to hit all of the pinnacle points in my journey with OCD. I focused on events I feel helped the progress of the illness along the way.

Each chapter is a key section or episode in my life, and the story is written as seen through my eyes. I have also added what I call an "Under Chapter" which analyzes what I think has been happening during the episode in light of what I now know about OCD, what I've learned from therapy, interviews with hundreds of other OCD and anxiety sufferers and what I've gleaned from literally thousands of hours of research on the web and in the offices and labs of some of the world's leading researchers on anxiety disorders.

I am not a scientist or a doctor by any means. I do, however, have an important story to tell as an OCD survivor. I have learned a lot and pride myself on helping others stop the cycle of madness that no mortal should have to endure. I'll try to keep the biological and psychological jargon to a minimum and make the explanations simple. Ideally, you'll come away from each chapter comprehending it well enough to explain it to somebody else. A lot of somebody else's out there have OCD. About one out of every fifty people in the United States alone has OCD.

Preface

That's more than five and a half million people. All of this, in just one country.

In other words, you're not alone, and you are certainly not crazy. No matter what you think or feel at this moment, help is available. New treatments, new medications with fewer side effects abound even for those with little or no medical insurance. They work. We will investigate them, and explore other options, some of my own creation along the way.

I think the hardest part for most people with OCD is taking that first step. Believe me, I know. I assure you that it's a lot harder to get treatment for the first time than it is to keep OCD under control. I think one of the most important tools I used along the way was my spirituality and faith in the power of positive and healthy living. The belief system I used kept me from killing myself as so many with this disorder ultimately choose to do. I want to share that powerful, positive thought process with you because it kept me alive during some of my darkest hours.

I have also provided a bibliography at the end of the book, which includes many of the websites I've found to be so helpful so far. Who knows? At the rate we're learning about it, new information could lead to a permanent cure! That's my goal, educating the masses about OCD. On line, you might be interested in taking one of the many OCD evaluation tests like the one on my website. This will help you to determine if you should seek further professional help. OCD is a very serious disorder. However, if you're afraid that you might be a slob, that's not going to be Obsessive Compulsive Disorder. It's obsessive disorder compulsion and you're reading the wrong book. Take out the garbage, put your dirty clothes in the hamper and get on with your life already!

Throughout my life so far, I have come to realize that when you feel like you might be going seriously crazy, a sense of humor is priceless. I firmly believe that humor can extend one's life and may be the strongest weapon in your arsenal of sanity. It's for this reason that I am dedicating this book to one of the most insanely crazy and funniest people I know, Mr. Hollywood Squares himself, Marty ("Hello Dere") Allen. He has made millions laugh around the world for over five decades and has inspired me in my professional career as an entertainer. It is with great pleasure I consider him a close friend and thank him for all those smiles around the breakfast table while sailing the high seas as we performed on the same cruise ships from time to time. "Uncle Marty," as I call him, does not have OCD. He just looks like he should have. I couldn't think of a more perfect poster child for any mental disorder.

That having been said, I hope you are ready. We are going to go through some pretty intense episodes in this book, just as you have gone through some pretty intense episodes in your own life. The good news is that we're going to get through it okay, and that life as you knew it, is over. The bad news is, it's going to be a very rough ride. At the end, your questions will finally have an answer.

OCD, Depression, Stress and Anxiety you're fired! We're armed and humorous.

Steven Diamond

On the beach in Honolulu, Hawaii 2003

CHAPTER ONE
The Calm Before the Storm

Even at the beginning, things were a little different for me. My mom says I was born with a magic wand in my hand. Okay, in both hands. Sideways. Over my head.

I think that's her figurative way of saying it was a rather difficult birth. On Tuesday, October 1st, 1968, in Portsmouth Virginia, Wilton and Shirley Mosley had a son. Robin and Shelia Mosley finally had a baby brother, unexpected, as it were.

The next morning, while Dad was at work, the doctor came into Mom's maternity room with some paperwork. "Mrs. Mosley," he said, "I don't see a middle name for your son for the birth certificate."

"We don't have a middle name for him yet. For now, he's just Steven Mosley."

This didn't wash with the good doctor. "Well, he needs to have a middle name."

Apparently, at the time, Virginia had some sort of rule that a baby must have a middle name. Okay, a baby's gotta have what a baby's gotta have. (In case you didn't know, Virginia itself is a little quirky. Ask any native Virginian. We're not from the state of Virginia. No, we're from the Commonwealth of Virginia although we are a state. You figure it out.) So, pen in hand, the doctor asks Mom another question. "What street do you live on?"

"Scott Street. Why'd you ask?"

"Just curious."

The next day, Mom gets my birth certificate. Steven Scott Mosley.

It's gonna be an interesting life.

I was an insatiably curious little kid. I absorbed everything like a sponge. I wanted to know how everything worked. I got bored with unbreakable baby toys very quickly. I wanted to take everything apart, figure it out, and put it back together. Well, sometimes I put it back together. I got this from my father for sure.

Bill, (as Wilton preferred to be called) Mosley was a simple truck mechanic. When I was little, he worked for somebody else, but as I grew up, he started his own company and was highly successful. Eventually, he grew from the owner of a small gas station to the head of a thriving truck repair company with government contracts. He specialized in fixing those big rig diesel trucks. We never wanted for anything. Dad always provided for us well. However, it came at a price. He was rarely home.

Meanwhile, my mother had her hands full at home raising her two daughters and preventing her youngest son from disassembling the high chair, the playpen, the TV set, the dog. Being my mother and having survived that venture earned her a Medal of Honor in later years.

The television. I knew there was a lot of magic in that box. I devoured "Sesame Street" and the Muppets as if the world was coming to an end. Sure, Mister Rogers was okay, but the Muppets and "Sesame Street"! Wow! When Ernie sang "Rubber Ducky," oh joy! Not only was it the beginning of my lifelong love affair with ducks, I was also utterly hooked on the Muppets and especially on their creator, Jim Henson. I didn't know how at such a young age, but I seemed to have understood that magic occurred behind the scenes. I had to know. I had to find out what it was, who it was and how it worked. That was the beginning of my first obsession. I was hooked on learning the secret workings at that point. My dream at that time was to meet Jim Henson. I wanted nothing more. Sadly, our paths never crossed before his untimely death. I was devastated. I still remember how I felt. I vowed to finish what he started by entertaining the world.

Obsessive Compulsive Disorder can begin as early as preschool. At that stage in my life, from about age three on, I was seriously obsessed with the Muppets and "Sesame Street". Especially Animal on "The Muppet Show". "Sesame Street" aired on weekdays, not weekends. During the weekends I would often worry about remembering to watch "Sesame Street" on Monday. I had to be there. Couldn't miss it.

I remember the worrying and wondering as if it was a trait I inherited. My mother is a constant worrier to this very day. Research is inconclusive as to whether OCD is genetic or not, but there is evidence that kids from families where either or both parents have OCD tend to get it more than other kids with normal parents. (As if any parent is normal!) Let me put it this way. So far, researchers have not been able to isolate a gene that causes OCD, but they do know that children of OCD parents are more likely to get it. From my own personal experience, I'd say it was probably heredity and the environment in which I was raised. My sisters and I didn't realize that my mom had OCD until the year 2000.

In retrospect, that explains a lot about her constant worry and depression while we were growing up. Does that prove she inherited OCD from her parents, and that I inherited it from her? No, but it is possible. Now, when I say environment, I mean, experience. If you have seriously unpleasant experiences, really traumatic experiences, a mountain of evidence shows that they can trigger OCD. Here's where research can make the argument that it's not necessarily inherited, because many OCD sufferers do not have any family history of OCD. No OCD parents, no OCD grandparents. No OCD great-grandparents, either. In other words, the jury is still out on this one. An interesting thought occurs to me. I wonder if there have been any in-depth studies on the number of reported cases of OCD diagnosed after the September Eleventh terrorist attacks. Have they increased? If so, are there more cases in people whose families do have a history of OCD? Just curious. That could be a PH.D thesis for some clever grad student out there. Go for it! I'd like to know.

I believe that people with OCD, specifically people with anxiety disorders, would tend to manage a sudden crisis somewhat more effectively than the population at large. Where most people become completely overwhelmed by the unfolding tragic events, the person with OCD lives with trauma every single day. The very nature of OCD is a relentless mental effort to process and prepare for life's most extreme scenarios. One researcher in the field of OCD recently made a very good point during a conversation I was having with him. He stated that the OCD anxious mind compels people to mentally anticipate the worst possible scenario and not the negative outcomes which life typically delivers.

Our usual world predominantly delivers circumstances to us, which don't come close to matching the level of negativity that people with OCD consistently prepare themselves for. So in other words, people with OCD might be able to handle an event like Nine Eleven a little easier than, say someone without it because of the simple fact that the anxious OCD'ers are prepared for such events in their own lives on a daily basis. They have those skills already in place because the world they live in is one of daily major traumatic events anyway.

So you might be asking, "Well, if it's not inherited, how do you get it?" Fair question. Some researchers believe OCD has shown up in kids after they've had severe strep infections (Strep is short for streptococcus, which is the first name for a humongous number of bacteria species, most of which can infect you and make you pretty sick. Ask my sister Shelia. She gets it every year.) even when there have been no previous symptoms of OCD in their families or in themselves. Other researchers think it might be caused by a virus or viruses as yet unknown, or by any number of chemicals in the environment.

Since there's so much as yet undiscovered about the causes of OCD, I wouldn't be surprised if it turns out it's a lot like cancer in that respect. We know that some cancers tend to be inherited, some are caused by viruses, some by radiation, and some by chemicals in the environment. (Of course, you would think with all the media hype, that everything causes cancer!) So it's possible that OCD may have a number of causes. If that's the case, then it's also possible that some people genetically predisposed to get OCD might have their symptoms triggered by a strep infection. All in all, though, I'm much more interested in how we can treat OCD than in how we can prevent it because it's almost impossible to prevent something if you don't know its causes. It's like trying to figure out a magic trick by believing everything the magician tells you.

The Calm Before the Storm

I was a bright kid. Even before kindergarten, I already knew how to read. I started making my own puppets. I began creating my own puppet shows. I would write the scripts, make the puppets, create the puppet stage and carry the whole production around with me where ever I went.

I was always putting on shows for my family or anyone who would watch. Sometimes, they were forced to watch me. I felt magical, special, as if I could do anything! This feeling called wonder is a magical sensation, a state of mind that I would learn to chase for the rest of my life.

One of my favorite places in the whole world is beautiful Colonial Williamsburg. It's not very far from my hometown of Portsmouth, Virginia. My father loved that place. It's living history. Highly skilled artisans in period costumes at a Colonial Village go about their business in a perfectly preserved 18th Century town, as it was over two centuries ago. That was very magical to me. It fascinated me to no end and was as close to a trip back in time as I could get as a young boy.

And Busch Gardens Amusement Park. Wow! The Old Country is the theme here, being right next to Colonial Village. It was springtime, 1976. The U.S. was celebrating its 200th birthday, and I was seven years old. My daddy was taking me to Opening Day! Was I excited? I was about as laid back as a rubber kangaroo on springs.

An extremely hyperactive child, I had more energy than any child, (or adult, for that matter) ought to be allowed to have. The wry parental observation that "Insanity is hereditary: you get it from your children" comes to mind here. Is hyperactivity in little kids a precursor to OCD? Maybe. Maybe not. Several of the studies I've read say that OCD may cause disruptive behavior, and it might exaggerate any other symptoms the child has; i.e., trouble concentrating in school, dyslexia (all of which I had), those conditions so many parents get worried about. Those conditions that we lump in the category called learning disorders, a term I so dislike it drives me crazy. The operative word from the research I have discovered is *may*. OCD *may* cause disruptive behavior. Not necessarily. Perhaps you're a parent of a small kid or kids and you're concerned. Well, as a magician, I've observed a lot of small kids at parties, in schools and through literally thousands of live shows all over the world during my twenty-five years on stage. I believe this *may* qualify me as an expert on the subject of kids. I have some important information I'd like to share. Parents, small kids are crazy.

This is normal. Most of them will outgrow it before you die. However, my mother is still waiting. Some kids will end up with OCD like me. So what! Don't worry. They can be successfully treated and live happy, productive lives. The trick is early diagnosis. Are you still worried? Relax and picture your three-year-old's birthday party. The little guests, ages two to five, are really excited.

They've had their cake, cookies, ice cream, candy and punch. The magician has survived and left with all but one of his props. And what do you observe about this room full of normal little kids at your three-year-old's birthday party? That's right. They're all psychos! I still laugh at actor-comedian Dennis Leary's description of such an occasion. "It's like being in a room full of drunken midgets!" And he's right. They are high on life and they should be. Give them room, let them grow and play hard. Most will turn out okay. The rest will end up in show business like me.

Hyperactivity in children does not necessarily mean they're likely to get or have OCD or Attention Deficit Disorder, for that matter. Speaking about all of this ADD brouhaha, well, I've got to get this off my chest. Personally, I think a lot of what passes for Attention Deficit Disorder today is mainly a crock of psychobabble. When normal little kids are growing, their brains are growing. Growing brains are the most powerful things on the planet. They are by nature hungry to learn, insatiably curious and full of energy. Of course they're not gonna concentrate on one thing at a time for very long. They wanna concentrate on everything at once! And they can! So they do! But, being older and too tired to keep up with them any more, we can't! So we adults pretend it's the kids with the problem. I see this a lot. We are just trying to cover our own butts instead of admitting that when it comes to energy, we lose, and they win. ADD really ought to stand for Ass-Draggin' Dinosaurs!

I'm not saying the condition doesn't exist. It can also be a very serious disorder in and of itself. I just happen to think it's too loosely diagnosed and widely overused. A lot of children out there need a good whack where it counts. Many children simply need new parents altogether. But I'll have to leave that one for Oprah to figure out. Personally, I think we should use Ritalin on the parents and teachers who can't cope, not the kids. End of sermon.

I bounce past an exact replica of that most famous playhouse from Elizabethan England, London's Globe Theater. The theatre of William Shakespeare. Who?

I don't exactly know who Shakespeare is, but I know he's been dead for a long time, is very famous and likes to write mushy stuff according to Dad. I gazed up at the octagonal half-timbered walls of the Globe replica, and I was awestruck. It was huge!

(I return for a visit in later years only to see how tiny it really is. Growing up sure takes the edge off first impressions.)

A banner hangs over the entryway: "Mark Wilson's Magic at the Globe Theatre". "Daddy," I say, "What's magic?" He gets a strange expression on his face. Bending down to talk seriously with me, he says, "Well, it's a show where all kinds of wonderful things can happen and you don't really know how or why, but it's fun to see." He continued, painting a vivid picture in my thirsty young mind. Even Ol' Walt Disney himself would have been proud.

I don't know what magic really is yet, but I knew that I had to see it. I had to find out what it was all about. And boy, did I find out! We were about to see my very first magic show! The fact that I was jumping up and down, begging, pleading, wheedling, insisting, and demanding that Daddy take me might have had a little bit to do with it as well. It was eleven in the morning. First show of the season for Mark Wilson's Magic at the Globe Theatre. First show of five performances for that day. We went inside.

What a magical place!

To this day, it gives me a wonderful chill every time I enter that theater.

The lights dimmed. The place went dark. It was spooky. Okay, this wasn't a part of the deal, Dad. I was having second thoughts. Suddenly, eerie lights played on a giant spider web. Now, I really had the creeps.

AAAAAAANH! A GIANT SPIDER WAS COMING DOWN THE WEB!

The lights came up. The giant spider turned into the magician himself in a puff of smoke. Abject terror became tension. Tension became confusion. Confusion became release. Release became laughter. Laughter became joy. Not just for me, but for everyone in the audience. I knew it instinctively. They felt what I felt! Listen to them! The laughter, the cheers, the applause. All inside of thirty seconds. In half a minute, this "magic" takes the entire audience and me on an emotional roller coaster from sheer terror to absolute joy. We are one. I am hooked, too, like an addict with a fresh needle. Magic became my drug and I only wanted more. It was my epiphany. From this moment henceforth, and forever more, I was irrevocably hooked on magic. I was beaming. As the applause died down, I told my father my future.

"You are what your deep, driving desire is.

As your desire is, so is your will.

As your will is, so is your deed.

As your deed is, so is your destiny."

This was not exactly what I said to Dad at the time. It's a passage I once saw from the Brihadaranyaka Upanishad IV.4.5 .

Pretty profound words, which have proven very true in my life. It explains clearly what I view as the cycle and inner workings of obsessions and how they manifest in our lives. When I say I became seriously hooked on magic, I mean seriously obsessed. Think about it. Only seven years old and already I had two major obsessions: The Muppets and magic. Does that mean I had a clue that I was OCD? Of course not. I wasn't correctly diagnosed with OCD until I was thirty years old, and the doctors told me I had symptoms going all the way back to my childhood. This means that I suffered with OCD for twenty-three years before I found out what the problem was, and the first seven doctors I saw missed it altogether. They were simply wrong, which isn't uncommon at all. If there's any good news to come of this, it's that most OCD suffers only have to wait nine years and go through four doctors before they find out what's really wrong with them. Although they generally don't start trying to find out what the problem is with themselves until eight years after their OCD symptoms begin. Confused yet?

Let's see, nine plus eight equals seventeen, twenty-three minus seventeen equals six, so most OCD sufferers find out six years earlier than I did. So, yeah, good news for them. Kinda. Sorta. Why so long? Do you have eight years of undiagnosed OCD?

Actually, it's much faster now that many physicians are beginning to recognize the true symptoms, moreso every day. Doctors are receiving training on how to spot the real symptoms as we learn about the disorder. I expect that the attention this problem receives through efforts like mine and other books, research and television programs, pushing this issue out in front, the better educated people will become and we will find that the diagnosis time will greatly shrink. I never had a clue that OCD existed, much less that I was suffering from it. It pains me greatly to know that right now, there are millions of people like me walking around suffering, without a clue.

The Calm Before the Storm

It wasn't long ago, when we didn't even have email? Then a few years later, everyone knew of email, although not many people had it. Now, we can't remember how we ever survived without it. It's all about spreading the word. As people learn and become aware of OCD, more people will find their suffering ends. That is what I am all about now. No one should have to live with the inner torments that I did for so many years. Especially now, when we have such wonderful medications that can in some cases make symptoms simply go away. Later we will talk in detail about the medications, my feelings about them and why I was so against taking even a single pill.

"Daddy, I can do that!"

He smiled. "You're right son. You can."

All too soon, the show was over. I was only seven, but I was walking among the gods, high above in the clouds, looking down upon the rest of the mere mortals on earth. "I can do that." Like an instinct born within, I knew my destiny from that moment on. Because "As our will is, so is our deed. As your deed is, so is your destiny." Nothing was ever so clear. Time had no meaning. The lights, the sights, the sounds, and colors of three-quarters of an hour had come and gone within subjective seconds. Dad saw my altered state. He kneeled down. "So what'd you think of the show, Steven?" No hesitation. "Daddy, I wanna be a magician!" It was as if someone turned on a light switch. "Son, if you want to be a magician, and you work hard enough at it, that's exactly what you will be some day. You have to dream and work hard to be a great magician or anything else you choose to be. You can be anything you want, if you work hard enough." These vivid words for the young mind of a child haunt me to this day. Little did he know how profound his words would be.

So what did I do? Well, I dragged Dad back in four more times. That's right, we saw every single show on opening day! I studied that performance inside and out, doing my best to figure out how they did everything, burning every detail into my brain.

When you're a seven-year-old professional magician, you've got to do your homework! A week later, Dad came home with a gift from People's Drugstore. A gift for me. In a green and black plastic box, was a genuine Junior Magic Kit! Let's get down to business. The next thirty days was full-on magic tutorial. Neither Dad nor myself had ever done something like this before, so we learned together. He seemed as eager as I was to learn. We read the instructions. We took things apart; we put them back together again. We practiced. We learned. Somewhere in the process of learning, my Dad changed. He realized I really was serious about this magic stuff. He bought me a second magic kit. He believed in my dream!

What a wondrous moment for a child of seven: the approval of a parent. It would be the true gift given to me that day, one that would only take me another twenty-five years to appreciate.

I began to see that Dad was more than just a mechanic. He was also a dreamer. I get that from him, but I also think I bring the dreamer hidden deep within the mechanic to life.

Now don't get me wrong. When I said Dad was a dreamer, I didn't mean he was a flake. He busted his butt to make my dreams come true. He told me not to know the meaning of no, to follow my heart, to work hard at it and never to let anything keep me from my dream. Not many fathers are like this. Thankfully, mine was. Though the roof over our heads and the food on our table came from his skills as a mechanic, I saw in many ways he lived his dreams through me. I felt that by encouraging my love of magic, he steered me away from the practical choices he had to make. Sure, he was a damned good truck mechanic, but I knew had been holding his own dreams back to raise his family. After I grew up, dad later told me that he saw magic as a way of keeping me occupied and away from the trouble in the world. It worked; I rarely ventured out of the deep secret layer my father used to call my room. I was always buried in a magic book. I was learning to create wonder.

Sometimes I heard parental discussions about my goals. My mom was a very practical person. She loved me and therefore worried as any loving mother would. Could he really make a career out of magic? She thought Dad encouraged me too much. I was only seven for Heaven's sake! Her concern boiled over and planted a seed of doubt in my mind when I heard her say one night, "Bill, you're leading him down the wrong path!" Wrong or not, it is the path I will never leave. That I know deep in my heart. Mom was protecting her baby boy, her only son, the boy magician.

Hearing Mom express such worry and negativity about my obsession with magic made me worry, and set up the classic OCD vicious cycle: obsession leads to anxiety, anxiety leads to compulsion, compulsion leads to relief, relief leads to obsession.

You can begin this pattern very early in life, and it will stay with you if you don't learn how to break it. I will show you how later.

At Lakeview Elementary School, David, Scott, Donny,

and Danny were my best friends. Girls were yucky, but that was okay. Everybody thought I was the coolest kid in the first grade, even the girls. At the end of my street lived two of my closest friends. Scott Turner lived with his mom and dad, Jan and Freddie, and his sister Penny. I think I spent more time at their house then I did at mine. Scott and I were always out in the garage building something for some hare-brained scheme we had invented. His mom and dad were like my adopted parents. Like it or not, I was the one who adopted them. Oh, they fought once in a while like any family does, but Jan and Freddie really loved each other and their kids, too. It was something you could easily tell. The relationship they had was the kind I wished every day that my parents would someday have. The Turners treated me like one of the family. Scott's mom made the best peanut butter and jelly sandwiches for miles around. They were always ready for whomever Scott and I might have brought home that day. Our best pal, Donny Bell, lived one house down. I never spent much time at Donny's house since it regularly caught on fire. They always rebuilt and started over. He was a regular around the Turner house as well. I think that every neighborhood has a gathering point like the Turner household. I did many impromptu magic shows in their den. In fact, some of the very first audience members I ever had sat in that den and watched me perform the trick of the day. They were without question, my extended family and became a safe house for me whenever things at home became too much for me.

    I had adopted grandparents, too. Well, they weren't actually my grandparents, but they acted like they were. Gent and Mary lived one door down from my house. Whenever I wasn't at the Turners, you could usually find me at their house playing with their real grandchildren, David and Kevin. I had never felt more loved in my life than when I was with either of these two families. My own mother began to grow distant, bitter, and seemed to be angry nearly all the time. My dad was always at work. Without the unconditional support of those families, I think my upbringing, a lot of which those families are responsible for, would not have been as smooth. They say that it takes a village to raise a child, and mine certainly did an honorable job. I am eternally thankful as my world began to grow very dark.

Not only had I been practicing my magic over the summer, I had also been keeping up with my puppetry and ventriloquism as well. I could make any inanimate object talk. This drew a lot of attention. A very addicting drug, attention. Remember that famous TV commercial with the talking margarine tub? "Butter! Parkay!" Well, I could make my sandwich talk in the cafeteria. Kids, howling with laughter at my antics, surrounded me. Making people laugh always came easily to me. It was something natural inside. I discovered this very early on and learned to use my ability to create laughter.

It's hard to say how many times my parents got calls from my teacher during the school year. You know, the "Mr. and Mrs. Mosley, Steven is a very bright child, but..." kind of calls. Didn't my teacher realize I was a serious performer, polishing his craft? Apparently not.

Second Grade. My teachers had a new strategy. Unconditional surrender. "If you can't beat'em, join'em." They couldn't stop the kids from liking me, and I couldn't stop getting better at what I did. So I started putting on puppet and magic shows for school assemblies. I got even more popular. No self-esteem problems here. A natural born leader. Always thinking of how to make things better, I was starting to get a little bored with puppets. I wanted to move more and more into the realm of pure magic. I loved it because I could set my mind free and dream of the many wonders I would someday perform. I drew every idea on any piece of paper I could find. My sketches were cryptic diagrams of tricks, illusions, or anything else I created. From this early age, I felt the need to write it all down. Piles of dreams... some of which I still perform today.

The school librarian had an idea. "Steven, why don't you do a show where all of your puppets tell stories to the class?" BINGO! Then I had an even better idea: I won't do magic. I'll have my puppets do magic! The very first magical puppet show!

It was a huge hit! They loved me! Time to expand; I built a theatre in our garage. I became head of a pint-sized production company. I was designer, choreographer, director, writer, and producer. Oh yes, and Dad was my shop guy, electrician, rigger, engineer, carpenter, gaffer and best boy. Not to mention my loan officer. Dad built me a full-on puppet proscenium stage in our garage. I designed it, of course. A big, humongous, glorious wooden thing you needed a forklift to move. It was so big, it couldn't come out of the garage. Heck, it filled the garage!

Dad built a dimmer switch box and rigged the stage lights to it. He painted the light bulbs to my exact color specifications using auto body enamel, since it could withstand the heat of the bulbs better than most other paints. Well, kind of. During rehearsals, the garage often filled up with a horrible smoke from the painted bulbs. That was how the neighborhood knew another

Mosley Magical Production was about to be unveiled.

During rehearsals, my sisters and our dog Kenny were my audience. They coughed at the smoke, but they loved the shows and didn't want to leave. Especially Kenny. He might have looked like a brown mutt, but he thought he was a human. So did I. Any dog that loved my show was a friend of mine. Sometimes, he was in the shows. Whether he liked it or not. After school and on Saturdays, the neighborhood kids filled the driveway. Dad solved the smoking light problem by lugging the stage up to the front of the garage, with the kids outside. Ventilation solved the problem. The show was a hit. Boy, did I love showbiz! My first company, Mosley Magical Productions was officially born.

Summer of 1977. Busch Gardens again. Now, I was a sophisticated eight-year-old, seeing my second magic show, but by now, I knew the cast and crew by name, and they sure knew me. I saw their first show so much that they practically made me their mascot. They taught me more and more skills. I learned more and more about magic, getting to watch many of their performances from backstage, a fact that would make Mark Wilson's skin crawl had he ever found out! (Sorry, Mark.)

I was flying high with the knowledge that I was the coolest kid in the school, what with my puppet shows and all, but now, seeing and feeling like I was working with real pros, I began to lose interest in puppetry. When I returned to third grade, I wanted to perform pure magic! I began to learn sleight of hand, the art of close-up magic. Miracles in the palm of your hand. That would really wow them! I was getting so excited by the prospect, I began to think that if I enjoyed myself any more, I was gonna get a fun cramp. I practiced and learned and studied all summer long obsessively. It completely consumed me for months. And then, I saw a rare television appearance of a man named Uri Geller. Time stopped.

It was another one of those moments when you could remember exactly where you were the night when... kind of things. He could bend metal with his mind. If he could do it, then so would I. What? He could stop your watch by looking at it? Well, then, I would aspire towards that as well. And I did. Before long, I was twisting metal objects without touching them, stopping clocks, moving objects by simply looking at them and more, feats I continued to practice for years and years to come. I learned through sleight of hand, books, and by creating my own secret methods to accomplish the very same things that I once saw the master, Mr. Geller, perform. Uri, however, well... he was a horse of a different color. Some say he is the real thing. Some disbelieve. I say, what a wonderful experience it is to watch him, ponder and wonder. That is the true magic in life. It happens so rarely the older we get. When it did happen, I cherished the moment forever.

Third grade. I did get a fun cramp. Boy, did it cramp my style. I hadn't changed, but my friends had. Was it pre-adolescent cynicism? I don't know. David, Scott, Donny and Danny -- and Danny! My best friend since kindergarten! He – they -- they didn't want to hang around with me as much any more. Suddenly, I had become seriously un-cool.

OCD loads you with feelings you can't control, and you don't know why. It's the most difficult part of my entire experience with OCD. I hate it. You feel as if something is controlling you inside, telling you things you don't want to know or hear. I love those T-shirts I see today that say, "I listen to the voices in my head and they don't like you!" I know exactly what that feels like. To me, it isn't funny at all.

Instead of actual voices, it was more of a feeling or a very strong urge that conveyed to you these things. It was overwhelming. You could not avoid it or NOT do it. I love the people who say, "Just stop doing that," as if they knew what they were talking about. Unfortunately, it doesn't work that way. You are not in control here. My world was growing dim. From the inside out.

At age eight though, I had no idea this was typical OCD behavior. I was forever feeling a general sense of unease, a kind of paranoia that I was not good enough, but I didn't know why. So I tried harder. At such a young age, I didn't have the skills to distinguish what it was, so I buried it, tried to ignore it. But I couldn't. The worry fed on itself and grew. Feelings like insecurity, fear, self-doubt, anxiety, depression and anger are not uncommon expressions of this inner paranoia hiding deep inside. It was at this age that a deep and all consuming depression began to engulfed me seemingly for no reason. It was beyond my control. I didn't understand these feelings and had no one to talk too. It was a very dark place I would come to know well though out my life.

No matter what age you might be, all of this leads to more worry, sometimes when there are no outward signs of trouble. You might develop frequent chest pains untraceable to physical illness or injury. You can become very tired easily and have serious trouble sleeping at night, waking up in the morning with a body that is constantly tense. Sound like you?

Well, get ready for the NOT- so- perfect storm. It's not going to be pretty and you're going to get wet.

CHAPTER TWO
The Not-So-Perfect Storm

By the way, Mom and Dad divorced in the summer of 1977. A small detail I forgot to mention. Here I am, starting Chapter Two, thinking it didn't happen until the summer between fourth and fifth grade, and then wham! It hit me. I've blocked a lot of stuff out for a very long time. You see, that's another one of the brain's default systems at work. It's actually a good thing for the most part. Until, of course, those memories decide to come back at the most inopportune moments life could offer. I've always said that if you don't deal with those issues early on, those issues will deal with you when they please.

Blocking traumatic events from memory is a typical human reaction. For small children, finding out that your parents are divorcing is one of the worst things that can happen. Blocked memories are very typical of Post Traumatic Stress Disorder (PTSD), but they are not thought of as being typical in OCD sufferers. (Blocked memories are also known as repressed memories.) Since all human beings come complete with a free set of personal problems, it's not that unusual for some of us to have more problems than one. For example, some of us (like me) might have what I call the "Un-Happy Meal Combo Deal". That's a healthy dose of PTSD and OCD or OCD and severe depression. Throw in a little ADD and a new insurance plan and you're a shrink's dream come true. Left untreated, it can be a lethal cocktail to say the least.

In situations like that, it's much more difficult to diagnose OCD, because the symptoms of one condition often mask the other. This is the principal reason why most doctors have so commonly misdiagnosed OCD. Remember that I went to seven different doctors before lucky number eight spotted some of my repressed memories and realized that OCD could be the root of all the evil.

He was right. Finally! It's extremely important that your physician understands clearly every symptom you may have, since you may have OCD and one or more other conditions as well.

You have to help him in his diagnosis by giving him as much information about what you are feeling and about your symptoms as you can. Prior to your visit, you might want to keep a Symptom Journal. I spent a couple of weeks writing down one symptom at a time (or whatever I was feeling) on a sheet of paper and then took that in with me during my visit. This helped me to remember in as much detail as possible all of the emotions, feelings and concerns spinning about inside me. It can be tricky for your doctor to see the true problem at first and even more difficult for us to remember all we have felt in the particular mental and emotional state we might be in. This is true for any anxiety disorder, not just OCD.

I suggest visiting a doctor specializing in OCD. However, this may not always be very practical depending on where you live. In this case, I would start the conversation out by informing the good doctor that you feel you might have OCD and why. I think it's important here to point out that unlike me, doctors are not magicians. They need your help. You have to give them as much information as possible and in the greatest detail that you can in order for them to do their part of the deal with the greatest accuracy.

The third, fourth and fifth grades became progressively worse in every way. The downhill spiral began to pick up speed. Then, I got a big break sometime in 1977 just before the divorce. One of our next door neighbors had a birthday, so Mom and Dad had a little get-together for him and his wife. Earlier, Mom threatened my life if I was not a good boy until they left. So there I sat, very un-amused at how dull adults can really be -- until all hell broke lose, that is.

The front door burst open, slamming against the wall, scaring the daylights out of everyone in the room. "MOM! HELP ME!" My youngest sister, Shelia, a sweet seventeen, was being carried in her boyfriend's arms. She was hysterical. He looked like a train wreck. Something was very wrong. Suddenly, my night began to look a little brighter and I perked up to see what was going on.

"I'M PREGNANT!" Shelia screamed. I was delighted as could be, glowing in all the trouble brewing before my very eyes. This was great stuff! My mother jumped up and lost control. Dad remained as calm and reassuring as ever. "Shelia, we will work through this -- you'll be okay," he said. Seeing they didn't understand, Shelia screamed, " No! I mean I 'm gonna have a baby right now!" as she collapsed in advanced labor. Shelia and Eddie had been hiding a nine-month secret. Oh joy!

The next door neighbors graciously thanked Mom and

Dad for the party and decided that perhaps now would be a good time for them to go home. They took their cue and exited stage left. In a flash, a pandemonium trip to the hospital ensued. At eight years of age, I became "Uncle Stevie" to my beautiful new niece, Brandi. As I peered in the window trying to see my niece among all the other annoying crying brats, a weirdly comforting thought occurred to me. No matter what I did from now on, no matter how badly I screwed up, I could never get into more trouble with my parents than the trouble Shelia was in right now!

It was a beautiful day after all.

By the summer of 1977, magic has been my passion for over a year. I also began to use it as an escape. An escape from the mental, emotional pain I felt. I was not a happy boy as a boy of eight should be. Something was not right between Mom and Dad, and that bothered me too. Whatever that something was, it led to the divorce I mentioned earlier.

When I say that magic was my escape, I mean that in the same way that a drug addict or an alcoholic uses chemicals to ease pain and escape temporarily from real-life problems I used magic. To me, magic became more than a collection of tricks and books of secret instruction. It was my only friend. In my mind it was a living entity not unlike the imaginary friends younger children will sometimes play with when left alone. I used my magic as a safe sanctuary. Magic became my safe place that I controlled. A place without pain or disappointment, without things I didn't understand. Whenever I found myself afraid, when the OCD cycle whirled about in my head, I would enter the secret world of magic and lock myself inside. This retreat from the real world is true of any addiction.

I'll tell you a quick story. While working in Australia in 1998, I spent a lot of time as a volunteer at an extraordinary outreach center for drug addicts called The Wayside Chapel in Sydney. It changed my life. There you find nothing but people trying to escape the reality of their own existence in some form or another.

It was there I saw heroin addicts, sometimes with needles still in their arms, talking to their drugs as if they were a living entity. For them, they were. It was no different for me with my magic.

I could completely understand the addicts and the emotional pain they were dealing with inside everyday. The endless mind loops that play over and over again. The compulsions that force you against your logical will. I understood their pain. But for the needle, I was no different.

Here is something else to consider. Drugs and alcohol can make the pain go away, but it's only temporary. The pain always comes back when an addict sobers up, and if OCD symptoms are not treated properly and you take drugs, you're adding the additional burden of substance abuse to your own set of problems. It's only downhill from there.

I'm very lucky and very thankful in that my magic addiction is a lot healthier than drug and alcohol abuse. I never went down that path. How and why I didn't remains a mystery in my life to this very day. You will understand better in a later chapter. I make a very good living entertaining people with my magic. As of yet, I have never met anyone who's become wealthy and successful from being constantly stoned and until I meet Keith Richard's of the Rolling Stones I likely never will.

When you travel down that long and hard road you usually end up right back where you started. Nowhere!

Here's another danger. The OCD sufferer, who starts out abusing drugs or alcohol as a way of preventing the pain of OCD, may end up getting legitimate medical help for OCD, but not the drug addiction! Sometimes it's the other way around. I have seen it too many times. OCD therapy involves not only behavior modification, but also various legitimate prescription medications as well. Any addiction is a serious matter. If you don't kick your other addiction, it could end up killing you. That's not my idea of a successful therapy. Death, insofar as we know now, is not curable.

My father was very civil in front of me, which was not the case with my ever-screaming mother. At night I could hear them fighting behind closed doors. It was hard to hear what they were yelling. I strained to hear. I covered my head with the pillow. It made me feel crazy inside. I sang to myself sometimes. I tried to reassure myself that maybe every family was like this. It didn't help much. It still hurts. I cried myself to sleep a lot when they fought. I wished my magic could make them stop, make them love each other like regular people did. Like the Turners. I learned a hard lesson. Even my magic has its limitations sometimes, and that hurts, too.

I began to see the gradual and ever-so-slow descent of my mother's mental health. I knew something was wrong with her, but I was too young to really put my finger on it. Instead I watched her, and heard her endless screaming and yelling. She was angry. Always unhappy, she began to hit and be abusive. One night, she kicked me in the stomach. As I lay on the floor, she continued to kick and kick me hard. I would later vomit. I didn't understand then, and still don't know why even today. All I knew was that it must have been my fault. I had enough going on inside of me, so I blocked it out. Somehow, the pain went away and I fell asleep in my room, alone on the floor.

She became extremely negative, a little more distraught every day. Her façade was cracking. I did my best to avoid her, not to disturb her. I stayed in my room and lost myself. Deeper and deeper I went. I didn't want to burden my mom. I mean, I was a handful to say the least. You never knew what I was going to drive you crazy with next. One time I saw something on TV that made me think you could turn a rubber ball into silly putty by cooking it. I drove my poor mother nearly insane until she finally gave in and was soon trying to fry my rubber ball in a pan. She was right. It didn't work, but she also knew that until she fried that ball, (with butter, no less) that I wouldn't leave her alone.

I remember going shopping with my mom one day and getting a little too crazy with the cart. It was on wheels. To me, that was reason enough to climb on board and take it for a test drive. I was off to the races! Mom was at one end of the aisle, peacefully choosing her canned goods, and I was at the starting line down at the other end. My engines were revved. Suddenly the light turned green and I sped off down the raceway in a cloud of smoke. The crowd went wild -- and then, out of nowhere, I hit reality in the backside, and down she went. Laid out across the floor among several cans of green peas and corn was Shirley Mosley. She was down for the count and I wasn't about to get anywhere within striking distance. All I remember is her screaming and bunches of people from everywhere running over to help.

I was a frozen statue with a look of sheer terror upon my innocent little face. Someone pulled the cart off my mother and the only thing I could think of to say was, " Mom, I'm sorry -- I couldn't find the brakes."

Never mind the front-loaded steel cart piling into her back at sixty miles an hour. That wasn't the bad part. When she got up, her hair was a mess and we were in the grocery store. That could only mean one thing. Shirley was going to commit murder that day if I didn't keep my eyes peeled, and I knew it!

Eventually it came to pass, that awful moment when your parents call you into the living room and say, "Son, we need to talk to you. We want to explain what's been going on…" Their words blurred. I didn't even know which parent was talking anymore. I felt as if I was drinking ice water really fast, only I was drinking it into my heart instead of my stomach. Now the ice water filled my head, my arms, my legs, and my chest.

"…So Mommy and Daddy are going to live separate lives now…"

The ice water settled in my brain.

"… But we love you as much as ever…"

The ice water hit my lungs.

"…So you'll have two places to live now…"

If I wanted to live at both places I could? What did that mean? It was all a blur. It was not logical because I was eight, and I didn't know what it meant to be logical. Grownups were logical and right now my mommy and daddy were logical and they were broken because that's the way it was. I didn't want to be logical. I wanted to be magical instead. Deeper and deeper I went. I was drowning in ice water by now, and I was dying of thirst. Mommy and Daddy were getting a divorce.

By 1977 I realized that it was a good thing Dad didn't buy the house I grew up in until after I was born. Otherwise my name would have been Steven Leonard Mosley. The only house I knew, my only home ever, 307 Leonard Rd, was going to be sold. Coming home from school one day I saw a sign in my front yard, another one of those moments you never forget as long as you live. I stood there for the longest time staring at it and wondering why. What had I done to make all of this happen?

Dad eventually got his own apartment. Mom found one, too. By now, both of my sisters were grown up enough to be out of the house. Okay, it was gonna be apartment life for a while, a thought that didn't thrill me at all. I had always lived in a really nice brick home in a nice neighborhood with a backyard and a shed. That's the way I wanted to keep it. I liked it there. Well, except for Creepy Norma the evil husband-beater who lived next door. She was so old, her watch ran faster then she did! I mean, she was really up there. The candles used to cost more than the cake on her birthday! Anyway, she hated kids. I always got the feeling she was looking at food whenever she gazed at me. The point was, Norma or no Norma, I didn't want to leave. I really liked it at 307 Leonard Road. To me, that was the only place I could call home.

Christmas 1977 finally rolled around. I was nine and I didn't know much about Virginia custody law, but the judge said I had to make a decision.

The only thing I knew was that making the best of a really bad situation meant moving in with Dad. Whether my feelings had anything to do with it, I didn't know. The next thing I did know was that Dad and I were living on the ground floor of a two-bedroom apartment in the middle of town across from Manor High School where my sisters went to school and graduated.

We had our own Christmas tree and a lot of furniture from the house. It didn't really feel like Christmas to me. I missed putting up the lights on the outside of the house with Dad. It was always such an important part of Christmas to me, but not that year. I didn't remember what presents I got, and maybe for the first time, I didn't really care. I soon discovered that Dad and I were not very good at cooking or decorating a Christmas tree. I think that year Charlie Brown's tree looked better.

We visited Mom. She was now a homemaker without a home. All I knew was that where she lived was horrible. She had next to nothing. Not even a Christmas tree. She had the barest of bare necessities. No rugs. Just wooden floors. A bed, a table and a few chairs. The most shocking thing of all was that even a television was no where to be found. It was a very cold and stark place and it scared me.

Neither parent spoke of the divorce again. It was like a grave-site with no headstone. You wondered who was inside and what happened to put them there, but you would never know. I did know this: There were no absolutes in life. Everything was relative, including your very own parents. It was a hard lesson to learn at such a young age. And there was more to come.

A bit later in 1978 I learned about the term nervous breakdown. First hand. Mom had one and was taken to a nearby hospital. I can still see her in her hospital bed. I was utterly terrified. It shook the very soul of me and un-stabilized the last of the anchors tying me to planet earth. I begin to have an overwhelming and most horrifying fear of death. No child of eight should have such thoughts. But I did. Every night she was there, I would often cry myself to sleep.

Hey wait a minute! I was a big kid now! How come I was so scared Mommy was gonna die? I didn't understand. I began to worry that my thinking these thoughts might actually make it happen, and so the cycle began. I quickly realized that not even my magic could help her. Not the most powerful trick I knew.

There was nothing I could do. I was a young magician with a broken wand. Nothing I could do would make her any better. I had never felt so horrible. Lost and completely alone.

I had never really thought of death and dying before my mother had her breakdown. Seeing her in the hospital was another trauma that triggered the OCD anxiety cycle. Before long it fired up again, and I was an emotional mess inside. In my case, the constant fear of her dying was overwhelming. A normal child would be very concerned, scared and worried as well. However, with OCD it is often one extreme or the other. Usually there is no middle ground. In time, as the mother would get better, a normal child would not worry much more about it and move on with life. I was far from a normal child. I took it hard. I internalized it and really felt that it was a problem that I myself had to solve. I believed it was my fault. I had to find a way to help her. I basically added the additional burden,-- a fear of death -- to my OCD anxiety cycle.

It's too much for a child of that age to handle. The more

emotional you are about something, the less control you have over the situation. Think about that. This is true with anything in life. It particularly applies to people suffering from OCD since that the main issue at its core is control anyway. You are fighting to regain control over your life once again. OCD takes that control away from you. My fear that she might die created an emotional state that clouded any reasonable logic I had left. My decision-making abilities, my reasoning, and my ability to see the facts before me, not my own perceived facts were completely shot. All I could think of was my mother, what put her in the hospital and if I had anything to do with it.

    I tried to think happy thoughts. Yeah, I hoped this would work, like Peter Pan told Wendy. Think happy thoughts and you can fly. I remember laughing out loud at the time when I was sitting in the back seat behind my mom while we were driving down the road going somewhere one day. I had been blowing bubbles with my Bazooka bubble gum and popping them with a most ear-shattering noise that my mother really enjoyed while driving. At once, she gave the command to throw the gum out the window. Reluctantly, and knowing that my mother's right hand was well-trained in the art of rear seat-smacking, I cracked the window a tiny bit and attempted to throw out the gum.

    But instead, it hit the window and bounced right into my mother's up-do! I said not a word. I knew that every move I made would be life or death from this point on. You see, my mother's 1978 hair was a work of fine art. You didn't dare touch it. It took her three hours and two cans of heavy-duty lacquer to perfect. Since the gum was in the back of her head, I though my chances for survival were looking pretty good, so long as no one else noticed it either. I had to keep people occupied. Which is where I first became introduced to the finer points of misdirection.

My dear Mother was very ill and I didn't know what to do. I had no answers. Everyone around me seemed too preoccupied with the situation to give me any attention. I found myself in a very lonely place in life. It was almost as if I became invisible. All the while, I was drowning in that ice water, dying of thirst.

A few months later, I actually had my own set of keys to the apartment. I was beginning to feel the "cool factor" again. I went to Lakeview Elementary School by this time and I had keys. Wow... I felt powerful somehow. At nine, I didn't know the term workaholic yet. But I did know one. My father was out of the apartment by six-thirty a.m., seldom back before six-thirty p.m. on a good day. It was okay, though. I knew how to fix my own breakfast, and of course I had enough lunch money for the cafeteria. After school, there was this wonderful lady in the apartment complex across the street from mine. I played with her kids a lot. They became my new friends. One boy was about my age, the other boy was a little older. I only wish I could remember their names.

She was really kind. I guess she knew my mom was not doing well, that it was just me and Dad, and Dad didn't get back until late. So after school, she fixed me snacks and sometimes dinner as if I were a boy of her own. We watched TV; we played games and always had a lot of fun. Her husband wasn't around much, but that was okay because neither was my dad. It was the way it was. But, I still can't remember their names.

I told Dad about her. He was glad she was such a nice lady. One time during amusement park season, Dad came up with a great idea. We would take the boys with us to Kings Dominion in Richmond, Virginia.

Kings Dominion didn't have a magic show so it was my second favorite amusement park. Then, when we came home it would be late so the boys could sleep over at our place and we could have a pizza party! How cool was that? I couldn't wait!

The fun day came and went in a flash. Just like that, it was gone and we were heading home. It was very late at night and the three of us slept most of the way in the back seat of the car. I always knew when we were home because of the speed bumps in the parking lot. They would always wake me up. They did, and when I sat up, we were passing the complex that my friends lived in. There, on the front lawn stood his parents and they were screaming at each other. The entire complex was watching. I mean, they were having a really bad fight. So my dad said we shouldn't interrupt them or something and we went into our apartment and got ready for bed.

By this time, we were way too pooped for pizza.

It wasn't long before their mother was knocking at the door. She thanked my Dad for the wonderful day and told my father she thought it was best that the boys went home for the night. "Are you sure?" my dad asked. "They are perfectly fine here," he said, thinking that maybe she and her husband needed to be alone for the night. "Yeah, I'm sure," she said as she thanked us again. They headed back across the street. We saw them through our giant picture window of our ground floor apartment and once they made it home safely, we went to bed.

The Calm Before the Storm

What a great day it had been. I just can't remember their names.

It must have been five in the morning. It was still dark. The commotion outside wakened my dad and me right up. We met in the hall as we came out of our rooms. We headed for the living room to see what all of the fuss was about. As we were coming down the hall, we saw flashing lights everywhere and heard all of this serious-sounding noise. Something had happened. We rushed to the big picture window. Several ambulances, a fire truck and police cars were everywhere. A big satellite television truck from the local TV station rolled up and stopped right in front of our window. It blocked everything. We couldn't see. Dad took my hand. Holding it tightly, he led me outside. We walked around the satellite truck. People looked worried. Scared even. You could see it in their eyes. Firemen, policemen, reporters, medics, all hurried about.

Dad led me through them, seeking information. He finally stopped and began talking with a policeman. Absorbed by the facts he received, he unconsciously loosened his grip on my hand.

At that moment, I noticed that all the important-looking people were coming in and out of my friends' apartment. What was going on? I decided to investigate and quickly disappeared, heading around the back way. Up the stairs I went. No one noticed me at first. My size, my speed, my curiosity, all conspired to plunge me, unready, into the surrealism of the real world. Death and destruction, what I feared most, were now before me. Running in, I splashed. I splashed. A red splash. Time stopped once more in my young life. Time stopped in a splash of red.

Fifteen seconds or less. Those fifteen seconds changed

my life and me forever. Suddenly, I was scooped up from this charnel house of red splashes I would never forget and raced back to my father. I would remember the smell forever. A very few seconds of horror seemed to last an eternity. I gained a video of the mind that would play itself over and over for many years to come.

Dissociation set in. I didn't see it. He saw it. But wait. I was he! He was me! What did I see? What did I see? Why do I still see it? And why can't I remember their names?

I write this over and over in this chapter because I can't. I've tried very hard, I've wracked my brain, but their names are still lost to me. I believe this is how I've coped with the trauma of seeing their mother's dismembered body. If you can't put a name to something or someone, it becomes less real in your own experience. On some level within my mind, I think this means that if I do remember their names, the recollection will become more painful, something I'd rather not relive again.

Think of it this way. Even on television, witnessing the horror of the World Trade Center Towers collapse on 9/11/2001 was bad enough, but for those of us who did not have family members or friends killed in the attack, the pain subsided over the next year.

Then came the anniversary and the memorial at Ground Zero, in which the names of each person killed were read aloud. It took more than two hours to finish. If you watched as I did, you likely felt that loss all over again. For many of you, I'll bet you were surprised at the depth of your own feelings a year later; and if so, I'll bet it was the simple act of naming the victims which brought out your feelings with so much more intensity.

To name them was to know them, a task too big for me to handle.

Somewhere, there is a part of me that wants to remember the names of my friends and their mother, but I think that the part of me that was horrified by seeing the body is not ready to recall yet, after all these years. Today, I am much better. I can talk about it now. There was a time when I couldn't even think about it without feeling sick and having nightmares.

When you have OCD, and add the reality of a genuine horrific experience to the unreasonable fears already whirring incessantly about in your mind's OCD cycle, it gets even harder to break. It occurred to me that the reason why the mother insisted her sons should come home with her that night instead of sleeping over at our place as planned was chillingly simple. It was her hope of self-preservation. I am convinced now that on that fateful night, she knew her life was in danger. I also believe she thought he wouldn't kill her if the boys were home. Unfortunately, she was wrong. I know they both loved their sons. I guess she wanted so desperately to believe there was enough good in her husband, enough humanity under his rage and violence, to bring him to his senses. My little boy's mind didn't know the word cynicism back then. As for today, well, I still don't like it. Even with all that has happened to me, I want to believe that there's more good than evil in most of us. We all have the same basic good set of qualities when we enter this world. Innocence, honesty, love, a perfect heart, to name a few. The challenge is that we are not all born into the same situations when we enter into this world. That makes a big difference. It's the luck of the draw and how you choose to deal with the cards you have been dealt. Life isn't always fair, but don't dwell on it.

I believe that people live much happier lives when they don't worry too much about that stuff and get on with life. I always say "Just relax and let life flow." There will always be bad people in the world and this woman's husband was certainly one of them. Life goes on. Like it or not.

Learning to control my OCD has helped me to see people more objectively and reinforces my faith that people are, for the most part, good. Even the Dalai Lama thinks so. I know because he told me himself. I know that when the time is right for me, the names of my friends and their mother will return. In due time.

I have no idea what traumas you've experienced, but I am talking about trauma the likes of which most could never dream. I am talking about fifteen seconds in the apartment of my best friends. A place where I had eaten many meals, played for hours on end and peacefully fell asleep on the floor as we watched afternoon cartoons on TV. A safe place I enjoyed nearly every day.

I splashed into the blood of the kindest person I knew, the mother of my friends. I didn't know if there were millions of pieces of her, I only knew that there were far too many pieces of her and I saw them all. She had been disassembled with a violent blade that was right there next to her. There was enough of her not chopped apart for me to recognize a face I had kissed goodnight hours before. Her lifeless chunks were everywhere. I saw the story in her vivid red hand-prints. She had clawed desperately to live as her life was taken so horridly from her. She didn't have a chance.

When Robert Oppenheimer, the chief scientist of the

Manhattan Project, witnessed the first Nuclear test, the Trinity atomic bomb detonation at Alamogordo, New Mexico in 1945, he quoted from the sacred Hindu scriptures, The Baghavad Gita. "I am become death, the destroyer of worlds." As a third grader, I was not aware of Oppenheimer. But the impact I felt in those fifteen eternal seconds was as powerful as that atomic blast ever was. I saw something that will never leave my soul for so long as I shall live, not unlike the frozen shadows of those poor people stopped in time and forever burned into that bridge in Hiroshima, Japan. As long as the bridge remains, so will the image of those innocent people. And so it is with me. Violence became a nuclear detonation of the psyche.

Death, the destroyer of worlds, ground zero in your brain. It explodes at will, beyond your control every day. The glorious fun-filled day at Kings Dominion would turn into the most opposite of opposites in fifteen seconds. That sight has never, and likely will never, leave my mind. Ever.

After I had been returned to my dad, he lifted me up into his arms and held me very tightly. He saw my white sneakers were covered in blood. He wrapped one arm around me, and with the other, he pulled the sneakers off my feet. They dropped to the grass below and we headed home. It was the last time I saw those sneakers.

I looked back and heard muffled screams. Coming down the stairway from my friend's apartment was a very strange sight. Four police were carrying two heavy loads. Cop, sheet load, cop; cop, sheet load, cop.

I recognized the screams. It was my two friends. I became furious. I wanted down. Why were the police hurting them? I tried to break away, but my father restrained me. It seemed that it was the only way they could get the boys past the remains of their mother without them seeing the carnage, they explained.

The killer? Their own father. He was arrested the next day. Sitting at a bar, drunk, he struck up a conversation with an off-duty traffic cop about what he had done.

I still can't remember their names.

OCD tends to be a pre-existing condition in the overwhelming majority of people treated. However, from what researchers can tell, Post Traumatic Stress Disorder may help trigger OCD symptoms without actually causing them. In other words, you might have had OCD all the while and never showed any signs. It was lying dormant awaiting its cue. This very well could have been the case with me, because I know I got a lot worse after this tragic event in my life. Then again, who wouldn't?

Two weeks later, their apartment has been emptied, cleaned out and sterilized. The carpet had been rolled up and left in the dumpster, under-matting side out. The stain still showed through. Huge brownish-red stains. My two friends were institutionalized. Their mother dead, their father in prison, they went quietly mad. We visited them.

The older boy eventually recovered enough to be released; the younger one, the boy my age, is still hospitalized. I never knew if he recovered.

In deep shock, the only stability I clung to was my magic. I disappeared in my room for hours, days on end, concentrating fiercely and obsessively on my craft. If I had any sanity left, this was it. Reality was no longer a concept I was able to understand. My father began to think about moving, buying a farm, remarrying and putting me in military school. At this point, I really didn't care. My mother was still in the hospital. Death was on my mind from every angle. I became emotionally numb to survive. It was a comfortable state of mind. I liked it and decided to try it for a while.

I never talked about what I saw that day. I never really could. Not until I was twenty-seven years old.

I went into my room, shut the door and locked it. My safe place. The only place I wanted to be. Physically, mentally and emotionally it was a place I would stay for a very long time.

CHAPTER THREE
School Daze

Fall of 1977 wasn't any easier for me. Most days I could only be found in my room in the apartment, locked away studying magic. I had surpassed the days of simple magic tricks and was beginning to create original concepts from my own imagination. Weekends and holidays I seldom come out at all. I missed meals. I forgot to bathe sometimes. I called my room The Land of the Lost. What was lost here was all track of time. For me, it was the security of another world.

I came back to school and suddenly I was no longer fashion conscious. My parents' divorce rendered much of what used to be cool meaningless to me. I was numb. I didn't care. I had new shoes, but I forgot to wear them. I put on whatever was in the closet. Meanwhile, my classmates seemed different. The guys were starting to talk about girls. They were wearing hip new clothes that I didn't recognize. When I went in the bathroom, the guys were snickering. They were looking at a few pages ripped out of a *National Geographic* . I guess you could say that it was the *Playboy* of my third grade confreres. We called it *National Pornographic*. They were ogling a picture of an African woman nursing her child, giving your general guttersnipe guffaws. I didn't get it. Was this what it meant to start acting grown up? About this same time, our bodies were beginning to go through the proverbial changes, which meant that on top of everything else in my life, I now had hormones to deal with. Girls, giggles, growth and now testosterone. My friends were beginning to act weird. I hadn't changed much, but they all sure had. I couldn't figure it out. Something was really different. They were all a bunch of goof-balls. Was it something in the water?

I kept things bottled up and obsessed about them privately. I knew I was very different from my friends. I mean, except for the trauma of my parents' divorce, my mom's breakdown and the murder scene, it was not like I had to tell anybody something was wrong with me. Even so, no one really noticed. I was simply a mess, both inside and out.

I wasn't doing a very good job keeping my personal appearance up to snuff with the other fashion-conscious kids. Not only did I feel different, I guess I looked different, too, nerdy, disheveled and unkempt while obsessing on magic. Forgetting to eat regularly, I stayed physically smaller. Small kids, like wild dogs, could smell fear. Since the small kids who were my former friends could sense my weirdness, I was easy prey and easily attacked. I wasn't cool anymore. Making fun of me and rejecting me was, on the other hand, very cool, very easy. It was as if they knew on some primitive level that I had PTSD and OCD. It made sense in an almost Darwinian way.

In nature, the weak and defective don't survive very long. The wild pack makes sure of that. In a pack of children, the normal kids sense the abnormal one and isolate it. This, I suppose, was out of fear that the abnormal kid might mess up their normal social behavior. They instinctively didn't like to be around weirdness. A perfectly logical, innocent cruelty. So much for childhood friends. OCD was not my friend, but it certainly was my constant companion. It did keep me focused on my internal problems and made me easy to dislike. What to do in defense? Shut down and go on offense.

In those days, my feelings of isolation and loneliness were such that I decided not to have friends after the fact. By that I mean, since the kids had already told me they didn't like me any more, I'd go along with it. Sort of like the classic sitcom plot:

"You're fired!" the boss said.

"Oh yeah? You can't fire me, I quit!"

That way, the rejection didn't hurt as much. Uh-huh. Sure.

So my brain had the new fuel of rejection to feed the OCD cycle's engine of obsession-anxiety-compulsion-relief. I'd disappear into magic even more to make them like me. That didn't seem to work, so I'd worry more about it, and practice my magic harder than ever.

I had all these great new tricks to show them, but they don't really want to see them any more. It seemed that I and my magic were now passé. Magic was so last year. I kept trying to join in, to fit in, but the harder I tried the less they seemed to care. I felt so empty, alone and completely rejected. Just what I needed. It would be the first time I would seriously begin to wonder if there was a place for me in this world at all? I didn't know.

By the spring of 1978, I had pretty much given up on trying to fit in with my former friends any more. I was an introvert. Lonely, I decided to make it a way of life. What else could I do?

After being stripped of all my previous popularity, it was emotional self-defense. What was most confusing to me was that I was very popular everywhere else. The town locals all knew me as "the magic kid". I was performing everywhere, at big festivals like Harbor Fest and the Chesapeake Jubilee. I was doing corporate shows, even on local TV at times. Everyone knew who I was. Still, my classmates seemed to reject me and it really hurt. I couldn't grasp why adults loved me and my friends wanted nothing to do with me. "What's wrong with me?" I thought. Like a broken record, that phrase replayed itself over and over endlessly.

I made a decision. No more friends. I had my magic and that was all I needed. It was the best friend a friend could have. My favorite companion. I knew that it would never reject me. Deeper and deeper I went. No one really noticed what was going on inside of me. Mom was busy getting better and Dad was never around. I was a great performer, too. My acting skills were Oscar-worthy. I could hide things inside when I wanted. My grades started heading downhill. Didn't I use to have perfect grades? Not any more. I become the class clown. I got sent to the principal's office more than any other kid in Lakeview Elementary.

To my surprise, Mr. Hill, the principal, did think I was funny. He still had to call my parents, divorced though they were. I begged him not to call Mom. Dad, I could schmooze over, but my mother would knock me into the middle of next week, plus the fact she didn't need this on her as well. My father got the call.

My mom sensed that something was wrong. She might

not realize that I didn't have friends any more, but she certainly knew how to read my report card. My parents tried to help me with my homework, especially math. I hated math. I still hate math. They finally took me to see a specialist. I had learning disabilities.

I was really disruptive. I didn't care if I was the center of attention any more, as long as I could spout off some nonsense that would stop everything else dead in its tracks in class. Some kids would laugh; some would be upset. I suppose I was more interested in vengeance than attention, after all that rejection. Rejection as a child is very hard to take on any level. The problem did come to a head though, and the adults were sure I needed help.

The specialist my parents finally took me to was a child psychologist, Dr. Welloy, as I remember. She told my parents I had a learning disability, because I was having trouble focusing, that I was extremely hyperactive and that I had a mild form of dyslexia. Suddenly, I wasn't allowed to eat chocolate and sugar, and she wanted me to write a letter to myself every night, then seal it in an envelope, and open it and read it a year later. I did it and this turned into a daily journal, which I still keep to this day.

I saw Dr. Welloy once a week for a year, after which she told me that I seemed to be okay, and didn't have to see her anymore. I was relieved, because I'd been angry about having to see her in the first place. I don't remember her using the terms Attention Deficit Disorder (ADD) or Attention Deficit Hyperactivity Disorder (ADHD). I don't remember if those terms were in common use back then.

I have tried unsuccessfully to find Dr. Welloy. Because I

don't have her full name, I can't find her today. I wanted to get a copy of my records. Would my current doctor agree or disagree with her findings? I wonder. I guess I always will. I don't remember if she prescribed any drugs for me. Did she determine that I was suffering from PTSD? I don't know. One thing I do know, is that what was known about OCD, PTSD, ADD and ADHD more than twenty years ago was probably a lot less than what we know about them now.

ADD and ADHD seem to be similar to OCD in the sense that they're all caused by biochemical imbalances in the brain. The ADD kid has a hard time concentrating on one thing at a time for very long, and the ADHD kid lets everybody in the class know that he's not concentrating! You can't help but notice the hyperactive ADHD kid. He's the one bouncing off the walls, the one the teacher wants to wrap in duct tape from head to toe. That was me for sure.

It was in the spring of 1978 that I first heard the words *Special Ed.* What's that? For all I knew it could have been a talking horse with a harelip. I cringed. I've heard of such a place except we called it "REEE--TARD class! And now, I was in it. Could it get any worse? Yup!

Fall, 1979. Fourth grade. Special Education Department. I called it *Das Spezialen Kinderstalag 17*. Barbed wire, searchlights, guard towers; *Wehrmacht soldaten* with Walther PPK 9mm pistols and bolt action Mausers, bayonets fixed. German shepherds patrolled, hungry for blood, and the sounds of "Lili Marlene" on *Sturmbannfuhrer* Schultz's harmonica.

Okay, maybe it was not that bad. But it was in that section of the school that all the other "normal" kids knew about.

And I was put in it.

"Didja hear about Steven?"

"Yeah, he got put in Special Ed!"

"Hee, hee, hee, hee…"

"Yeah, what a REEE-tard!"

Later on I became known as "REEE---tard the Magician."

I knew why I was there. I was being punished. Punished for wanting to do what I loved. I was a performer wasn't I? Wasn't that what performers did? We entertained? That was all I was doing and for that, I got this pint-sized concentration camp. I hated it. Although I knew that it was my fault, I hated it. I had to get out of there. I was determined to get out. But how?

I'm-being-punished was another OCD loop in my head. I obsessed over the fact that it was my behavior causing the punishment. To seek relief from the obsession, I practiced my magic and performed even harder.

The catch, of course, was that as I practiced my magic, I developed my stage personality, too. So where did I first try it all out? In the classroom. Was it well received there? Not by the teachers it wasn't.

With OCD, it is common to worry excessively about harming yourself or other people, and to immerse yourself in feelings of guilt about such behavior. Now, take that worry and kick it up a notch, because your behavior actually was disruptive! Bingo! More justification for the continued OCD cycle. It was suffering at its best. As the great Indian scholar Shantideva has said, "If there is a way to overcome the suffering, then there is no need to worry; if there is no way to overcome suffering, then there is no *use* in worrying." The sad part is that people with

OCD would never be able to fully grasp such a truth. In really bad cases, they might recognize this truth but be unable to do anything about it because of their state of mind.

Home from school and right into my room. Into that Lost Land, my one true friend. By the summer of 1980, I had survived the worst school year of my life, the fourth grade. It devastated my self-confidence. I was the butt of cruel jokes. Not behind my back, but right in my face. I sank ever deeper into the very pit of my room, learning, practicing, and creating. I thought by this time I knew as much magic if not more, than most magicians. I kept thinking that things had to get better that fall. I was gonna be in the fifth grade. I thought positively in good faith that all my hard work would pay off. "They'll like me now, you just wait and see." For whatever reason I had it in my brain that the better I became at magic, the more powerful and mind-bending tricks that I knew, the more the kids would like me. It was not true.

Fall, 1980. Fifth grade. The bastards still had me in Special Ed. However, I comforted myself with the knowledge that nothing could be worse than the year I had survived. Lenny decided to make me reevaluate this perception.

About Lenny. Well, he was the school bully in the fifth grade. Every school had one and he was ours. He was a mean sucker, a towering giant compared to the rest of us who had yet to receive our growth spurts. Lenny seemed to have gotten his early and more than his fair share.

When I stood next to him, I felt like I was one foot one, three pounds, and he was thirty foot nine, seventy tons. Perception is reality when you no longer have any self-esteem and no friends.

In retrospect, he was tall and skinny with braces. That was irrelevant to scared, small, even skinnier me.

Lenny considered a day wasted if he didn't have an opportunity to beat me up. I was desperate enough to turn to my divorced parents for advice. I got the classic equation for a bloody nose.

Dad (fight back) + Mom (tell on him) = contradiction = inaction.

So I did neither.

That conflicting advice from my divorced parents was enough to send my OCD cycle through the roof, as well as place me in a state of extreme anxiety out of my genuine fear for my own safety. So then you had a kid with ADHD, PTSD, and OCD who was also depressed. I worried about harming others, harming myself, fighting back, not fighting back. You name it, I was worried about it. Someone once told me that worry is the interest you pay on trouble before it's due. If that is true, I hate to think what trouble really costs!

Now here's another gift that OCD hands your worried brain, an obsessive worry that you'll lose control of your aggressive urges and really do serious damage to somebody else. Some OCD sufferers have the compulsion to check things over and over, such as light switches, or look around the corner a certain way, or wash their hands over and over. It can be any one of a million stupid behaviors that waste time and accomplish nothing. In my case, it was practice, practice, practice that magic, checking to make sure that each trick was perfect. The irony here was that on stage, practice does make perfect, but in OCD, practice makes you feel imperfect. A cruel game at which you are bound to lose and your brain is the only winner.

As a budding magician, I did my best to disappear. Disappear from Lenny's sight. I was pretty good at it, too. If it were baseball, I'd be in the Hall of Fame. Five days a week, I managed to completely avoid him at least eighty percent of the time. That's a lot of work.

Can you imagine batting 800? Of course, this merely served to annoy Lenny. So did my calling him Lenny! He was only batting 200, but when he connected, it was a home run every time. He knocked me out of the park at least once a week. Once a week, I returned to the apartment bleeding. Quickly, I cleaned up before dad got home with time to spare. I had to come up with some tall tale for this week's injury.

My father thought I was a complete klutz.

Spring of 1981. As long as I'm using baseball analogies, let me get you up to speed on my growth spurt. It was finally starting. I was getting taller and filling out a little. My testosterone must have been kicking in, too, because I was starting to get really pissed at being the butt of jokes and a bully's punching bag. I was about to discover the joy of teenage violence.

My rage was going from simmer to boil. We were in P.E. class, playing baseball out in the field. It was a really nice day, warm, and the sun was shining bright. I was at bat, wearing the number 8, which was three points higher than my batting average. I was bad at baseball. I mean, if I got two hits in a row, the ball was sent out for drug analysis. Lenny was the catcher that day. He started razzing me. He didn't know he had also switched on my rage alarm. I could see it flashing in my mind, like a red light with one of those Ah-Hoo-Gah! Ah-Hoo-Gah! klaxons you hear when there was a flight line scramble at a Strategic Air Command base in one of those old movies from the Cold War Era starring Jimmy Stewart. My rage squadron scrambled. They were armed, fully loaded, taxied into position, and ready for takeoff.

My studies of magic provided me with a lot of knowledge about physics. I knew about arcs, angular momentum, positioning, velocity and timing. I positioned myself just so at the plate. Lenny continued his razzing. I was precisely positioned. When the pitch was thrown, it would look like an accident. A perfect, premeditated accident.

The pitch was thrown. Rage squadron, you are cleared for takeoff. Full throttle. Vengeance roared down the runway, and lifted off. As I swung, the arc of my bat carried cleanly behind me in a follow-through which took the side of Lenny's face and his mouth into the realm of retributional physics.

The crack of my bat was the crack of his cheekbone shattering. The impact left a perfect impression of his braces in the wood. He dropped like a stone. He was out cold, bleeding. The braces saved his teeth. My swing taught him a vicious lesson. He would recover, but he would not mess with me again. I stood over him, peering into his eyes as they put him on the stretcher. No words were exchanged. None were needed. He got the message loud and clear. I experienced the fiercest of joy. I looked fear in the eyes, and for the first time, fear was afraid of me. On this day my warrior within was awakened.

I could have killed the guy, but luckily, I didn't. Is this typical OCD behavior? No. An OCD personality would obsess about intrusive thoughts of doing violence to somebody, but usually not act on them. People with OCD are generally very gentle, not aggressive. I was provoked to the extreme over a long period of time. I suppose a clinical psychologist could opine that in retrospect, Steven was acting out of repressed rage from the traumas of his past. Whatever. You know what I think? I think I'd finally had enough and did what any normal preteen developing his own personal supply of testosterone would have done against a bully. Fight back.

The moral here is that not every event that happens in an OCDer's life is due to OCD. Freud once said that sometimes a cigar is just a cigar. Well, that is, unless it was a gift from Bill Clinton. Lenny would send his friends after me in the future, and though I would not start any fights, I never again turned and ran. I stood and fought. I might not win, but I would always give as good as I got or better. The scared little boy was gone. The magic was beginning to work.

Where is Lenny now? In prison for domestic violence. Life sentence.

CHAPTER FOUR
The Time of My Life

This is not going to be an easy chapter for me to write, but it's really important to my story since I believe that it did the most damage in my life. I have labored in thought for many months over putting this in or leaving it out altogether. I must admit that I am still afraid of what people will think about me and how it might affect my professional career in the future. I am concerned about my future, mainly because that is where I am going to spend the rest of my life. For me, these were among the very darkest of days in my life. To this day, it is still my single most life-changing experience. One I think about, feel, and still am angry over even now. It was very personal, painfully so. I am releasing it here so that I may release myself and finally breathe the fresh air of my own freedom.

That having been said, I finally decided to leave it in for one reason. I survived.

It was the end of innocence for me. In light of some of today's top headlines around the country regarding this matter, I felt that my story might hit home with others out there still trying to survive their own *Life among Secrets*.

In early summer, 1981, I was twelve. By then, I was starting to make some pretty good money with my magic, although I was a kid. I made it performing all over town. I was really in demand. Obsessed as ever with getting better and better at my craft, I jumped for joy at what was coming to Norfolk over the Fourth of July weekend: The IBM Convention.

No, not that IBM, but the International Brotherhood of Magicians' Annual Convention. For those of you not familiar with Virginia geography, Norfolk is right across the Chesapeake Bay from my home town of Portsmouth. It's either a bus ride over the bridge, or a fairly short trip on the ferry. I was still living with my Dad in the apartment, and it was not even an issue as to whether or not I was going to the convention.

It was a done deal. Not only that, but Dad gave me four hundred dollars to spend there, not counting the stash of cash I had that he didn't know about! My dad! What a guy! I was so excited I could hardly ride my bike.

Every magician in the galaxy showed up for one of these conventions it seemed to me. It was a four-day event at the Norfolk Omni, with countless display booths in the exhibition hall, seminars, tricks to buy, acts to see, famous magicians to meet in person. Holy moley! I was happier than a cat in a tuna patch! There was a rule though. Dad wanted me home from the convention every night by six. Since the exhibits and shows don't end until nine, I would miss a lot. I wondered if there was a way I could stay later.

On the big day, I rode my bike to the Portsmouth-Norfolk terminal, chained it to a post, and caught the Portsmouth Ferry to what I knew was going to be the greatest event of my life so far. We docked, and I was at the Omni before my brain could even catch up with my feet. FANTASTIC! STUPENDOUS! AMAZING! I must have been possessed by the ghost of P.T.

Barnum. You might be tempted to think that giving four hundred bucks to a twelve-year-old magician at the IBM Convention is a bit like giving whiskey and car keys to a gang of teenaged boys, to paraphrase P.J. O'Rourke. In all fairness, though, I had a plan of moderation. I would limit myself to spending only one hundred dollars per day of the cash Dad gave me. I would pace myself. I would discipline myself. Yeah, right!

How could I already have spent four hundred dollars? Poof! Like magic, it simply disappeared . Pretty soon I had to leave for the Ferry Terminal and get home! What to do, what to do? What's this? A message board? Hey, this is neat! It's a bulletin board where people who don't have a reservation can leave a message asking if anybody wanted to share a room so they wouldn't have to leave the convention! I guessed it wouldn't hurt if I wrote a message. I posted a room request on the board in my twelve-year-old scrawl.

It was getting late. I had to leave and catch the ferry unless there was a reply to my room request. Hey! There was a reply! It said someone had a room at the hotel and wouldn't mind sharing it. I was to meet him in the exhibition hall at booth such-and-such.

I got to the booth. I couldn't believe it! I was him! "Jeff!" (Not his real name.) It was the magician who did the famous Soda Can Trick. Wow! I was a big fan of his!

I introduced myself, and although he was famous, he seemed like an ordinary, down-to-earth nice guy. Everybody knew him, and he was really funny, too. The rooms were pretty pricey for a twelve-year-old, but he said I could bunk with him for only twenty bucks a night. Sounded like a fair deal to me.

Fantastic! I just had to convince Dad.

Dad wanted me to call every day and check in with him and I'd already made one call. Now I had to call him again and convince him to let me stay. It wasn't easy, but I succeeded. I CAN STAAAY! I CAN STAAAY! YAAAY!

I ran back to the booth where "Jeff" (Remember, not his real name.) waited, and told him the good news. It was pushing six P.M. He handed me a set of keys to the room and told me to make myself at home, drop my stuff off, come back to the exhibition hall, and hang around with all the other magic freaks and finger flingers till he got off. The hall closed at nine, so he would catch up with me later. My brain buzzed with happy overload. I thanked him and headed up to the room. It had been a long, wonderful, tiring day. Even for a twelve year old.

It was a nice hotel room with two beds. I picked one, and plopped my sack full of magic loot on it. Four hundred dollars worth of new tricks to learn forward, backward, inside and out. AND THEY WERE ALL MINE! It was like Christmas in July. I sat cross-legged on the bed, spread them out methodically. I would go through them one by one.

Time had no meaning. I didn't realize I hadn't eaten dinner yet. Huh? It was already nine at night? Wow. I savored the moment. How could life possibly get any better than this? I was in magic heaven for sure.

I barely noticed that "Jeff" had come up to the room. I was deep in the New Trick Zone. He asked if I was hungry, and suddenly I realized that I was. I told him I would go down across the street to Burger King, but he saw that I was torn between going out to eat and skipping dinner, so I could stay and keep learning.

He came up with the solution. He would order room service. His treat. Gee thanks, man. What a guy! Now then, where was I? Oh, yeah, right. I re-submerged in the New Trick Zone.

The food came. I suppose I ate, but I didn't really notice. I was still zoning. "Jeff" ate quickly, and announced that he was going to take a shower. Mm-hmm... Background noise from some place near the New Trick Zone. In one ear and out the other. He stripped methodically. Right in the room. Right in front of me. The full monty. I didn't want to be rude, so I kept my eyes down. Nobody walked around naked in my family, but maybe his family did. I didn't know. It didn't really matter much anyway.

Three was the charm. The divorce, the murder, now this! This was the beginning of another horrible event. I didn't know what was about to happen. The combination of my innocence and OCD behavior made me ignore what would probably have been obvious to a normal kid. I wasn't comfortable that he stripped naked right in front of me, but that's where my OCD behavior insulated me from reality. I was utterly and completely obsessed with learning the new tricks I'd purchased, so the small portion of my attention that was pulled away from learning them by his nakedness was quickly shut down. My brain was working on full-tilt. Ignore it. It'll-go-away mode. Because I felt uneasy, I obsessed in my magic ritual all the more. Any worrisome thoughts I had would be taken care of if only I would practice my magic harder.

I was still in the New Trick Zone. And it was his hotel

room. Maybe that's what grownups did in hotels.

He mumbled something about going to take his shower and went into the bathroom. Mmm-hm. Fine. Still in the New Trick Zone. He didn't close the bathroom door. A lot of steam fogged up the mirrors. He came out of the bathroom, drying off. He was not a dangler. He was a towel rack. I had no idea what gay meant. I was only twelve.

He threw the towel away. He sat beside me on the bed. He tried to kiss me. I pushed him away and laughed it off. I moved quickly to the other side of the bed. I tried very hard to get back in the New Trick Zone.

My sense that something was wrong had been jarred into consciousness by his attempt to kiss me while naked and aroused. I was actually annoyed as well as uneasy, because it was very disturbing when something broke the rhythm of an OCD ritual. There I was, deep in magic, and he was really intruding on the mental reality I'd been creating. My laughter was out of nervousness and confusion. It was very important for me to shut out his advances, and get back into the mental comfort zone that my OCD magic ritual provided. It was more important to do that than to get the heck out of that room!

He went back to his bed. He had a little black leather bag. He opened it and pulled out a bottle of clear liquid. He opened the bottle, poured some of the liquid into his hand. The New Trick Zone had evaporated. I was in a horrible present moment. This guy was acting really weird. I had to ask. "What is that?" He answered, "It's lubricant. It feels good." I panicked. I had to get out of there. He was much bigger than I was. I couldn't get past him. He shoved me down upon the bed, ripped my pants and under-shorts away. His full weight was on me.

Time stopped again.

I mean it stopped the same way it had for me when I walked into that tragic scene at my friends' apartment. I still have chunks of memory blotted out from this attack. For example, the time. Ten, ten-thirty, eleven? I don't remember what time it actually was. What happened to those missing hours is a blur. I'm not really sure I want to know anyway. To go through this with a grown man when you're a twelve-year-old boy is unimaginably horrific. When you're already suffering from OCD and PTSD, it gives hell on Earth a whole new twist. Imagined anxieties from OCD become mingled with the actual atrocities visited upon you, and it intensifies the OCD cycle into a virtual mind storm.

Somehow, at some point, I found strength. It must have been the pain. I screamed, and screamed and screamed. Finally, I bit him as hard as I could. Even today, I can still hear my own screams sometimes, not unlike Agent Starling and the lambs she was never able to silence.

In the hallway I was naked, bleeding, screaming inside. Somehow part of my rational mind resurfaced. I remembered one of my friends and his parents were here at the convention, in the hotel. I remembered their room number. It was on this floor. I found myself in front of their door. Pounding, screaming, terrified. The man that raped me was in the hall, too. He was coming after me. I screamed and pounded the door harder. My friend's mom answered the door. She grabbed me and pulled me into their room. I was in shock, but I was also embarrassed. I didn't want her to know what happened. I didn't want my Dad to find out what had happened. If my Dad found out, maybe he wouldn't let me come back to the convention. I couldn't let that happen. After all I went through, I still couldn't let that happen. Magic was still my only real true friend, my only real companion.

For whatever reason, they didn't tell my Dad. Maybe they didn't really know what has happened to me. Maybe I convinced them that nothing really bad had happened to me. Maybe they did know, but they didn't want to tell him, or they didn't want me to know that they knew. I don't know. They didn't call the police after lots of pleading on my part. I got very busy burying the experience as deep in my mind as I could. I had a lot of burying to do. I told my friend's mom I had been locked out of my room. All my clothes and new tricks were in there. Her husband quickly assessed the situation. He put on a robe, headed into the hall and before too long was pounding on "Jeff's" (Not his real name) door. I heard my friend's dad yelling at him. I heard loud words, very sharp words. I don't know if they exchanged physical blows.

By this time, all the guests on the floor were awakened by the commotion. They opened their doors. My friend's dad is a take-charge kind of man. He told everybody to go back in their rooms and they did. He came back to the room with all of my stuff. I didn't know if hotel security got involved. I only knew I was in a lot of physical pain and I couldn't tell them. It was almost one in the morning. I slept on their floor.

From then on, I commuted to the magic convention. I think I told my dad that if I stayed overnight, it would be less money for me to spend on new tricks. Something like that. All I really knew was that he never found out. Or if he did, he never let me know. I worked hard on burying the mental pain and ignoring the physical pain, which in time would heal. One day I missed the last ferry and took the bus home. On another day I missed the last bus, and Dad came to get me. He was pleased that I was getting so much new magic. To him, I was more interested in magic than ever before.

The only bad thing about the convention was "Jeff" following me around the exhibition hall whenever he saw me. I was furious with him and avoided him at all costs. He had betrayed me. He acted so nice, so apologetic. He was so sorry, so sorry. Oh he was sorry alright. It would never happen again. He swore it.

I was only twelve. I wanted to believe him . I used to look up to him. I would still like to look up to him. Kinda. Sorta. As a magician, as a teacher. The fact that he gave me close to a thousand dollars worth of free magic tricks helped me to believe he was sincerely sorry. Didn't it? Kinda. Sorta. I was only twelve.

At this point, PTSD and OCD worked hand in hand. They formed a partnership designed to make me believe that everything was all right. The moments too hideous to remember were locked tightly by PTSD in a mind vault with 128-bit encryption and a combination I still have trouble remembering. My OCD cycle worked overtime to soothe everything else in its own strangely calming, familiarly painful way. Mental scabs became mental scars.

Over the next several years, I saw Jeff at other conventions. The word *anger* does not even begin to describe the rage I feel inside for him. The very sight of him makes me physically ill. Yet I hold it all in.

He will never know the pain, suffering and mental psychosis he has caused me. That is, until he reads this book. I was more than happy to mail him the first free copy, autographed of course.

The nightmares, the sheer trauma this single moment in time would cause me in later years is simply overwhelming. Never mind the fact I have OCD. For so many years I was ashamed of what happened. It was the darkest place I knew. A secret so guarded that a person would do anything it takes to keep it, even if it meant having to create a brand new identity. A new me, because the old me was used and dirty, full of sin and very ugly. It was the natural thing to do in my mind.

Start over. A new beginning, a simple way to repress and hide, to block out every detail for years to come. All so I wouldn't have to deal with the pain. I had to focus on magic. I couldn't let anything stand in the way of that. I would forget about it like it all never happened and move on. If only life worked that way.

A diamond begins its life as a dark, dirty and unwanted piece of carbon. It's only after many years of great pressure and stress that it one day emerges, a brilliant, precious jewel sought the world over. To me it was very symbolic of everything my life had become. I was determined to make it and emerge a very successful magician and entertainer. No matter what. I felt that as long as I did that, then whatever I had to go through to get there was the price I would have to pay, the cost of doing business.

I believe that it was at this time Steven Mosley quietly faded away, and Steven Diamond was born. The door to the past was sealed shut, locking away its truth, its horrors and its pain in hopes of a brighter future to come. What I didn't understand was that regardless of when you deal with the past, you WILL deal with it, some day, at some point in time. Nothing in the universe goes unchecked. Nature has a perfect accounting system and keeps track of everything, including what you have tried to forget.

You generate your future by the choices you make every moment of your life. The choice I made to repress, block and hide this event in my past came back to really raise hell in my life in later years. It would have been much wiser and easier to have sought professional help back then. To have dealt with the situation then and there instead of so many years later would have made life so much easier down the road.

Whether you like it or not, everything that is happening in your life right now is a result of every single choice you've made in the past. Stop and think about that. Put this book down and think. You will see that it's a very powerful fact of life.

It applies to everything you do. My father used to tell me, "The problem with wisdom, is that by the time you get it, you're too old to use it." I think my father had it wrong. I believe that it's never too late to use wisdom although it may only benefit other people.

CHAPTER FIVE
How You Gonna Keep Me Down on the Farm?

It was the fall of 1981 and Virginia was spectacular. People came from all around for a Sunday drive in the hills during the fall. When the leaves turn colors, nature puts on quite a show for all who want to see. Especially in the good ol' Smokey Mountains!

By 1981 I was a seventh grader, a skilled semi-professional magician by this time. I didn't get picked on so much these days. My adolescence commenced at W.E. Waters Junior High in Portsmouth. More magic to learn, more skills to polish, more money to be made doing shows around town. Too busy to let those traumatic memories surface. Keeping them buried with things like magic, schoolwork and becoming a member in the "Able and Ambitious" performing Arts program. Mrs. Heath, who would later become my music teacher in high school, Mr. Griggs, the program's director, and Olga Morales, choreographer, were going to be very busy with me, because I wanted to be on that stage in their productions no matter what it took. I was going to be a star!

I would make the auditions, get in and go on to become one of the singer/dancers in the show. I lived for that program which taught me everything I needed to go on to produce my own productions in later years. It was Harriet Heath who would touch my life more than any other teacher I would ever have. I think that "Momma Heath" as I called her was the first to teach me about morals and respecting yourself. Though I didn't realize it at the time, she was always there for me to talk to. She was the only source of strength and honesty I had. Momma Heath never let me get away with any of my craziness and could spot a lie before the sentence was even finished. I never met anyone more honest, loving and true to herself than she was. Many years later, in therapy, I would learn how important her influence really was in my life. She taught me things that money can't buy and she did it with her actions, not her words.

    I recently went back to Portsmouth, Virginia, to visit with her and her husband Eddie for the first time in too many years. She hasn't changed a bit. I found it amazing how someone like a simple music teacher could affect one's life in such a massive way. Mrs. Heath was my role model although I don't think either one of us really knew it at the time. When I was in therapy I was asked the question "Who would you select as the most influential person in your life and why?" It took me nearly a month to figure it out. I thought about it hard. I really wanted the answer to this question. It is an important question for everyone to answer. So I sat down and made a list of everyone I could think of and the reasons why I thought they were in the running. After finally reviewing my list, my choice was clear to me from the amount of notes I had written under her name. I went back to inform her that I was going to be talking about her in this book and also to thank her for all that she instilled in me when I needed it most. If this world could only have more teachers like her… The reason we don't is that the teachers in this world are grossly underpaid. Her actions in and out of the classroom are what taught me most. I can never thank her enough, and I am a better person today for having crossed her path.

Summer, 1982. Dad was still a workaholic; he had his own Master Mechanic's Business called Victory Truck Repair named after the street it was on, like me. He also had his own cardiac insufficiency episode, the first of many coronaries to come through the years.

I remember being in Tower Shopping Mall with my dad one day when I was young. He began to look a little blue in the face. Suddenly he said that he needed to sit down.

He did. I asked him what was wrong, and he told me that he had heartburn really bad and that he needed a minute to catch his breath. So I sat there next to him and looked through the magic book he had purchased for me, while my father suffered a mild heart attack. A while later, he said he was ready to leave and we went home. His doctor had warned him to slow down. More than that, the doctor told him after one of his serious heart attacks that he'd better reduce his stress levels or he would be facing an early grave.

They checked his heart and discovered that my father, who had a very high tolerance for pain, had suffered several mild heart attacks prior to this one, which he mistakenly believed was heartburn and gas. He told no one, and his silence could have killed him.

Any normal person is naturally going to be very worried and scared if his or her dad has a life threatening condition, and so is anyone with OCD. Of course, the OCD person is going to respond with the built in Obsession-Anxiety-Compulsion-Relief monkey on his or her back, and the results will take them deeper into the cycle, regardless of the health of the patient. In my case, I thought that if I worked harder on succeeding in show business, it would provide my father with a sense of well being, which might help to make him better. That's completely illogical, of course. At the time, it made perfect sense to me. I was desperate to do anything that might help my father feel the slightest bit better. I was quick to provide him any good news I could muster.

As time went on, Dad was not getting any better. He was getting worse. Obviously, to my OCD brain, the fault was mine. In reality, it didn't matter what I did. He would have gotten worse anyway, but that's not important to the OCD mind. The only thing that registers in the OCD mind is to do whatever ritual you do and do it harder, longer, better. If things aren't improving, it's all your fault because you're not trying hard enough! Although the rational portion of your mind knows this is a complete pile of steaming cow poop, the OCD sufferer can't do anything to stop it, not without therapy and medication. Any event seemed overwhelming to me. I began to fall apart inside.

My father was my strength. I suddenly realized that I might not have that solid pillar to lean on any more . Everything I had known was threatened, and I became very angry. "THOSE DAMN DOCTORS ARE NOT TRYING HARD ENOUGH!" I said a million times.

All this scared the hell out of me. I'd had enough stress in my life so far that I certainly didn't want to lose my dad at thirteen. I experienced that horrible feeling all over again, the same feeling as I had when my mother was in the hospital, a feeling I knew all too well.

In the summer of 1983, the doctor decided that he didn't

like the way my dad was handling his business with all the stress that typically comes with owning your own company. My father was good at what he did. He loved it too. He was a workaholic because he had a family to take care of, a secure future to build for those he loved. His thriving business paid for all of that, and caused his second massive coronary.

This time, it was too much. The doctor told him he might well die if he didn't sell his business and retire. For the first time, my father took the doc's advice. Our lives were about to make a major change, one that my crystal ball couldn't possibly have foreseen.

Portsmouth may not seem like an urban center to someone from New York City or L.A., but it was a big city to me. It was my home, and I liked it there. When Dad sold his business, he decided to go back to his roots. You see, his dad was a farmer, so how hard could it be for him to join that pastoral way of life? Not very, he figured. He bought an old farmhouse on a sixty-acre spread outside of Lynchburg Virginia in a little town called Phenix, Virginia. Being fourteen, I moved with him, and I was not amused.

Phenix, Virginia. That's not a misspelling. Phenix, not Phoenix. Population 250, of which about 210 are related. "Fer" example, Jeb's husband-in-law is his second cousin half-removed, 'cuz granny's sister is her great uncle, unless it's de other way around. By the way… could you help me unhitch my house?

Just think of the movie "Deliverance" without the banjo soundtrack.

Now I am talking about some laid back, real time, country

folk here. No question about it, these good people had no place to be anytime soon. Kind of like riding Greyhound.

I remember hearing my father telling a story about our next door neighbors. They lived a quarter of a mile up the lane. You see, in the country people lived the quiet life, yet everyone knew everything that happened within a hundred-mile radius. Not much got them really excited either, except "Coon Hunting", beer and gossip! Sounds like a country song.

The story was that one night the old lady of the house was unhappy because her old man wasn't paying any attention to her. To get him interested again, she ran past him in the nude as he watched television. He didn't move. Returning a few minutes later, dressed again, she asked him, "Did you see something go by?"

To which he mumbled, "Yeah, and whatever it was, it needed ironing!" Which explained why he slept at our house that night.

That was Phenix, all right. Always plenty of gossip going around.

The townsfolk joked that Phenix was too danged small to be able to afford an "O" in the name. When I got up that first morning, I was awakened by the sound of cows in the front yard. They moo a lot.

In the fall of 1983, at age fourteen, instead finishing at Manor High School in Portsmouth as a sophomore with a thousand other students, I found myself being ripped out of Manor and entering Randolph Henry High School in Charlotte County. There were only eight hundred kids in the entire school. Now, I'm not a country boy, no sir. I'm a city slicker from Phenix.

Reality began to settle in. If only I could shut up those darned cows!

Still deeply engrossed in improving my skills as a magician, I was not too caught up with making many friends my freshman year, either. I had been through that and didn't need the bother. Word soon spread though-out the countryside, thanks in part to the gossip hotline, that the new kid in town did magic. Before I knew it, I was a full-on local celebrity. I was getting a lot of gigs around the state, too, and Dad was happy to drive me around to them whenever I needed his help. I was getting a good professional reputation before long, too, thanks in part to the *Charlotte Gazette,* the local newspaper that did several articles on me. It was great for business. The phone was ringing off the hook. No one else had ever been so popular in that part of the woods.

Although I was the new kid at a pretty much rural school, it was not too bad. I began to like all the attention. Nobody was picking on me any more, and the students were actually kind of impressed by my skills. They even voted me Most Talented in my high school year book. How cool was that?

Where I got picked on was at home. Dad had re-married. To one of his two secretaries, no less. It's time for you to meet my Step-Monster, Nancy, the Beast from Hell.

You might think me a little harsh to call my dad's new wife my step-monster, but then again, you didn't know Nancy the way I knew Nancy. At just under five foot tall, weighing one hundred fifty pounds, Nancy was the pint-sized equivalent of a menstruating Tasmanian devil with a smile. I was never able to see what attracted my father to her. She wasn't the prettiest horse in the barn, but not the worst, either. I guess my father was lonely and since we all need someone to hold, she became the object of his affection because she was around him all day at work. She was there.

Back in the days when my father still had his business, he had decided that the one person he could not move away from was his secretary, Nancy. He fired the other one. Nancy was sweet as pie to everyone around the office, and to me so long as were in public or when Dad was right there with us. When it was Nancy and I alone, however, the story of Robert Louis Stevenson's *Dr. Jekyll and Mr. Hyde* came to mind. This woman was the Mayor of Nutburg. Totally certifiable. I begged and pleaded with my father not to marry her. Anybody but her! She hated me from day one. A long-time employee of my father's, we had known each other since I was about eight years old. All my pleas were to no avail, of course, because Dad never saw anything but the softer side of Nancy, a side I never found.

I could see right through her as clear as day. So why couldn't he? I couldn't grasp this concept. It made me worry.

In autumn, 1984, I was fifteen years old. If I could hold on for a little longer, I could get my driver's license and drive myself to my own gigs. Don't get me wrong, it was not that I didn't enjoy having my dad drive me around; it was that Nancy was now a year crazier. If I could drive myself, maybe she would back off me a bit. Now she had graduated from verbal abuse to physical. Still sweet as pie though when Dad was right there.

Along with the name-calling and torrents of invective, the woman (and I use that word loosely) liked to slap me and throw things at me. Having quick reflexes, I was pretty good at dodging what she lobbed, so I didn't have any obvious injuries to show Dad as proof. Even when she slapped me, it was not the sort of thing that left any marks. She was cunning and careful. I suppose I should have learned to lean into the line of fire when she tossed something at me, and got some sort of bodily evidence, but the thought never occurred to me.

For me, summers, holidays and weekends were always a great time to make money. In 1984, I was averaging $350 a show. A three-show weekend made me over a thousand bucks. I was making some real money, even by grown up standards. And the places I went! State fairs, big cities, little towns all over the Mid-Atlantic Seaboard from West Virginia to South Carolina, and from Maryland to Pennsylvania.

I still have fond memories of Dad's beat-up old yellow Ford pickup truck with the black cattle rack, loaded down with all my gear in the back, and additional stuff crammed in the cab. Meanwhile, Dad sat behind the wheel in his blue jeans and a plaid shirt, while I sat next to him in my pastel blue tuxedo. I couldn't have asked for a better roadie, stagehand and chauffeur. If only Nancy didn't mind.

That hot and very muggy summer of 1985, I was sixteen years old. Nancy still minded. She was quite the expert at hitting and spitting now, taking her psychotic resentment of me to an even greater level. This made her want to pee a lot. Okay, maybe I should explain. You see, the old farmhouse was constructed in such a manner that the only way Nancy could get to the bathroom was through my bedroom.

When Dad was not in or around, Nancy loved to burst

open my bedroom door, hoping to catch me doing something – anything -- that would allow her to go off on me. Although I was a teenager, I was not a druggie or a sex fiend, so there was nothing she could reasonably catch me at. This only fueled the fire. She was looking forward to the day when I got into some trouble, and she would have a real excuse to kill me. Finding me innocent, she muttered about having to use the facilities, and gently murmured that perhaps one day she'd poison my food. It was time for me to get my driver's license.

The thought here was that if Dad was not driving me around to all my gigs every weekend, then Nancy might cool her jets and not resent me so much, right? Right. And the executed Saddam Hussein might be next in line to the Pope at the pearly gates! So I finally got a car. My dad had a long-time friend, a veteran of WWII, that he met during the Korean War. I grew up calling my father's friend Uncle Guy. According to Uncle Guy and the pictures he kept in his wallet, he was a former boyfriend of the famed female pilot, Amelia Earhart who vanished without a trace. Amelia and Uncle Guy both served as fighter pilots together at the same time. The story went that my father saved Uncle Guy's life during the war, pulling him from the wreck of a crashed plane in the Korean jungle. He was the only survivor. They developed a very close friendship that continued to Uncle Guy's dying day. Uncle Guy was pretty old by then and finally decided along with the help of the Roanoke Virginia Police Department that he no longer should be on the roads behind the wheel. So the next thing I knew, he gave his car to me.

My first car ! A big old green nineteen-sixty something Cadillac. Lovingly, I called it The Tank. And it was, too. On one level, because it was so huge and the amount of gas it could drink, and on another, I suppose because, if I was inside it with the doors locked, it would protect me from Her Imperial Madnessty, *Psychotica Maxima*, the High Empress of Derangia.

October, 1986. I was seventeen years old. Raging hormones. My senior year in high school. Another year of better magic, more shows, bigger shows. I had illusions now and I worked with a guy who owned some tigers. Siegfried and Roy, look out boys, I've got tigers in my act! Not just tigers either, but lions and bears (Oh my!) as well. I could make a beautiful girl gracefully transform into a real leopard. I pulled an eagle out of the very flames of fire and I could fly. All around the stage, too, long before that other magician -- now what's his name … uhm…David-something-or-another, even thought about it. (Just kidding, Dave.)

I was hanging upside down from dizzying heights while strapped in a real straitjacket, selling out public shows at the State Theater in Farmville, Virginia. I was on my way to the big time. Nothing could stop me now. Nobody else had tigers in their act at eighteen. I began traveling up and down the East Coast. I was on the road a lot, making good money, making a name for myself, skipping school to do a show here and there. Okay, I wasn't the perfect student. Not even a good one. I hated school, but loved the people in it. I was away from home a lot, too. No doubt Nancy was pleased when I was not there. Then again, who did she have to scream at when I was gone? I was pretty sure the cows didn't listen to her, either.

Perhaps it ate at her, not being allowed to blow up at anybody. I didn't know. I did know that it began to feel really good to be away from the farmhouse. Now that I had wheels I was rarely home.

Nancy had two kids. Ronnie was the younger and most daring of the two. Sharon acted more like an adult than Nancy did. Her own children used to get tired of her and would stop talking and visiting her for extended periods of time more often than not. Instead of it bothering her, I discovered early on that Nancy only simmered and waited for my return, savoring the buildup of her pre-eruptive state. This is not an exaggeration. I have witnesses. I told anyone and everyone who would listen, including my own mother and sisters that Nancy was a mad cow, long before there was such a thing.

That fact that I was well known for many miles around did not help matters either. It turned out that Nancy had plenty of help in remembering me when I wasn't around.

I made it a point to give an annual show at Randolph Henry High and waive my talent fee. Instead, I donated the proceeds from the ticket sales to my class so they could have a party or whatever might be needed. By my senior year, it was part of the funding behind the senior class trip, a trip I never got to attend. I was performing that weekend, of course. It made me even more popular at school and I certainly didn't mind being popular again. It helped to make up for the living hell at the farmhouse.

Nancy heard about my popularity wherever she went. "Oh, you're the mother of that wonderful magician aren't you?" and "You must be s-o-o-o proud of him! We just lu-u-uve Steven!" Nancy began telling people what she thought of me whenever they would speak to her in the store, in a parking lot or wherever she was. People would come to me all the time and ask me if I had done something to her. It was making me look bad. I grew tired of having to explain myself when I was the one dodging flying items from around our house.

One event that really put her over the edge was the day I became a published author and the local newspaper did a story about it. "The Key to Being a Teenage Success" appeared in *Magic Manuscript Magazine,* a private magazine for the everyday conjuror; it was an international publication. I was on cloud nine! Higher then the highest roof in all the world. I bounced around the house screaming and yelling, jumping for joy when my issue arrived in the mailbox. My dad was so proud. he framed a copy and joyfully showed everyone who came into the house. Word of my success had spread throughout the magic community, and I was asked by the magazine's editor to write a feature article for other kids out there like me trying to make it in magic. So I did.

Nancy was not happy. Nancy wasn't happy that I was making $350.00 a show, plowing most of my profits right back into stupid magic tricks and buying more illusions. Nancy wasn't happy that I had a pulse.

A sense of contentment is a key factor in attaining happiness in this world.

Being jealous and/or filled with hate, about anything, for whatever reason, will never allow you to find the happiness that is rightly yours. Nancy would never be happy. This became clear to me.

I finally realized that no matter what I did or didn't do, her happiness was not something I could fix. Not even with magic.

It was something only she could change and it had to begin with the heart. Therein lay the problem. Nancy's heart, for reasons still unknown, had grown cold.

During my senior year, Dad got increasingly more frail from his heart condition. He was laid up in bed a lot of the time, forcing Nancy to become his only caregiver. With perfect whacko logic, taking care of Dad made her hate me even more. She let me know it when I got home one day. When Dad was asleep or out of earshot, Nancy came after me. Not just slapping, spitting and throwing things with all kinds of beautiful and artistic four letter words flowing from her mouth like Shakespeare on a bad night, she now liked to chase me with a kitchen knife.

At first, I thought it was funny, seeing that I had finally realized that she was mentally ill and it wasn't me that caused it. She was a screaming, one hundred fifty pound, four foot-something banshee with a knife, and she ran funny across the yard. It was quite humorous for a split second. I could always run faster and so I never feared her when she was like that. I leaped out the nearest door, and she would come after me right on cue. Often she would come in the house and take a nap having worn herself slam out.

For years, I obsessed about what I had done to make her hate like she did. I couldn't understand why she was like she was.

The humor wore off quickly when I suddenly realized and become very afraid of the fact that she might come after me while I was sleeping one night. I did not believe that Nancy ever had OCD. She was very violent and clearly displayed every symptom of a serious mental illness.

So what happens if someone you know has OCD or you think someone has it? What do you do if someone you love, even a parent or other family member seems to have what you believe to be OCD? What do you do? How do you intervene?

Whatever you do, do it gently and in a very positive way. It's no one's fault. The individual will likely have a very low self-image already. The more critical you are, the more depressed he or she will become and the deeper he or she will go. Very often people with OCD do not realize that they have a specific biochemical disorder that can be treated. They may think that they are slowly losing their mind or, as in my case, actually going crazy.

Start out by learning as much as you can about OCD. By now, there are plenty of websites, including mine, containing a wealth of information, all for free. I have on my site a link to a question and answer forum with experts who'll be glad to answer any questions you have on line. If you're not computer savvy, go to your public library and ask the librarian to point you in the right direction. Most libraries have computers on line now, and will be glad to show you how to use them. I suggest doing research on the internet first, because that is where you will find the most up-to-date information. Some older books I have read contained outdated information. I will recommend some of my favorite up-to-date websites on OCD at the end of the last chapter.

Once you have researched OCD, and realize to some extent what the OCD sufferer is going through, you'll be better able to broach the subject. You've got to read the situation. How well do you know the OCD sufferer? What is likely to make him or her cooperate and listen to you? You must also consider the fact that the sufferer may not want help. As a general rule in life, if people aren't asking questions about a certain topic, they usually do not want to hear what you have to say about it. So tread lightly.

You certainly will not make any headway if you confront an OCD'er aggressively.

An in-your-face "Hey! You've got a problem, and you're gonna get help whether you like it or not!" approach is only going to push the sufferer deeper into the OCD cycle. What you need to do is make them want to get help themselves. Making them think that getting help is their idea if you can. Maybe, be seen reading this book, or try leaving some OCD literature around the house where the OCD'er will find it. As a rule, the more you push, the farther away what you seek will be.

There is an excellent booklet called *Learning to Live with Obsessive Compulsive Disorder* by Barbara Van Noppen and others which you can get through the OCD Foundation website listed in the back of this book.

Your OCD'er might not even know that help is available. I didn't. Information is the single most important key to opening up the sufferer's world and stopping the cycle. The wisdom of revealing that information in such a way that the OCD sufferer will welcome it, is what you need to have. It takes a lot of courage on everyone's part. I once heard that "Courage is not the absence of fear. It's acting in spite of that fear." How true this is. Whatever you do, don't give up on your friend or family member. The result is a living hell for the OCD sufferer and possibly for you, the friend or family member. No one deserves to live like that as I did for well over twenty years. It's too much and it can make you lose your will to live. Trust me, no matter how bad it may seem, life is worth living.

You do have a purpose and you are here for a very specific reason. Finding out why is half the fun. It's all a matter of personal perspective, and we will discuss this more a bit later.

I told dad about Nancy's increasingly violent behavior towards me, but either he didn't believe it or he didn't want to believe it. I even talked to her own children about it. They believed me! They both confirmed that their mom was a wacko. That's why they stayed away from her. I decided to get out of the house as soon as I could.

Here it was a year later and my rational self knew full well that getting out of there once and for all -- permanently -- was the only real solution. Instead, the cycle had me enchained, telling me, " Work harder, do more shows, get your own car, push it all out of your mind and then she'd like you." It would never happen that way. How long would I keep going there? OCD wouldn't let me do the right thing and get the heck out of Dodge, although I knew it was the only way out.

This illustrates a complexity that can happen in anyone's life, not just in the life of an OCD sufferer. Sooner or later, you're bound to encounter some person who can make your life miserable for whatever reason, and there's nothing you can do to make things better except to get away from that person. What happens if you don't know that?

I'll tell you what. Did you know that another person's misery can kill you? Well it can, and it has for many who are no longer here. Other people's emotional states are like infectious diseases. Sometimes, like in the movie "When Harry Met Sally" you'll want to have what she's having. But not when it comes to OCD. As an OCD survivor, I am quite happy now and living a peaceful life relative to me. However, when I was suffering, I experienced complete misery. I drew misfortune upon myself 24/7.

Personal growth is most painful when we resist. I resisted everything. Nothing flowed in my life. Everything that came about in my life I instantly labeled as good or bad. This is a powerful and completely negative force, a whirlwind that will suck anyone nearby into its jaws. You will go down with them if you're not aware and very careful. Love with detachment.

Shortly before my father died, seventeen days to be exact, he wanted to talk to me about life and what he had learned in life. I thought what he had to say was very profound. It was the most serious conversation I ever had with him. He knew his time was up.

He told me that there was no "good news or bad news," only news. How you choose to perceive that news determines whether you view it as good or bad. He told me that I had to stop labeling everything in life, and that if I didn't, I would never find peace of mind. He told me to take care of my heart and to exercise it every day, a lesson he learned in the most difficult way. He told me to be careful what I dwelled on because that is what I would attract in my life. He told me that there would always be problems in my life, that they were my teachers, and not to be afraid. He said I would have problems no matter how much money I had, no matter how much success I attained or didn't achieve. Problems were going to be there. If I changed the way

I viewed problems and began to see them as teachers and challenges that kept life interesting, I would always continue to grow as a human being.

He told me that until I changed the way I viewed my personal disasters in my life, they would continue teaching me the same lessons over and over until I finally got them and moved on to the next one. He said to embrace change in my life, to be flexible and let life flow as it might. Because, he said, "Life will always win."

Most importantly, he told me to love. He said that love, forgiveness and compassion might be the most powerful lessons anyone could ever learn.

I never realized how wise a man my father was until that day. I don't think many people really did. He had never spoken in such a manner before. He was the quiet type who didn't say very much, especially towards the end. But that day, it was as if he had been spoken to by a higher power and was passing on the message to me. It would take me many years after his death to understand the full impact of all the wisdom he gave to me the last time we spoke.

Getting out of the house and away from Nancy became my only goal, the only thing I could focus on. But where would I go? What would I do? What would people think? I worried and worried and knew that I had to find the strength to do what scared me most. Leaving home. Leaving my dad. Leaving the only life I had ever known. I didn't know if I could make it. I grew very scared. Fear took over. I began to shake inside when ever I thought about it. In spite of it all, I started looking for the right solutions.

CHAPTER SIX
Him Again

August, 1986, New York City. I was growing up, not a shy little kid any more, to outward appearances. I was a pro. A professional magician. I was earning more money than my dad did. Even so, to the International Brotherhood of Magicians, I was still a junior magician, and would remain so until October first, my eighteenth birthday. After that, I would be in the big leagues, finding out what it was like to compete with the real pros.

This is analogous to the switch you make from high school to college. In June, you're a hotshot senior; in September, you're a lowly freshman again. Before I made the switch, I wanted to find out if I had what it took. I wanted to go head-to-head against my peers. I entered the Junior Magic Competition. I would be up against more than five hundred of the world's best junior magicians, from every corner of the globe if I made it to the competition.

I knew my stuff. I had over ten thousand hours worth of experience under my magic belt, and my version of the Floating Light Bulb Illusion (first made famous by the great Harry Blackstone) was a killer! By the time I made it to this contest audition, I had already rehearsed my routine ten hours a day for nearly three months. I won admission. I was going to the Junior Magic

Competition! It was being held at a military school campus on Long Island. I was psyched up! I was psyched out! I was both!

In this case, OCD was a double-edged sword. My obsession with magic made me very good at what I was doing, but my obsession also prevented me from enjoying anything else in life. I had pinpoint focus, sometimes called tunnel vision, and could see, smell, hear, taste and feel nothing else. Though I loved performing magic, the downside was the compulsion to practice for endless hours. Nothing could stop me. Nothing else mattered. Not food, not water. Nothing.

Without OCD, I would probably have enjoyed it more, because the horribly unpleasant cycle would have been out of the way.

Dennis and Terri were the husband and wife team who ran the competition. Dennis was a long-time professional magician, and Terri was one of the best professional magic clowns I had seen. She was a real sparkler. They were wonderful people and made me feel right at home from the very second I arrived at the airport. Once we reached the camp, I told her my name and she beamed. "Oh, you must be the Steven from Virginia!" She searched over her clipboard for my name. "Ah, here it is."

I felt great. She handed me my packet, which gave me my dorm assignment, and a bag full of fun magic stuff. Could life get any better? I headed upstairs to find my room. I couldn't wait to meet the other campers and my camp counselor! As the thought was running through my mind, I came across my room. I took a deep breath, turned the corner and went in. Suddenly, I felt the ice water in my lungs. Staring me in the eyes, with a sick smile was my worst nightmare. "Jeff" (not his real name). He was my camp counselor! My elation vanished faster then a kangaroo can sprint. I stood there, cold as ice, stunned and completely unable to move. I was in hell. This couldn't be real. I had worked so hard to be there. It was all I had dreamed of for many months. All the rehearsal was lost at that very moment. I wanted to go home, and I hadn't been there a full hour.

This was his *modus operandi*. He was a full-fledged molester who preyed on young boys. He should have been a priest. He got young boys' confidence at magic conventions, shows and other functions and seduced them with his fame in the magic world. Everyone had seen him on the covers of magic magazines and had bought his little tricks. It was easy for him to do. He lured them to his room, molested and raped them, bribed them, and kept them quiet, because after it happened, he seemed so sorry, so nice, and he promised he would *never* do it again. His victims wanted to believe him. They looked up to him. I had. His sick smile made me realize that he knew I was coming. He must have taken a special perverse pleasure in seeing if any of his victims were going to be there each year. Hell isn't hot enough for people like him.

He came over to me. "Hey, Steven! Come in, man. Good to see ya again. Hey, what's wrong? You look like you've seen a ghost." He laughed. I remembered his laugh. I could barely move. Some of the other guys came over and began talking to me. They asked me what was wrong. "Oh nothing, just reliving an old nightmare." I guess it broke the ice. I went inside, but I wouldn't be staying very long. I wanted out.

The list of campers! He saw the list! He had arranged for me to be in his room. He knew exactly who I was and that smile told me he had been expecting me. So that's how I had the honor of meeting him once again. I began to wonder if any more of his victims were present. I was going to find out.

I found myself badly shaken. I tried to pull myself together. I kept thinking about what that bastard did to me. Flashbacks of my very first IBM convention began to make me weak.

I needed to find a way to get my mind off of this. I tried hard to talk to Dennis, but I couldn't bring myself to get it out. That would mean telling him what happened before, and I couldn't tell anyone. They wouldn't like me anymore. So I returned to the room. Ignoring Jeff (not his real name), I talked to all the other guys. Before I went to bed, I thought. I reminded myself that I was far from the scrawny little twelve-year-old he raped in that room at the Omni five years earlier. I was a very street-smart, muscular six-foot young man. If he tried anything this time, I would take him out. The anger came rushing back as if the rape had happened yesterday. I was angry, but I had to calm down. I had to sleep. I finally fell asleep really late, long after all the other guys, exhausted from a very stressful day.

These do not at first glance appear to be the words of an OCD sufferer. But remember, this guy raped me when I was twelve. It was violent. At that time, he added Post Traumatic Stress Disorder and severe depression to my OCD cycle, making it all far worse than it was before.

Speaking of PTSD, doctors and researchers have found that roughly one third of the patients being treated for OCD who don't improve are also discovered to be suffering from PTSD as well. Sometimes the PTSD symptoms are so bad that they interfere with successfully treating the OCD symptoms. If this is true in your case, make sure your therapist is aware that you might be suffering from Post Traumatic Stress Disorder as well. You need to be treated for the PTSD before the OCD can be successfully dealt with.

Here's a great analogy. Let's say you need to change your car's oil, but you get a flat tire on the way to the garage. You'd better fix the flat first, because you're sure not going to get your oil changed on the side of the road! PTSD is the flat tire. OCD is the oil that needs changing. Oh, and while you're at it, clean the windshield, too…

My OCD kicked into action the second I laid eyes on Jeff (not his real name), acting as a trigger. It rescued me, shielding me from my PTSD and depression. It had been hard not to think about what happened to me for the last five years, and every time it came up, I would redouble my efforts to bury the memories by retreating deeper into my OCD cycle. It was horrible, and it would continue for many more years.

When I encountered him this time, the mere sight of him brought back a flood of horrid memories, as if I had my eyes shut and was watching a movie on the back of my eyelids. For a few seconds I couldn't see. I could only hear, feel and remember all over again. I smelt fear. I knew I was in great danger. Sort of like being in a dark room, not being able to find the light switch, when suddenly, you get that very distinct feeling that someone is in the room with you. Yet you hear no sound. It makes the hair on the back of your neck shoot straight up! I felt the need once again to retreat deeply into the OCD cycle. Although I didn't know it was called OCD, I did know enough to recognize its old familiar confusion, and realize that if I was to stand a chance of doing well, I had to muster enough self-control to either ignore it or coexist with it. This time however, there was a very big difference in what I was feeling. It was called anger, something I didn't feel the first time around. I was angry. Anger can be a very powerful motivator to protect yourself at all costs. The fact my body was completely filled with my own newly produced supply of adolescent testosterone helped in getting me through it. I knew I had strength. I was tall, and angry enough to confront King Kong if that is what it was going to take for me to survive. Keep in mind that all of this I have described happened within a few blinks of an eye. This flood of rage hit me all at once and it stunned me for a few seconds.

The more I look back at it, the more I feel this represents the first time I actually had my OCD under some degree of control. Without a clue as to what OCD was, without any medication, I knew it was essential to control myself and not the other way around. Unless you have OCD, you'll never quite understand how difficult this can be.

The rational part of my mind wanted to win the competition, and get even with the S.O.B if possible. Then as now, using the rational part of my mind to set goals for myself kept me ahead of the cycle. It wasn't easy, but somehow I managed. Barely.

I knew that the minute I lost sight of my goal to win the competition, fear would take over and OCD would jump back in my mind and become master to the slave. As we know now, OCD is not curable, but it is treatable, if the OCD'er learns how to live with it and control it. You can control it. In essence, I was doing the right kind of therapy on myself back then, without really knowing it. Of course, it would have been so much less painful and easier if I'd known what OCD was and had the proper therapy and medication.

I use the same sort of mental discipline today, but thanks to therapy and the aforementioned medications, it is much easier to coexist with OCD. Jeff (not his real name), didn't try anything until the second night. Asleep in my bottom bunk, no longer on guard and having ignored him all day, I began to feel strange. Was I dreaming? I woke up in the dark. He was in my bed! I shoved him violently away. I jumped up, swinging and yelling at the top of my lungs, still in the dark. I found the door and ran into the hallway. I was pissed. I was filled with adrenaline and dared him to come one step farther into the hall. The hall instantly filled with people from every room. "Steven? What's wrong? What happened?" they all asked. Noticing the fear and anger on my face, the other counselors ushered all the campers back into their rooms.

Jeff began to laugh it off. He started his verbal tap dancing, doing the side step shuffle. "Hey, C'mon man…it was just a joke! I was trying to scare him," he said. "A JOKE?"

"YOU WERE IN MY BED YOU FRICKING PERVERTED CREEP!"

As unbelievable as it may seem, they believed him. They settled me down. I returned to the room and lay down. I noticed the looks on the faces of the other guys. It wasn't a game. They knew something. Jeff was called out of the room. We campers began to talk. They all asked what happened and I told them. I saw two of the guys begin not to look so good, but they said nothing in response. One of the five other guys said, "I have heard he's gay."

"GAY?" I responded, full of rage. "He's not gay. I assure you all, he is a monster with a charming smile, looking for his next victim." I had gay friends by this time. Some had attended my high school. I had met gay people doing shows all over the East Coast.

Show business is filled with some of the most wonderfully colorful and talented personalities I have ever met. There is a very big difference between being gay and the irresponsible idiots (who happen to be gay) who choose to live their lives wrapped in the public drama we all hear about and see in the headlines. Respectable people who are homosexual are not like that. They are your friends, neighbors, coworkers and (Yes, Mother) even attend your church. They are normal, everyday people living their lives and making a living like everyone else in society. Nine times out of ten, you'll never know and shouldn't care about their private lives. I grew to like the later group, and they have never so much as looked at me the wrong way. They are great people, productive members of our world and highly creative, who have taught me much about the real world we live in. They have sometimes helped me in my career. Hollywood and New York would come to a full stop if they all suddenly disappeared, as Jerry Falwell wishes every day of his hypocritical life. My definition of a hypocrite is somebody who sets a good example only when there is an audience around. Actually, I shouldn't give him such a hard time. Jerry has been on TV for years preaching that there is great comfort in religion, and he proves it, too, every time he drives up to his multi-million dollar

Lynchburg home in his limo! Makes me wanna start a church. Anyway...

Jeff was not like the other gay people I know. He was sick, mentally ill, and no different from any other molester. The sex of his victim was irrelevant. These kinds of sick people are completely different. Something I didn't even have a name for. Out of respect for my friends, I wouldn't allow the campers to label him gay.

Suddenly, he walked in the room. Everyone got quiet. The light went out. They all drifted to sleep. Except for me. I was not closing my eyes for a second during the rest of the night.

At seven the next morning I was up. I took my toothbrush and shaving kit into the dorm shower. It was one of those big, open-tiled jobs with no individual stalls, just multiple shower-heads on the walls. No privacy at all. This bothered me at first. After the previous night, it really creeped me out. Still, it was the only place to take a shower, and I wanted to wash every last trace of that pervert from my skin. If only I could have washed him from my mind.

In high school physical education class, I hadn't used the showers next to the locker room. We had the option of taking our showers at home because it was the final class of the day. Since I never felt comfortable in a communal setting, I took advantage of the home shower choice.

I took a deep breath, told myself to do it. Other guys were in there, and they were not self-conscious, they were taking showers. No more, no less. So here I went. I dropped my towel, and I began to feel guilty again. I didn't know why. I laid my toothbrush and toiletries on one of the shelves, and put my towel on a hook. One of the guys in the shower looked older than everyone else. He must have been a counselor. Wait a minute. I knew him. I read his columns every month in the magazines! It took me a minute, but I realize d I was next to another famous magician. He was a pretty high profile comedy magician from the West Coast. He was a member of the famed Magic Castle in Hollywood! He recognized me. "Hey, are you the young man from Virginia who wrote that article?" Wow! I couldn't believe it. HE knew who I was! He said, "I was very impressed with your article, and I heard you were coming. It's nice to meet you." All the other kids looked impressed. Tom (not his real name) knew who I was. It was a moment of glory, but it was short lived.

"How did you know that I was coming, Tom?" Another kid asking about one of his routines interrupted him. As he talked to the kid behind me, he had his head under the shower, washing his hair. Suddenly, I got the impression that he didn't think I had two eyes because the only portion of my body he was making eye contact with was below my waist.

Okay, enough of this crap, I thought. I'm out of here. I rinsed off, grabbed my towel and began to split. When for some reason, I stopped, turned around and said, "Tom? How did you know that I was coming?" He smiled, turning off the hot shower. "My good friend Jeff told me!" I turned and left the room.

I decided it was all too much for me to handle all over again. I had come to the camp for one reason and one reason only. To win! To go home with the gold or whatever they were handing out for the top spot. I had to refocus and make up for the lost time. I decided to go and watch some of the other acts rehearse. I dried off and changed. Heading to my room, I was back on track, refocusing my mind to accomplish the mission at hand. I watched some acts, rehearsed a little bit and talked with some really cool, normal folks. An hour or so later, when I went back to my room I realized that I had left my toothbrush and shaving kit on the sink in the shower. I returned to get them only to find that Tom (not his real name) was still in the shower. Still checking out all the junior magicians who had awakened late and went to get clean. It took a lot of self-restraint to prevent me from doing physical violence to him. I had another idea. I was going to talk to my new friends and find out what they had heard about Tom (not his real name). Was he the same as Jeff (not his real name)? Was I making all of this up in my head? Maybe he wasn't looking at me funny. I didn't know anymore. I knew one thing for sure. I was going to ask my roommates to come clean, even if it meant telling them about the day I met Jeff. One by one I talked to them all, and they each had a lot to say. Especially this one guy named David.

  The camp and competition was a week-long event. As I made my inquiries, I heard the disturbing rumors. "David is the one to talk to," they would say. "He knows everything." It turns out that David had been molested the year before. Not by one, but by both Tom and Jeff at different times. One attack happened at the camp, the other at a convention. He reluctantly told me his tale. He didn't really have to. It was a story I knew all too well, and I told him so.

  We talked for hours about our new common denominator. It bonded us and we instantly became the best of friends. I wasn't going to let anything happen to him this year, and we agreed to watch each other closely.

Every day I would turn a corner and there Jeff and Tom would be. I ran into them all the time, (Thank goodness I don't walk backwards.) and they were always chummy with me. Where was Lorena Bobbit when you really needed her?

I talked with a lot of guys and found out these two were out of control. There was an entire list of kids who had been inducted to the fan club. I discovered that these same kids had a list of other men in magic they knew of and avoided at all costs, one of which would go to jail in later years for molesting a child in the kid's own home with his parents in the next room. Guess what? He's now out and free as can be. Still doing children's birthday parties. Isn't our legal system great?

I was in shock. I couldn't believe this information was so widely known and accepted. I also found out that Jeff had been sent home from the camp in prior years for mysterious reasons. There was no mystery here. We knew. What I didn't expect to find out was that the owner of the Camp knew about these two. He had personal conversations with at least one of them concerning such matters. Why were they allowed to come back to a wonderful educational institution like this camp? With the exception of these two, it was a brilliant organization that inspired and taught future great entertainers who would carry on the traditions of our historic art. There was nothing wrong with the camp! I loved every second of it, except for the moments I stood in the same room with either one of the two magical molesters.

It took some time, but I finally got a real answer to my question. "Why are they still here?" The reason, sadly, was money.

The simple fact that they were going to be at the camp pulled in enough new kids every year to justify the risk, I was told. People admired these two along with all the other stars of magic who would pop in and out of the camp during the week. These two were advertised as special guests along with other well-known magicians and were guaranteed to be present.

However, it was a crap-shoot as to who else would show up. People like Harry Blackstone Jr., David Copperfield, Doug Henning and so many more of the true professionals would come and share all they had to give with everyone there. You never knew who would show up unannounced. It was a chance to mingle, talk with and get close to the real leaders of our craft. For most, it would be the only chance.

You had to learn all you could from the masters because in the blink of an eye, they would be gone, back to work, entertaining the masses, living the lives we all dreamed of leading someday. It was a true honor for me to get tips on my floating light bulb from the great Harry Blackstone Jr. He remembered me from a show I had attended a few years earlier and was more then happy to sit down and talk with me and share his vast experience. Why couldn't the magical molesters have been as wonderful as Blackstone or Copperfield? David spent hours on end talking with me on several different occasions whenever I would see him. He personally answered the many letters I sent to him over the years. Doug Henning invited me into his private trailer and offered me a sandwich while his crew set the show one time. Never had I met more wonderful and special people to admire. They used their fame and power in the right ways. They were happy to see someone serious and passionate about the art of magic.

What made Jeff and Tom go the other way? It baffled me. It still does.

I finally decided that somebody had to do something. I remembered seeing a program on TV about a serial killer, New York's famous "Son of Sam", and how he kept getting away with his crimes again and again. To me, this sicko Jeff was no different. I strongly believed that the list of victims would grow longer if I didn't stand up and do something about it. I thought about my father pulling Uncle Guy from that crashed plane and what would have happened had he kept going. So I was convinced. I could make a difference. I went to the camp's owner directly and had a chat. Dennis and Terry didn't own the camp, they just ran it.

I told them all what was happening and what I would do if Jeff, the magical molester (now THAT'S his real name!) hung around one day longer.

Thankfully, they believed me. I found out that others had complained before. The next morning, Jeff was gone.

I went on to win. Not just first place out of all who entered and then against the ten finalists, but the judges gave me a very special award. This award wasn't given out every year. You could win first place, which proved you were the best of the competition that year, but you might not impress the judges enough to win the Creativity Award, a really coveted prize. A big Golden Cup given for inventive and creative risks successfully taken in one's act. It was one of the most memorable moments in my life. I was proud despite the fact that Tom, the-endless-shower-man was a judge. This shocking fact I learned after I had won and they put a spotlight on the judges.

The camp was finally over and soon I was back on a plane heading home. I had shows to do. As I looked out of the window cruising so high above the world, I felt proud. Mostly because I survived all the stress and pulled myself together, visualizing my power performance over and over long enough to sweep the top shelf of awards. It was good enough for me. I could return to Virginia a real winner! Proud and tall I would stand, for a few weeks anyway. I was most proud of the fact that I was able to gain such a degree of control over myself to investigate, ask questions of the other guys about the "magical molesters", and then go to the owner myself and spill my guts. I am thankful he had the integrity and courage to do what he did as well. He had not a second thought either. He did the right thing.

Dennis and Terri continue to help young, up-and-coming performers. They are great teachers. I still talk to them every once in a blue moon. They are both dear to my heart and always will be.

Now, I know full well that the magic community will give me tons of flack over this chapter. I will be the punch line of every joke at the conventions, and that's okay with me. After what I have been through, there isn't anything they could really say that would offend me now anyway. They will say this chapter portrays all magicians as child molesters. They are not. I give my readers more credit than that, anyway. There are always a couple of people in any profession who will mess it up for everybody else. You know who you are, and so do I. These few are ours. You should have no fear of hiring a good magician for your children's birthday party or any other event. My advice is to talk to other families or event coordinators that he or she has performed for and get a reference. If the performer is really good, you'll know it. Parents will tell you the truth.

Had I surrendered to the comfort of the OCD cycle during the competition, I would have been buried so deep in confusion that I probably could not have won. Worst of all, those two creeps would have still been at the camp to work their putrid perversions on the innocent.

As it was, though, once the competition was over, the need for such self-control was not nearly as strong any more, and OCD would rear its ugly self in my mind over and over again. After all, I had to return to the farmhouse, cows and Nancy.

My act? The Floating Light Bulb, of course. I have never done a show since without it. Ask my good friend Vinny D'Jew (as he is lovingly known) in Las Vegas. He keeps track of such things.

I never went back to another competition. I had proven to myself that I was good enough, at least among my peers, but I knew that magicians weren't going to be paying my bills.

I left that day with the knowledge that the only people who truly mattered were sitting in my audience. I guess that's why I never made it on the cover of any of the magazines I used to faithfully read every month. I doubt they know that I exist.

My new focus from this point on was not to become the most famous magician in the world. That was too narrow-minded for me. I was aspiring to become one of the greatest entertainers in the world. To me, it made more sense. I lost sight of other magicians and magic conventions for a number of years.

Him Again

Is there any doubt why?

I became a huge admirer of people like Sammy Davis Jr., Liza, Jerry Lewis, Marty Allan, Lucile Ball, Danny Kay, Milton Berle, Johnny Carson, Don "Bullet Head" Rickels, Waylon Flowers and Madam, The Osmonds, Bill Cosby, Tim Conway, Red Skelton, Chevy Chase, Eddie Murphy, Liberace, Tom Jones, Charlie Chaplin, Robin Williams, David Letterman, The Three Stooges, The Great Carole Burnett, Benny Hill, Mary Tyler Moore, Goldie Hahn, Leslie Nelson, Tina Turner, Edgar Bergen, Tony Orlando, Sonny and Cher, Miss Piggy, Crazy Phyllis Diller, Red Foxx, Harvey Cormen, Dick Van Dyke, Wayne Newton, Lilly Thomlin, Merv Griffin, The Jacksons, Rip Taylor, the completely innocent Pee Wee Herman, Jerry Falwell and many more on my World's Greatest Showmen and Women list. If you don't recognize any of these names, you owe it too yourself to discover their genius. They brilliantly entertain, above and beyond all else.

They knew how to make us scream with laughter, fall in love with a song. *What* they did was unimportant to me. *How* they did it, was what I studied.

Whether it was Marty with that crazy "Hello Dere!" hair, cracking people up with his amazing wit on Hollywood Squares, Rip with the never-ending stream of confetti, Tom Jones with his throbbing leather-clad hips, or Jerry Falwell on CNN's Larry King spewing forth his "I'm so righteous" routine. They all did the very same thing extremely well. They put on one heck of a show. Every one of them gave the audience much more then they came for. Each one of them is a unique master in how he did it, but each left the audience wanting more. Which in turn, is the reason they became the show business legends they are today.

I had finally put my finger on what I wanted to be. After all those years of rehearsing my sleight of hand, my act, developing my show, I had finally found what it was I truly wanted to be. Magic was the excuse to be up there on the stage. I wanted to entertain and become one of the great showmen of my time. I loved nothing more then to make people laugh. It came naturally to me. Comedy was my thing. I was good at it.

I wanted to learn all I could from the very best in the business. I never dreamed that I would end up working with several of the people on my list in future years. Others I got the honor of actually meeting and getting to know. A couple of them I knew quite well.

I will never forget bumping into Sammy Davis Jr. in a grocery store at three a.m. on a warm Vegas morning. He was buying coffee as I recall, and we talked for more then an hour. He invited me to see him at the Sands Casino and eventually would spend several more hours with me in his dressing room backstage after the show. There will never be another like him. I'm honored to have known him for the short time I did.

CHAPTER SEVEN
Viva Las Vegas!

I finally graduated from Randolph Henry High School.

Actually, now that I think about it, I think I graduated only because all the teachers got together and decided that they couldn't possibly endure another year with me. It's kind of like price fixing, only with grades. Hey, isn't that illegal? Well, I guess they figured it was worth the risk.

It would be the first time and the last, that I ever saw my divorced mom and dad together in the same place. Mom didn't want to talk to my dad. I think she was afraid of the step-monster, and with good reason. My father told me that he would have no problem talking to Mom if she came up to him. So, I tried hard, even then, to get them to talk to each other. I guess I saw it as my last and final hope.

With my new diploma in hand, I thought not a second about going to college. I knew my future would begin very soon as a professional magician, as if it hadn't already. The World Capital of Magic is without question, Las Vegas, Nevada, having more magic shows per street corner today, than any other place on earth.

So, Las Vegas it was! That's where I had to be although I had never been there. In the meantime, summer found me driving all over the place again, performing more gigs than before.

International performances, even. My reputation in the magic community was better than ever, thanks to my unquestionable victory at the junior competition. I met lots of great magicians who had either been to Vegas and/or had played there. They all told me about what I should expect, but as time would tell, they left out a few details. Major details.

Isn't it funny, when you finally make a clear decision and truly commit yourself to achieving something in your life, how things seem to suddenly appear? A door opens, you meet people who can help you find your way, someone knows somebody else who shows you a book you "have to read" and it gives you an idea that makes the difference! The ways and means to achieve your goal open up and reveal themselves to you unexpectedly and with the greatest of ease if you are open to receiving them.

There is a very old saying that says, "When the student is ready, the teacher will appear." Just like magic. Well, not really. There are some very strict principles behind making this "Life Law" work for you. First, you have to relax and let life flow. I have found that the more you push the farther off course you get. You must learn to pursue your goals with detachment. By that I mean pursue them with the flexibility to change should you need to. That's very important.

Don't get too close personally to what you want to achieve. Put it in your mind and let your mind do all the subconscious work for you. You will be amazed. The true power in this is letting it all happen. Have you ever wondered why rich people seem to get richer by the day? Detachment is the answer why. Oscar Wilde once said, "The only people who think more about money than the rich are the poor." And he's right! The less you worry about it, the more will flow your way. The more desperate you become, the less likely you are to find what you need. It's the way life is and nothing will change it. Don't even try to resist life, because life will always win and that is a fact. Don't try to understand how these things in life actually work. Accept the fact that they do and let them work for you. So what does all of this mean to my story? Well, read on.

I met a very nice young lady named Debbie at one particular gig. We became very close and I began to call her Deb for short. We did everything together. She could make me laugh so hard at times. It was great fun. I never could have imagined what was going to happen next.

You see, Deb had a boyfriend I'll call Christopher, who owned a private twin engine Cessna 401 plane. In fact, Deb was one of the first female professional pilots for a major airline herself. They were a perfect match. Well, sort of. Okay, not really. Anyhow, Christopher needed to do a cross-country flight to build time, and he invited me to join them on a weekend flight to Las Vegas! "Oh…. Twist my arm. Okay, I'll go!" Who would have known?

In the blink of an eye, off we went into the western sky, flying through the night and resting during the day at small airports and towns along the way.

A day later, late at night, we're deep into Nevada airspace, on final approach for McCarran Airport. There is no better way to see Vegas for the very first time than from the air at night. I was completely and utterly enchanted, totally Vegasized!

That night we hit the strip and walked all over this amazing twenty-four-hour town. At three am, as many people were on the street as at three o'clock in the afternoon. You could feel the electricity in the air. It was truly amazing. I couldn't get enough. Although I was completely exhausted when I got out of the plane, now I had more energy then ever before in my life. This was it! I was right and I knew I was. This was the town where I belonged! No question about it. I was Vegas bound as soon as I got home. This clear decision was made less than two hours after I arrived for the first time. The casinos were the most magical, captivating buildings I had ever seen in my life! I couldn't believe a place this wonderful really existed! No cows! Not a single one, except for the plastic cow on the roof of the Holy Cow Casino, and the ones standing in line at the buffets. (And that's no bull!).

Every where I went there was magic all around in every form in every way. I was beyond words. I didn't want to go back to the Cheesy Motel where we were staying. We stopped by a McDonalds on the strip heading to our room. Even the golden arch had more lights then you could count. I'd never seen a McDonalds like this before. They sure didn't look like this where I came from. I was in a dreamland, like something out of a movie. I had seen Vegas on TV, and in the movies and magazines, but I could never have imagined this! I found it funny that in every casino we visited I always overheard someone telling somebody else to "Give me the money I told you not to give me." Strange, but true. From that second on, there wasn't a doubt in my mind. This was my home. Truly where I belonged.

We went to see some shows. I got to see Master Showmen Siegfried and Roy for the very first time. I saw Lance Burton at the Tropicana doing the awesome act he won the gold metal for at the IBM convention where I met Jeff (not his real name).

Christopher knew lots of people in Vegas, and they got us tickets. I saw the legend himself, Mr. Frank Sinatra, Ol' Blue Eyes. We even went to see the "Lido de' Paris" at the world famous Stardust Hotel. It was there at dinner, that Christopher introduced Deb and I to the President of the Stardust Hotel, Mr. Burton Brown, a great and very powerful man who would become my personal mentor and closest friend in later years.

Burton had lots of connections all over town like any casino president would. He got us more tickets to watch some of the most amazing shows I had ever seen. It was four of the greatest days of my life, another one of those magical moments I will never forget. The last day we were in town, I got to meet the great ventriloquist, Sherrie Lewis. She had Lamb Chop in her purse. Could it have been more exciting? I didn't think so.

On our flight back, I thought about honing my craft, and figured I'd be ready for the Vegas big time within the next five, maybe six, years. It kept my mind off the size of the Cessna 401 we were in, that I loving called a human mailing tube with not quite as much legroom as the 747's I was used to flying on by any means. Talk about a no-frill airline. Before we took off, I heard Deb tell me to fasten my Velcro!

As I finally stepped out after we landed, and unkinked my crumpled appendages, I asked Christopher if the plane was made in Italy. He asked me why. "Oh nothing," I said as I walked under, swearing that I saw hair under the wings. I smiled, grabbed my things and said good bye. I had a Vegas career to work on!

"WELCOME HOME, SON!" My father greeted me on

the front porch.

"Hello, Dad! Nice to be back" I said as I hugged him tightly.

Suddenly Nancy walked out the door. Un-welcome home.

"Can I really last another five years on this farm?" I thought to myself.

In October, 1988, I was twenty years old. Maybe my Vegas timetable could be moved up a bit. I had finished one of the most successful performing years of my life. Then, too, Nancy wanted me to leave the nest, a fact she made known every day for an entire year although I was hardly there any more. She also let me know in another way, a more subtle way. You see, she came after me with a butcher knife, screaming like a banshee in heat. This time, my father had been at the store picking up a few items for dinner. He drove up in the drive and pulled up around the back of the house. She was screaming so loudly that neither one of us noticed. Dad stood on the back porch and listened. After a while the door swung open. In walked my father, and he's mad as hell! He told Nancy to shut up, words my father had never uttered before. So she did. She sat down and dropped the knife.

For the very first time, my father believed me. "Steven, son, I am so sorry that I did not believe you. I have never seen this side of her and I could never have imagined it was true. Maybe I didn't want to believe it. Whatever... I didn't mean to hurt you like this." I was crying. My father was in shock. The only thing he could say to Nancy was, "Get out of my sight right this very minute. I will deal with you later!" He embraced me and wanted to go outside for a walk to the barn. I read a lot from the expression on his face.

As the fear and anxiety of living with a crazy stepmother put my OCD cycle in high gear, so did my anger at myself for knowing that I wasn't really doing anything to make the situation any better between us. In my brain it was, "She hates you. Bury the feeling. Focus on magic. She still hates you. Tell Dad. He doesn't believe you. Focus on magic. She hates you even more." Repeat. It was a horrible mental recording that played over and over and I couldn't stop it, until I learned how. When my father heard Nancy screaming at me using every four-letter word she knew, and some she created herself, he finally knew the truth. It did not break the anxiety part of my OCD cycle. My knowing that Dad finally understood his wife was a wacko relieved me in the sense that I felt vindicated. My OCD replaced one anxiety with another. Instead of worrying that Nancy was trying to hurt me, I worried that she might be upset and embarrassed because she got caught. Because my dad knew she was crazy, she might try to harm him.

It was a very painful time for me internally, and I didn't have the skills to cope with all of the stress. I fell apart. I was never angry with Dad for not believing me earlier. I knew he didn't know that side of her. I always wondered what Nancy's true purpose in life was. I guess she was what happened when you never really get back on the right path. She certainly resisted life at every turn and she reaped the rewards of that choice, too. Have you ever noticed that an internally angry and unhappy person can suffer in silence louder than anybody else in the world? It's true. When Nancy was angry or unhappy, I was the one who would always know about it first. I remember my father calling

Nancy his greatest treasure one night at the dinner table. To which I mumbled, "Yeah, and she's worth her weight in plastic, too!" It added fuel to the fire. I had to get back at her if only through humor, which pretty much kept me alive most of the time. So it ended up taking physical danger to make me move my butt out of the house when I knew all along I should have done it sooner. I didn't listen to my heart.

My father wasn't a very emotional person. He never raised his voice, never said a bad word, never really spoke unless he had something important to say. Never hugged or kissed me either. "That isn't very manly," he used to say. If I wanted those things, I always had to go get them from him. This day, my father hugged me. It sent a very clear message to the High Empress of Insanity herself. She went to her room to pout. She had been caught, and she knew she had no way out this time.

The woman my father loved wanted to kill the son he loved. He would leave her if he could, but he couldn't. Regardless of what had happened between Nancy and me, she always took great care of my father. That I will admit on her behalf. I guess that my father's age and his ever-failing heart condition prevented his leaving. He needed her. She was his only caregiver. On our walk down to the barn for firewood, my father talked to me like he never had before. He told me how much he really loved me and how proud he was that I never got into all the trouble Nancy's son had.

I had never been arrested, never smoked, never drank a drop of alcohol, never gotten anyone pregnant and had never used drugs. He told me that out of all his children, I was the one he feared for most, but I had proven him wrong. He told me that he never dreamed that my magic would have taken me to so many places, and so far in life. He loved it, and encouraged me to continue what I truly loved because "as long as you are doing what you love, and you're happy doing it, not only are you ahead of most of the people in this world, but you're going to live a more productive life. Don't worry about the money, son. If you are good at whatever you do, the money will come. Just focus on being the very best." Dad had never before in my entire life uttered such great words of wisdom to me. I was in complete shock because I had spent my life trying to win my father's approval, always feeling as if I was missing the mark. All the while he felt I had surpassed it years ago. I didn't have a clue. It was as if someone had lifted the proverbial ton of bricks off my back.

"But son, I don't think it's wise for you to stay here any longer. You two are like oil and water and will never get along no matter what. I love you with all my heart, but you should think about leaving home." For my own good, I was being kicked out of the nest.

Actually, I knew I should have gone much sooner, but I was too busy to be bothered with it. The time had come, and I knew that Dad was right. So I spent a few hours making phone calls to my friends before gathering my things. I told Dad I loved him and he told me to keep in touch as I got in my car.

I never looked back as I drove down the half-mile long driveway. It was as if all the animals on the farm knew something was wrong. Animals have a way of sensing these things. They had all gathered along the fences that lined the driveway, as if to wish an old friend goodbye. It was one of the saddest days of my life and I never could quite figure out why.

God bless Reverend Don Simmon and his family at the Keysville Baptist Church, where I occasionally attended the youth group. Keysville was not too far from Phenix.

I called and told him what had happened. He invited me into his home for a few weeks until I was able to sort out what had happened and where I was going to go. He was an amazing man. A very young pastor, I might add. He was hip and was exactly what I needed to help me through the rain. Here again, the teacher had appeared, when the student was ready. I would talk to him for hours on end, days upon days, and he listened, sometimes jumping in with the proper wisdom needed at the time. He understood me.

He was the first person I think I had met that really did. He didn't judge. He didn't shove religion down my throat either. He really helped me. Most importantly, he told me that what I did with my life was my calling. He explained to me how I could help people with my magic, how I could really make a difference in the lives of all who came to watch. I had never thought about using my magic as a way to heal, but it made perfect sense to me. "Laughter and the art of magic takes people away from their daily burdens if only for a moment, and that is a form of healing," he went on to explain. His profound words shook me to the very core of my being. I wasn't here to exist or to make money. I was here to share my gift, to heal, to inspire. It was like the beginning of a new chapter in my life. I felt as if someone had finally turned the page. A thought I had never had before, when I thought I had had them all! I really learned something that day. It was another lesson life had to teach me, the principle that everything truly happens for a very good reason.

We, as humans, all wrapped up in the drama of our own lives, can't see it at the time. We don't need to. We need to know that there is a higher force at work with a plan and it's presenting a positive opportunity, sitting there waiting for us to discover. The choice is ours. We don't need to understand why or how. Just believe. "Seek and ye shall find," as the saying goes. We are, however, able to look back a year later and understand with perfect vision the course of unfolding events and why they unfolded the way they did. The universe sends us signals every day. Most of us are too busy to see them, to feel them or to simply listen. When we don't listen, life begins throwing us more difficult life experiences to endure. If we continue to refuse to listen, it throws us a catastrophe.

Isn't it perfect universal order how sometime it takes a stroke, a heart attack or a psychotic step-monster with a knife, to finally make people change their lives? Sad, but it's a fact. Reverend Don as I called him, taught me a lot, not only about myself, but also about my life and my magic. He encouraged me to continue doing what I loved to do and told me that if I would only learn to listen to my heart and never distrust what it said, I would always continue to follow the right path and discover all the rewards that come with it.

My sister Robin had her hands full, to say the least. She had remarried for the second time to a wonderful man named Charlie. From her first marriage to Mike, Robin had two beautiful children who needed a little special care. Jennifer was born first, a quick-witted very intelligent girl. She is the happiest person I have ever met, despite the fact that she has Multiple Sclerosis or "MS" and is wheelchair-bound.

Next came Jill, right in the middle of my birthday party, too. The phone rang and suddenly my mother screamed, "Party's over, kids!" and we whizzed off to the hospital. I didn't get to take off my birthday hat or open any of my presents! Not only do we share the same birthday, but also we seemed to develop our own language from the start. Jill is mentally challenged. Both of my nieces are beautiful angels that my family adores. Did I mention that Robin has lupus? As if she didn't already have enough on her plate, one day, out of nowhere, Charlie suddenly died of a massive heart attack while walking the dog, leaving Robin and the kids in shock and alone. So I couldn't possibly call her for help. She has never complained a single day in her life. She trusts that if this is the hand life dealt her, it is for a good reason, and she is going to play the ball where it lies. My older --much older-- sister, Robin, has been a constant source of inspiration all my life. I don't know how she manages so gracefully.

So I looked for other options. Remember my other sister, Shelia? You know, the one who came home and sort of interrupted things in advanced labor back in 1977? Well, she and Eddie got married. My mother made sure of that one. Brandy was ten years old and a striking young lady she was, too. I gave her and the cat, nothing but pure hell, though.

I chased them both from one end of the house to the other, terrorizing her at every opportune moment with pure joy! Nothing made me more crazy, than to fight with her beloved kitty cat named Miss Kal-Kal. The very sight of me brought a streak of fear in to Miss Kal-Kal, the likes of which no other cat had ever experienced. I have never seen a cat disappear the way that one did! What appeared to be a puff of smoke always became a pile of hair on the floor. She was gone! I nearly drove her insane, and used up at least seven of her lives in the process. Shelia and Eddie had just moved into a town house not far from where we all grew up in Portsmouth. I was dying to get out of the cow pastures and called Shelia with my woes.

It was good to spend some time with my sister. Well, good for me, anyway. A free place to stay and all the food she could keep in the refrigerator. I arrived back in Portsmouth in time for Christmas. Home for the holidays. Shelia worked at a local TV station and Eddie worked for... well, he worked for someone, I'm sure. I was so happy to be home I couldn't control myself. I was close to Mom and could visit her whenever I wanted. That really made me happy. She was out of the hospital, doing very well on her own. She had a good job and looked really good as well. I was happy for her. I felt relieved that finally she was going to be okay. Now if only I could have found her a boyfriend...

Christmas came and went. New Year, too. Soon I felt there had to be something else out there for me. I grew tired of doing the same old corporate events, parties and the usual shows I had been doing my entire life. It was time to change. Not just my act, but everything. I knew the time had finally come. The powerful urge down deep in my stomach that both scared me and made me happy as a hog in S***!

I was Vegas bound, baby! Outta here! Gone! See ya! But how? My tank wouldn't make it across the country. Hmmm... I knew. I had this friend in Atlantic City who had told me once he wouldn't mind moving away from the city. I called him.

It was a short conversation. Joey jumped at the chance to move to Vegas. He was a successful magician in his own right, having come from a well-known magic family, the Festas from Absecon, New Jersey. They were known all around to anyone who knew anything about magic. A really fun family, too. Some of the most giving folks I ever met. I first met them all back at the Omni Hotel at the infamous IBM Convention in Norfolk all those years ago. Joey and his sister were a performing team. They had won the Junior Competition that year. I was jealous of them then, but they never knew it. I helped backstage during the competition and became great friends with them all. I really liked them and was impressed with the act Joey and his sister did as well. We kept in touch through the years by phone and writing letters. No one had ever heard of e-mail back in those days. It was a perfect plan.

Let me tell you about Joey Festa. He was a real character to say the least. He was very Italian and all that goes with that. He had girls on top of girls wherever he went. Well, you know what I mean. A practical joker at times, too. I remember once he tried to get rid of me by telling me he had killed a guy and was going to prison for a very long time, and that he wouldn't be around anymore. Of course, I didn't believe him, but I let him believe that I did for a little while. Back in those days I could be a little too much for some people at times. Okay! So it was a lot to most all of the time! There! Are you happy?

I knew Joey, and I knew he couldn't hurt a fly. (There is a zipper joke in there somewhere, but I am going to leave that one alone!) Over the years and through my career traveling all over the world, the Festas came to my aid several times when I couldn't or didn't know how to bail myself out of the mess I was in. They were wonderful people. If you should look them up and give them a call, tell them I said hello.

Now, the logistics. Since my tank sucked up gas like Don Ho used to suck up mai tais, we decided to go in Joey's little Nissan Maxima. He kept it in perfect condition and would kill you for getting in the car without banging your shoes on the sidewalk first. There were only two things that Joey liked more than magic, dating girls and his clean car's stereo!

It was really loud. He liked rap music, too, and I didn't. It was logistically shaping up to be a very long trip. The Nissan was the only real choice. When I first thought about taking my car, I had visions of various pieces of metal falling out of the oil pan along the road until there was finally nothing left but a steering wheel, two seats, four wheels, twenty circling vultures, a turkey buzzard, a couple of Gila monsters and one grumpy rattlesnake in the middle of the desert circling our soon-to-be-dried out bodies. It didn't make a pretty picture so I decided to go with Joey and his spotless car although the road trip bookies in Vegas would have given the odds-on favorite to make it all the way without crappin' out on us to the Nissan. It was a no-brainer.

The real challenge was going to be fitting two illusionists into that car along with all the stuff that went with that sort of profession. It would take a lot more than magic to make this happen, for sure. Somehow, the planets aligned right and we got most of what we felt we had to have in and on that car any way we could. I don't think anyone had mentioned to us that Las Vegas was much more then two thousand miles away. It didn't matter. I had sold the great green tank and we were heading to Vegas, baby, and placing our bets on ultimate success! Move over, Siegfried and Roy. We were Vegas bound and Vegas had never seen the likes of us before! Or so we thought.

I couldn't drive a stick shift, which meant that poor Joey would be doing the driving the whole way. As if he would allow anyone else to drive his precious machine anyway. We slept in the cheapest of cheap motels, only when we had to. Joey drove for thirteen to fifteen hours sometimes, breaking every speed limit in every state along the way, because we wanted to hit Vegas as soon as we could. Three days on the road and we were nearly there. The car sounded funny to Joey so we pulled into a truck stop just outside of Phoenix, Arizona. (The one with the O.) It was freezing cold, and believe it or not, it was actually snowing! "Doesn't happen that often," the locals told us. We didn't believe them.

As the mechanic figured out how to drain even more money out of a couple of east coast rubes, Joey and I found a hill and looked out over the city lights in the snow. It was really quite charming.

Before we knew it, the car was ready and so was the big fat bill to boot. Who cared? We were on our way to Las Vegas and we were going to be rich and famous soon anyway? Right?

You can see it coming can't you? Now, don't get ahead of me!

Having been in a car for nearly seventy-two hours, we stank. I mean it was armpit city in that little car. We finally merged onto Interstate 15. It was nighttime, but we finally came over that last hill and saw the Vegas lights! A true Kodak moment. There it was, the show business Holy Grail. We were utterly exhausted, emotionally numb. This glitter might as well have been New Jerusalem after the Second Coming. It was here we would be received, accepted, and anointed. This we knew. We pulled into the very first place we saw that looked affordable, a Motel Six. Yes, they left the light on for us. Our fortunes would have to wait until the dawning of the new day. We got our room with double beds and a nice view of a trash dumpster and went to sleep. We were young, smart, talented, and completely clueless about the reality that lay ahead.

The innocence of one's youth is actually a good defense system we are born with to protect us. If we really knew what laid in wait for us, we would never leave the house. It's a fact. Innocence shields you from becoming too despondent at the very start and helps you to believe in your dream while the demons are busy gobbling up your castles in the sky through your wallet, usually. That innocence serves a very important function in our lives. It allows us to experience and explore life with wild abandon, and that is, in part, what makes life so very interesting.

The new day came all too quickly. We didn't crawl out of bed until about four p.m. that day. We got up and went looking for food and some permanent digs. We found a low rent apartment complex a few blocks off the strip on Flamingo Road called the Woodbridge Inn. We didn't see it as low rent, though. We were high on Vegas air.

Two beds in one room, a bathroom, a balcony, a kitchenette. We were in heaven! We were finally real grownups! We were the coolest beings on the whole planet! Our very own apartment in Las Vegas! It was too cool to be true!

Sin City! I'm talking a fantasy oasis in the middle of nowhere, full of dreams and a few nightmares. Fortunes were won and lost in a single hour here. The show business capital of the world was all mine for the taking. I was the new kid in town and there wasn't a doubt in my mind that in less than six months I would be signed to a major casino and become rich. It was the most exciting time of my young life. Everything was beginning, and it felt good to be alive. I truly felt like the king of the world, and it's good to be the king. I remember sitting with Joey in the hot tub out by the pool with a bunch of the other folks who lived there. We couldn't believe that it was real and that we had made it to the city of our dreams.

Self -help guru Tony Robbin's always says to think back to a point in your life when you felt truly empowered and learn to harness that energy to help you through the tough times. For me, this was that very moment he was talking about.

I still use this memory today as motivation whenever I need to feel strong.

Could I have been any more wrong? People, let me assure you that this is the undisputed reason that we can not see our own futures. Had I known the facts and fears that lay before the journey I so badly wanted to take, I would never have gone. There would be no life lessons for me to learn, no troubles to make me strong, no tears to teach me what I didn't know, and no adventures for me to discover. What a boring life it would have been. Stress and life-challenging situations make us better humans. A life without stress and struggle is not living, it's existing. Following one's inner urge to better one's own life will never lead you down the wrong path. It might allow you to detour down a road less traveled, but you'll always come out exactly where you are supposed to be.

I just realized something. Imagine for a moment that I didn't have OCD. This would have been the synopsis of the plot from "The Jazz Singer" and the parable of the prodigal son.

Remember that we continue to take the very same lessons in life until we learn from them and only then we are allowed to move on to the next one. It's all a part of the process down here. Those who "get it" seem to be lucky people. Everything always goes their way. And those who don't "get it" are dooming themselves to a life of hardship, resistance and misfortune around every corner they turn. I didn't get it.

The Vegas high we were on diminished in direct proportion to our lack of jobs and the dwindling of our funds. Reality began to assert itself over the next few weeks. We had lots of lessons heading our way. Joey was very fortunate in that he was not only a magician, but he had also been working real jobs whenever the magic biz slowed down. His experience got him hired by a window tinting company for his day job, while he dreamed of magic at night.

Me? Well, I didn't want a real job, number one. For number two, magic was the only thing I had ever done besides delivering balloons back home in my tank for my agent, Bobby McLamb, who owned a Balloon Company as well. I mean, surely I would be picked up immediately by all these Las Vegas bigwigs, right ? After all, I was the winner of the Junior Magic Competition! I did more corporate shows than any other act on the East Coast! I had trained and performed with seven hundred pound tigers, the big cats, including white tigers for many years !

For heaven's sake! Las Vegas had to dig me! I had video proof and a portfolio of spectacular pictures. I couldn't go wrong here. I was a real pro.

So why wasn't anybody calling? I had been pounding the pavement with my magic portfolio and videos all over town for a month. I interviewed with Siegfried and Roy until I saw the contract and learned that I couldn't work as a magician for the next ten years if I worked for them! I was using every trick in the book to get people to see me, too.

I had been trying to get into see one of the most important entertainment directors over at the old Dunes Hotel and Casino for a long time. He wouldn't take my calls, and I called every day. Finally, one day he picked up the phone and screamed, "What do you want, kid? I'm busy as hell!" I began to tell him all about me and he listened until I said the dirty word "magician". I explained to him that I had white tigers to which he exclaimed laughingly, "Well, make a tiger appear on my desk right now and then I will be impressed, kid. I gotta go. Sorry." Then he hung up. In less than a minute, he was gone.

So I called my freaky friend who actually owned a real tiger, and convinced him to do me a big favor. Any normal person would have realized the danger and stupidity of what I was asking of him and hung up on me.

But not this Vegas freak. He was a pot-smoking weirdo right out of the pages of some science fiction novel or, better yet, America's most wanted list, and he thought it was "way cool"! So we took his tiger down to the Dunes Hotel to make a house call of sorts. I had scoped the place out and there wasn't much security in the dying casino anyway. I knew exactly where the freight elevators were and up we went with a full-grown tiger partially hidden under a blanket. Believe it or not, no one noticed. Life is stranger than fiction sometimes and this was certainly one of them.

I marched right in to the executive's office, popped open his door and right in the middle of a meeting, pounced a huge adult tiger right on his desk. Papers went everywhere and a lamp crashed to the floor. I held out my hand and said, "Hi, I'm Steven. Your wish is my command." He was stunned and was unable to speak or move for a few seconds. His guests had all but vanished when they saw the cat. Finally the director of entertainment said, "Okay, you've made your point. I'll see you, but get that thing out of here before someone gets killed!" I told my friend he could leave, and he escorted his "kitty" back to the van he came in. I guess ex-con's are good for something.

Hotel Security suddenly appeared and were told that it was just a joke and everything was fine. "How the hell did you get that cat up here past security?" To which I replied, "Well, I am good at what I do, and if you put me in your show, I'll tell you!" He smiled, and I knew I had him! He liked me and it worked!

The story became a local legend, but I wasn't as clever as I thought I had been. I didn't get the job. He liked my videos, not to mention the fact that I could put white tigers into his casino. Which would cause quite the scandal, being that S&R was a few casinos down and famous for being the only ones with white tigers! He liked that idea. He thought it could be the ticket to pack that house every night, but there was a little detail I never counted on. You see, Las Vegas is a very small town. Everyone knows everyone else. Just like back on the farm, Vegas has its own version of the gossip hotline, too. It was at the end of contract negotiations with the Dunes when they turned their agreement with me over to the legal department for final approval. When they did, one of the lawyers (who was also the lawyer for a local magician across the street at the Aladdin Hotel) called magic boy and told "The Princess of Magic" as I so lovingly called him, all about my pending contract. The order was given to stop me at all costs. He had just purchased a crossed-eyed baby white tiger for his show and was planning the same scandal.

Karma got him back for me. The cross-eyed baby white tiger was inbred. It grew up to be bright orange, just like all the rest! He had been sold a regular tiger cub and convinced it had the very rare recessive white genes. Isn't life grand!

The next day, I called the entertainment director and was told by his assistant that "We no longer require your services, as there has been a change in our production plans." I was never able to speak with this director again. He refused to take my calls, and returned my letters. As quickly as it all happened, it was all lost. Like putting your last quarter into a slot machine, I was doomed by the underground show business mafia that ruled the strip at the time.

Now what? Where do I go? I had to find something. "Maybe I will have to get a real job, I had better start looking. I've got to try harder!" I told myself.

This is the part of hell on Earth that many OCD sufferers have gone through. It wasn't the OCD part of me that was getting scared, it was the rational part of me. OCD did its number on me by wasting my time when I really could have and should have been looking for a job, let alone taking the time to enjoy the beauty of life. OCD, meanwhile, was still running its try-harder loop in my head, while my rational self had to suffer the consequences. You who struggle with OCD know exactly what I'm talking about. Don't listen to your OCD cycle. It's not your friend. The comfort it gives you is nothing but an illusion. It's your worst enemy. It won't make you better if you listen to it. OCD will only make things far worse.

Not only does OCD rob you of your precious time, it steals time from those you know and love, from those who know and love you. You know what you have to do; so do it. Get help. Quit obsessing about it and get help. That's why you're reading this book. It takes great courage, but you have it in you. You are not insane or crazy. You need to learn how to control your specific case of the disorder from the people who know. Don't blame. It won't do any good. Accept the fact your life has gone the way it has and it wasn't your fault.

Defeated and greatly depressed, I began to fill out applications anywhere I could. But it was too little, too late. I walked into a local photo copy center at the end of a blistering 112 degree day, praying the whole time that this place needed help. UNLV was just down the road on Maryland Parkway and it seemed that every job in the town off the strip was taken by students. I was afraid this copy place was going to be another dead end. They weren't too impressed with my magic experience. They wanted a kid who could help customers make copies at the Xerox machine. They told me maybe they would have an opening next week. "Come back, kid, and we'll see what we can do." I begin to pound the pavement, trying even harder than before, going even farther away, looking for something, anything. I didn't care what.

Self-doubt took hold of me and I began to wonder if Mom was right. Maybe I was on the wrong path. Maybe I should go to college and get a real job. Desperation began to set in. I had about a week's worth of living expenses if I only ate once a day, and only if I could find fast food specials. What was I going to do? I had never been like this before. I had always had plenty of cash on hand. Where had it all gone?

I pulled my frazzled self together and thought, This is only a temporary setback. I know that I will be discovered soon if only I keep trying! I promised myself never to give up. I could give in and give out, but I could never give up.

The reality of the value of that new high school diploma I received began to become crystal clear. The only thing outside of magic that my diploma would get me was a chance to flip some burgers with a friendly, "You want fries with that?"

I had filled out what seemed like an unlimited number of applications and no body was hiring. I was getting frantic. I was about out of money. The rent would be due soon. Joey was only making enough for him at the window place. What was I going to do? Fear began to take over. I would have to ask him to loan me even more money until I got a job. He had been paying more than his fair share. I would ask anyway when I got back to the apartment.

I put my key in the lock and opened the door. Right away, I noticed that it was too quiet. Joey was usually home by this time. That was strange. Had we been robbed? Joey's stuff was gone! Wait a minute, what was this? A note from Joey. He must have gone camping with this girl he had been eyeballing at work or something.

Joey had left and wasn't coming back. I was less then a week away from rent being due with only enough money to eat on. No rent money, no home, no food. I was losing my Las Vegas high. In fact, it was all but gone. The letter was short but sweet. It explained that he was tired of paying more than his fair share. He felt that I was not out there every day looking for a job as hard as he thought I should have been, although I really was. He told me he had met a girl, "THE" girl. (Of course, they were all "The Girl" for Joey, the Italian Stallion.) He was moving in with her and he would contact me later. "Good luck with your hunt for a day job and the magic gig, too." No phone number, no way to get in touch with him. It was signed "Joe." He always hated me calling him Joey, but I didn't care much. Maybe I should have.

Standing on the balcony, looking down at the Strip, I told myself something I had been trying not to admit all along: "The lights in Vegas aren't that bright anymore, are they?" The neon was growing dimmer by the day.

CHAPTER EIGHT
Lost Vegas

I finally got a hot job prospect. After several days, that copying place now thought that they could use a good laminator, "if I was skilled enough" they said. They showed me how it was done and then I tried. Now, you would have to be a complete moron not to be able to do this. I quickly discovered how this copy shop really made its money and why they were so selective in whom they hired.

What I spent most of the day laminating were identification cards. Fake identification cards, mostly. These were really top-of-the-line fake ID's. They did a very brisk business providing bogus proof of age for college kids who wanted to get into the casinos and the bars. They took the orders through the Mexican Fleet as I used to call them, on the street and through others that worked the campus of UNLV. Additional orders came to a P.O. box they had advertised in the rag magazines across the country. They were $250.00 each in 1988, with never a shortage of buyers. In Vegas you have to be twenty-one to get into the bars. Most customers were young college guys wanting to get into the famous Las Vegas strip clubs. You know, girls, boobies and all that goes with that sort of place. We were providing a service, filling a need for a huge demand, it was explained. I was happy to be working, and I was really worried about paying my overdue rent, too. My first paycheck wasn't for two weeks. What was I going to do?

During my second day on the job, more of the same, really. I got off at four p.m. and headed back to the apartment. When I arrived, I noticed a big external lock on my door. Uh-oh.

I went down to the manager's office and there he was. Jabba the Hutt. Well, anyway, he was just about the same size as Jabba and nearly as charitable.

"Whutcher' apartment number, boy?" he said while chewing, his mouth stuffed with Purina Slob Chow. I told him. He half twisted in his groaning chair and gestured at a pegboard full of numbered hooks. Some had keys, a few had a red tag. Guess which one I had?

"Ya aint' paid ya rent, boy," he announced importantly. The man was a genius. I told him that I was broke, but I had a job and would get paid in two weeks. I also asked if I could go to my room to get some personal things. "Sure ya can, when you pay the rent, boy." We argued back and forth for a while. My OCD began to launch itself into a wild fury. "Yer stuff's mine till I get paid. I don't care about your hard luck stories, son. Now move on, I got business to tend to." Suddenly I understood what a prisoner condemned to death by hanging feels at the instant the trap door beneath his feet drops away. It is a rush of sheer primal terror.

I wandered aimlessly about. Outside, inside the hallways. I had no thoughts. I was blank. I was dead. I returned briefly to moments of consciousness. I visited the manager's office three times during the night. He wouldn't give in. Jabba the Hutt would not let me in, no way, no how.

Everything in the OCD cycle requires order, demands order, in fact. The ritual must be done just so. In my case, since magic was such an integral part of who I was, what could be more devastating than being denied access to it? Although I was successfully controlling my OCD now, magic was still a large part of who I was. I was a professional magician, a magic man who aspired to entertain the world.

Now, imagine what it must have been like when all I really lived for was my magic, not knowing that I had OCD. Instantly, I was cut off from the only thing in my life that I considered to be real and stable. How bad was it? Let me give you some insight. What I am about to say might sound hideous, but it's the only way I can give you an inkling of how horrific the OCD cycle can be when you're abruptly cut off from it.

I once read that several French doctors were curious about the physiology of decapitation. They wanted to find out if being beheaded was really a humane and instantaneous form of capital punishment. They received permission from several prisoners condemned to death on the guillotine to conduct post-decapitation experiments.

The results? The doctors determined that the terrifying moments leading up to execution caused the condemned to hyperventilate and secrete massive quantities of adrenalin. Their hearts were hammering in terror, with pulse rates well in excess of two hundred beats per minute. These physical reactions in anticipation of impending death meant their brains were supplied with far more oxygen than usual. Enough oxygen to allow consciousness after decapitation. One severed head remained aware and responsive to a doctor for more than twenty seconds. All the heads were aware and conscious after being chopped off. Can you imagine the horror in the mind of a severed head in the seconds before life was gone? Chop an OCD suffer off from his ritual, and think about what I've just told you about the severed heads! If you don't have OCD, but a member of your family does, and you're thinking about breaking his OCD cycle abruptly -- don't. You have no idea how horrifying it feels.

If you do have OCD and if someone or something has interrupted your OCD cycle, you know exactly what I'm talking about. You and I have felt the panic and horror we wish on no human alive or dead. You know well that it was that intense. Whatever the OCD ritual, be it the washing of hands, obsessive counting, extreme perfectionism, repeating a certain phrase over and over, or flipping the light switch on and off fifty times, it doesn't matter. If that ritual is denied to the sufferer, there is an overwhelming, uncontrollable sense of panic that can lead to hours, days, weeks or even months of very painful disorientation, fear and internal terror. Let's say that you do not have OCD, but someone close to you does. Maybe it's a brother or sister. You've had it with the way their disorder is messing up not only their life, but your life as well. You've had it! You're going to stop this damned OCD behavior once and for all! Let's say you haven't taken the OCD victim to a doctor yet for proper therapy and medication. What do you think will happen to him or her, in light of what I've just told you? That's right. A total disaster awaits you. Don't even think about trying to do something on your own. That is, unless you think it might be better to have a complete zombie requiring around the clock care on your hands. Sometimes your honest and most sincere effort to help only inflicts more internal pain in the sufferer.

They will remember that pain. It can make them terrified that whatever the doctor does, it will be far worse then what you did or what it will actually happen. In short, attempting to intervene before getting qualified medical attention and counseling as well as treatment for OCD will not help. It will make things much worse. That is why it is so important in my view for you to absorb as much information and OCD education as is possible before making a single move on your own.

Remember the guillotine.

Exhausted, I finally fell asleep in the hallway, leaning up against my door. The sun awakened me. I was still in shock, not thinking clearly. I continued wandering up and down the Strip. I wandered in and out of nearly every casino, trying to distract myself from what I was facing. I didn't know a single soul in Vegas except for Joey, but I might as well forget about him. He was gone and didn't care anymore. I didn't know what to do. My best friend was gone. My magic was gone. Literally. All my magic props, my whole act, was in that apartment. No money, no food. I got light-headed. I hallucinated about selling my soul to the devil. No deal. He told me, "Sorry, kid, you ain't got a soul to sell anymore." It was locked in that apartment. "Call me when you get that back rent thing cleared up." The devil was right. Without my magic, I had no soul.

When I was suffering this shock, I was unable to make any of the right decisions. Had I not been OCD afflicted, I probably would have called the police. In retrospect, I am sure they would have been able to assist me in getting some of my personal possessions back somehow. Was Jabba entirely within his rights to deny me access to my stuff? I really don't know. I can't help but to think that I would be entitled to at least my toothbrush if nothing else.

My fourth day without eating, except for a little popcorn some casino was giving away for a promotion. I ended up sitting on a bench in front of the Barbary Coast Casino on Las Vegas Boulevard. A kid with a Blue Mohawk haircut came up like it was his turf. He was tough, yet kindly. After a couple of minutes of sitting next to me in awkward silence he said, "What's your story?"

"What'd you mean?"

"I've been watching you go up and down for days, and you look like you don't belong here. Are you a runaway?"

"No, I came here on business. And I do belong here, buddy."

"Well, if I didn't know better, I would say you're homeless, dude."

I was a lousy liar. He knew this and laughed at me. It took me a second, but I finally gave in. I needed a friend right about now for sure.

"So, what's your name?"

"Steven."

"Hungry, Steven?"

"Yeah."

"C'mon with me, I'm going to get something to eat."

I had nothing to lose so I followed him down the street, in and out of back alleys and through a dusty field. We ended up at a pay phone outside a famous national pizza parlor. He had some change, enough for a phone call at least. He ordered two extra-large, super pizzas with sausage, mushrooms, pepperoni, olives, green peppers, and triple anchovies. I didn't have a clue as to what he was up to, but I knew that he didn't have enough money for all of this food he was ordering.

"So how are we going to pay for this? I don't have a penny. I am broke, man!"

He smiled and said, "Watch and learn, bro. I am the master at finding free food. It's a scam."

He seemed really confident. Through my hunger fog, lack of sleep and the general weakness from not having eaten in days, I sensed that I was about to find out what street-smart meant. We circled around to the dumpster behind the pizza parlor. There was a pickup truck nearby. We used the truck as cover so the workers couldn't see us.

There we sat and waited for a long while. We talked about nothing really. Just stuff. His blue hair, the rings in his nose, and the big scar on his arm, were among the hot topics. Just when I was beginning to think that all of this was pointless, an employee comes out with two extra large pizza boxes and tosses them in the dumpster.

As soon as he was gone, we ran to the dumpster, grabbed our dinners, and headed back behind the truck for a feast. I was not really wild about anchovies, so I picked those off. It was my first meal in four days.

"Get used to anchovies, dude," he told me. "That's why we are eating!"

He went on to explain that with any other order, they could keep it warm and probably sell it to somebody else within an hour. But with anchovies, triple anchovies to boot, the whole pizza reeked from the fish odor and no one would buy it. Bam! Dumpster City. Now I got it. Street smarts!

Our bellies were full, and I was starting to think about where to crash. It was getting dark, and I couldn't go back to the apartment. Jabba told me not to set foot on the property again without the rent money. The last two nights sleeping on hard, cold ground in the park had not been good for my health or my morale. Although Las Vegas is in the desert, it could get pretty cold at night in the winter. I wondered if it would be rude to ask my new friend about finding a place to sleep after his generosity in scamming a hot meal. So I asked. He told me he had a squat and I was welcome to crash there. I figured out immediately that a squat must be a place to stay. I thanked him for his generosity, but I still didn't know his name. The manners I had learned growing up in Virginia convinced me that I should introduce myself formally, but he abruptly held up his hand and stopped me. He explained that on the street, there were certain rules and a code of unspoken conduct, just as in civilized society.

Rule one, you never give out the location of the squat.

Rule two, never give your full name to anyone. Use an alias if possible.

Rule three, you never ask questions of a fellow street person about the past. Let him talk to you about it. Most importantly, never volunteer information about your own past.

Rule four, if possible, look out for your fellow squats in tough times that really count. Warn each other when the cops are close. If the place is burning down, be sure to drag the addicts out. Most of the time, they are in a corner somewhere, wasted, without a clue.

Rule five, never steal from the others in the squat. That could seal your fate.

I figured that I could handle all that. So he shook my hand and told me his street name. "I'm Spunky." I told him my street name: Steve. Nobody needed to know that my real name is Steven. Man, was I getting the hang of the street thing! Spunky led me to a boarded-up wreck of a house. It was officially listed as abandoned by the city and county, and scheduled for demolition at some indeterminate future time. As long as it stood, Spunky would put it to good and bad use. Spunk looked around to see if anyone was watching. When the coast was clear, he lifted a piece of plywood on a concealed hinge, and in we went. It was an enormous old place with no running water, no plumbing, no electricity, and it smelled.

Spunky showed me around and explained the house rules. He first found the place and was the squat leader. It had many rooms, a big two-story deal with a long staircase that ran around the walls up to the second floor. Each room had a candle in it. Candles had to be stolen from somewhere every day to keep the place lit each night. Being boarded up, the squat was dark as night inside all day long, except for the second floor where in one of the rooms you could see right through the roof. We called it the moon room. It was also the room in which most of the drug addicts shot up from time to time. Often they passed out with the needles still in their arms and a smile on their face. It was a freaky sight to see by candlelight in an old house with holes in the roof.

Squatters were supposed to use public bathrooms before entering the squat. If they absolutely had to go in the squat, they were supposed to pee in jars with lids and poop in plastic shopping bags and take the waste with them the next day. There was a special room for this activity. Ya see, this place wasn't like staying at Bale's. It was hard core.

So were the kids and others who lived there, wandering in and out only at night. In the middle of the night, stoned junkies sometimes forgot the squat rules of personal hygiene. The odors of their mistakes permeated the walls. At least it was dark enough that you couldn't see.

You also couldn't see the rats and the roaches. You could hear them, and sometimes felt them if they scurried over you. Spunky said that you got used to them and didn't notice them after a while.

Now, I was in the real land of the lost. A crash course in a world reality I'd never known. This was the old ruin I would be calling home for the next year of my life.

In the spring of 1988, I was living a late twentieth-century version of Oliver Twist. Spunky was Fagin to a never-ending stream of transient kids. Runaways, fugitives, druggies, prostitutes, you name it. I followed the rules; I didn't ask questions. Of course, being a magician, I was a pretty keen observer of human behavior, and after a while it was not hard for me to figure out which kids are being eaten alive by which inner demons. I kept those observations to myself. Sharing unsolicited insight or advice was a good way to shorten your life span. For the first time in my life, I was beginning to feel quite normal.

There must have been fifty or sixty kids in the squat on any given night. As new ones drifted in, old ones drifted out. Some never left. A few finally went home, some got arrested, a few died from drug overdoses. Some died of pneumonia, malnutrition, or AIDS; others ended up dead at the end of a bad deal gone wrong. A lot of death lived here. I didn't ask questions, I observed. To them, I seemed as indifferent to our daily struggles as they did. Inside my soul I absorbed all the horror. Inside, I thought their souls did, too. But I was not about to ask. I was too busy trying to survive.

Three months in the squat taught me a lot about street smarts. One morning I woke up only to find that someone forgot Rule Number Five. My wallet, all my ID and everything else I had was gone. Poof! Just like magic. It had been a tough week for me.

I was still working at the copy center until I got fired for telling the manager to stick it where the sun didn't shine, or something to that effect. Now I had no ID. I was screwed.

I had no way to prove who I was. So I learned how to become a dip. What's a dip, you say? It was a pickpocket in laymen's terms. Spunky was a great teacher. He taught me so well that later on I would incorporate my dipping skills into my magic act. Thank you, Doctor Spunky, Ph.D., Dean of the College of Street Crime, Squat University, Las Vegas.

One of the greatest improvements in my dipping career came the day the brand new Mirage Hotel and Casino opened in Las Vegas. Siegfried and Roy had built a special exhibit to display their royal white tigers to the public for free, when they were not performing. It was encased in thick glass and became the hottest attraction around. A huge crowd of tourists always stood in front of the glass window, pushing and shoving for the perfect spot to take their photos. It was in a small hallway off to the side of the hotel, packed with a hundred people or so. Sometimes however, there were several times that, trying to cram in. It was too good to be true.

Because there was so much pushing and shoving going on, it was the perfect place to make a few wallets disappear. It paid off handsomely. Especially with the older women, who had just come from a hot bingo game. They were easy to spot, usually having several bottles of ink in their pockets and big, open bags. They always had several hundred dollars on them. Sometimes I got caught and had to run for it. But the vast majority of the time, no one saw or felt a thing. I became very good at it. I knew what I was doing. It was called misdirection, an old magic term used by the pros to describe what happens when your attention is distracted for a second, allowing a clever magician to make the secret move, so to speak. For me, the tigers were all the misdirection I needed. I only had to blend in and find what I was looking for. Now, I am not saying I was proud of what I was doing. I knew it was very wrong. I didn't come from that kind of family. But when you are hungry, and trying to get off the horrors of the street in downtown Las Vegas, you do what you must to survive. If you ever ran across my path at the tiger display in the Mirage, I beg your forgiveness. You likely got your wallet back because I would only take the cash and put the wallets in the nearest mail box, hoping the post office would find your ID and return it to its owner. I never meant to hurt anyone. This is a part of my life that has caused me great guilt and pain in later years. Nevertheless, it was better then selling my body or trick'n' as it's called on the street. Most of the guys did it. Their clients? Mostly males.

Although my fellow squatters weren't gay and didn't enjoy it, they had to, if they wanted to eat. I would gladly have given up my life first before living that hell once again. I began to understand why they called it Sin City.

Over time, I got the honor of meeting and getting to know some of the other fine faculty members of Street Crime U. I learned every scam on the streets and was actually very good at them. My skills as a magician came in handy. There was a lot to learn in order to survive long term. Things like how to find stuff to eat that wouldn't kill you. The fine art of dumpster diving. It was cash I really needed. I knew that the only way to get my stuff back and start all over was to have a pile of cash on hand.

In Las Vegas, money talks, and it speaks loud and clear. Vegas is a very unique town. In fact, if you are a clever dude with a few simple skills, it's actually easy to survive after you learn the basics. For example, I once used my dipping skills to swipe a security badge from a hotel employee at the Flamingo Hilton. I had discovered that most of the casinos gave free meals to their employees in a private room. You couldn't get into this lounge unless you had a badge. Then, it was good eatin' time! Hot meals, with all the trimmings, too, including deserts that made my mouth water at the very sight of them. I couldn't believe it.

Most nights I was sneaking into the Flamingo's main showroom through an employee access door on the second floor balcony. The waiters used this door to serve the meals to the guests sitting up there. I had met one of the producers of the show. His name was George, and George loved chasing after me. He was a harmless old queen and I thought he was pretty funny most of the time. His business partner, Bill, was a sheer delight and the very picture of class, a real gentlemanly guy. He was not as crazy as George was and I liked him, too. I met George when he saw me walking down the street one afternoon and offered to give me a ride in his convertible. I hopped in and he took me where I was going. He gave me his card and invited me to see his show. I soon learned that he would let me see the show anytime I wanted, as long as he thought he had a chance. The rest of the time I sneaked in by myself. I was never scared of George who was a friend and was the one who showed me the employee's dining room. I ate there with him several times, being careful to map its location and its operation in my mind.

George and Bill both were wonderful old souls who came up in show business the hard way. They made it and inspired me to do the same. I always felt we had something in common. The show was called City Lights and it had one of my favorite magicians at the time, Joseph Gabriel. I was spellbound each night as I showed up on time to see his evening performance. Though his part of the show was only a few minutes, I knew to the second what time in the show he performed. Beautiful cockatoos flew around the show room in one of the most incredible shows to ever hit the Las Vegas strip. That show was my hope for a long time. It kept me alive. Every night I dreamed that one day, I would be up there on a stage in a show like City Lights. I had to get off the streets.

Another clever little scam I reworked, using my magic skills, turned into a regular gig where I and a partner would walk away with exactly ninety-nine dollars every time. I would dress as nicely as possible and walk into some small casino like O'Shea's, for example. I would find a bar out of the way with two bartenders and a bunch of folks around the bar and begin to do some magic. People loved it. Once the bartenders began to try and see what I was doing, I knew it was time to make my move.

I would ask the bartender on one end of the bar if he would like to see one of the most amazing and impossible illusions ever. Of course, the whole crowd wanted in on it, too. So I would have the bartender go to the till and retrieve a one hundred-dollar bill. This would always create big laughs from the crowd, but after a little confidence winning, they would always give in. I would have him sign his name neatly along one of the edges of the backside of the bill. This would allow him to identify this bill later on in the trick.

Slowly, and very carefully, with my sleeves rolled up and surrounded by lots of on lookers, I folded up his one hundred-dollar bill and made it simply vanish. I then began to talk about the laws of physics and how magicians used them to create illusions. Pointless babble that only stalled for time, nonetheless, I had the complete and undivided attention of everyone, especially the bartender. At some point I would ask the bartender if he would be amazed if the one hundred-dollar bill was now back from where it first came. Of course, when he opened the register, there it was, his signed one hundred-dollar bill.

The audience was blown away! I became a magical god. I had made a cool $99 bucks and it was time for me to disappear. Magic is a beautiful thing in that it can be used in so many ways. You are dying to know how I did it, aren't you? Well, okay. I'll reveal it here only so that bars everywhere will watch their cash a little closer whenever a magician comes to town. This scam is as old as time. It's been around in different versions since the days of the pharaohs. Here's how it worked: Using some of that misdirection I told you about earlier, I would slip the bill to my street pal posing as an onlooker, in a secret device that every magician has with him at all times. My friend, having never been seen close to me, would then go to the other side of the bar, to the other bartender and buy a cheap soda. He paid for it with the one hundred-dollar bill faced up. The bartender would then go to the cash register and put the bill in, giving my friend ninety-nine dollars in change. My friend would leave the casino and wait for me outside.

By the time the bartender discovered his register was $99 dollars short, we had been gone for hours. Now, aren't you glad I only use my powers for good these days?

There was another way we used to get free money. We never gambled, Spunky and I. Some of the other guys did, but neither of us saw the logic in it since we knew full well that the odds were always stacked in the house's favor. As my dear Professor Spunky would say, "Watch and learn." And I did.

In the nineteen eighties, the pre-computer chip slot machine era, the one-armed bandits were mostly mechanical and electronic. They didn't have random number generating integrated circuits yet. Some of the newer casinos like the Mirage never had the old machines. But most of the casinos still had them and we were mighty thankful they did, too.

Each electronic slot machine had a button on the front that read "CASH OUT". This was the button that you pushed to get your credits released in the form of coins. Grandma from Iowa would simply scoop up the coins and put them in her Dixie cup full of quarters, if she knew what the button was. Most tourists back then had no idea that they had any credit and would only scoop up the quarters that came out. It was a beautiful thing to see them get up and walk away with a blinking "CASH OUT" light on their machine. So Spunk and I used to walk up and down row after row, looking for lights on the empty machines.

We would hit the button, cash out, and move on calmly as if nothing ever happened. Security wasn't what it is today. We knew how to get around it and do our thing. Occasionally, we would get chased out of a bigger casino, but the small ones were the easiest of them all. Especially the ones downtown on Freemont Street close to where we lived. Those quarters meant a lot to us.

I didn't feel as if we were ruining someone's vacation. That was important to me at least. The money we collected meant that I got dinner, and Spunky got his heroin. Every night.

You know, it's truly an amazing thing, that while living at the squat I never did drugs. I never asked Spunky if he was a smack freak (street talk for heroin user). I didn't have to. I saw him shoot up enough times to figure it out. Remember the code? No questions. I saw enough drug use all around me every day that I guessed this reality that the user can't see, really sank in. It was not for me. I had enough problems without having to deal with drug use and all that went with it. I don't know how many people I saw dead or dying from drug overdoses during my tenure on the streets. It was a lot. I've blocked much of what I saw out of my mind. It was too much for a guy from a different world trying to live his dream.

Most of the ones who died never believed in dreams. They gave up and surrendered to the only friend they knew. I was not going down like that. I knew that somewhere in me, I had the will power and strength to survive. Oddly enough, Jeff (not his real name) became my strength during this time. I felt that if I could survive that, anything else life threw at me would be a piece of cake. I was only trying to save money that I had to bury to keep safe. I wanted my apartment back. If not that one, then another one. I needed to find the path I was once on and travel down that road once more. This time, I knew I could make it, if only I could get off the streets.

Around this time, I heard something about a law they have in Nevada. Basically it said that if I had not paid my rent within three months, the apartment owner had the right to sell my things, legally, free and clear. I told myself not to panic, so I did. What would I do if he sold my things? That was my act, my whole life's work, my future, my soul. I learned that it doesn't necessarily mean that my stuff would be sold right that minute. After all, who'd want to buy it? I didn't have enough saved to reclaim it. I needed to get another job. Life on the street had become too comfortable. It was too easy. Spunky and I were a great team. I would have to go back and check. I hoped old Jabba hadn't sold my things yet.

It was summer; I had been on the street nearly six months and all of that but four days in the squat. I finally had enough cash saved up to get my stuff back. Spunky had found some of the money I had hidden and shot it right up his arm. So it took a while to recoup from the loss. On the street, hiding your things and your money is a fine art. You have to keep very quiet. If people found out I was saving money to repossess my stuff, they would know it was not in a bank. It was either on me or hidden some place close. At that point I ran the risk of being robbed or killed. It was all very stressful. I thought that it was this kind of stress that made the kids in the squat look so old. Not chronologically old, because they were teenaged runaways mostly.

Teenagers made a living on the street anyway they could, -- dealing drugs, selling their bodies, smoking crack to escape the pain. They shot up, stole, and then shot up some more. Day after day for months and years on end. This kind of life can make you old really fast. Nineteen on the streets is very old indeed.

The don't ask, don't tell policy that Clinton began using in the Armed Forces was not a new strategy. It began on the streets of any town USA. By keeping that law I had survived. Now I had the money I needed so I headed across town to the apartment I once called home. I walked into the office. Jabba was still sitting in the very same chair as the last time I saw him. "It's too late kid. It's all been sold." Jabba didn't know who bought it and he didn't care. He wanted my money for storage fees. Realizing that it would take him several minutes to get out of that chair, I politely told him to stick it where the sun didn't shine or something to that effect as I recall. I walked out of the door with my money, but not my soul. I felt profoundly empty, profoundly desolate and defeated.

Even so, I wouldn't let it come through when I called my dad back in Phenix, Virginia. I was too proud.

My ego wouldn't allow me to declare defeat and return home to the cows and Nancy, too. My years as a performer enabled me to sound upbeat and positive, pursuing leads, working magic gigs here and there, prospects getting better all the time. Or so I told him on the phone. Every Sunday, I would call my Mom and Dad to let them know I was okay. "Dad, it's a matter of time until I get my own showroom!" I used to tell him.

A lie that hundreds of magicians in Las Vegas continue to tell themselves to this very day. It just doesn't work that way.

I knew that if I told him the truth, it would hurt him. I couldn't do that to him. He was in enough physical pain already. I got myself into this mess, and I was going to get myself out of it somehow, some way. I couldn't allow my family to know. That would be a very painful and a very slow death. At least, that's what I thought.

In September, 1988, I was still alive. I'd been in the squat for nine months so far. So much had happened that I felt like it was all a big blur. Spunky had developed a little side business in the last couple of months. He was now a pimp, too, running girls out of the squat as if they were a dime a dozen. He had so many girls that the chicks could be choosy about the losers they locked up with! Some of those girls had been on the street since they were twelve. A few of them had been out there so long, their panty hose had curb feelers! It was really sad to me. It put money in Spunky's pocket and in the girl's pockets, too. That's got to count for something. I guessed it was his way of moving up in the world. He sure was proud of himself.

The squat wasn't all drugs, horror and death. I had some fun times there. I met some people who were genuinely caring and kind. In fact, some of the kindest people I ever met in my life were the ones with the least to give. Of course, I can't give out their names, because that would be against the rules. Then, why do I spend so much time talking about Spunky? Doesn't this violate the rules? Not really. You will understand why soon enough. Keep reading.

I remember one time that Spunky and I were rolling in dough. We had plenty of money and sometimes shared it. We stopped by a convenience store to get a soda, sandwiches and some other stuff. Spunky got his usual carton of milk. We were sitting in the parking lot on the curb, laughing and talking about some of the day's adventures. Spunky took a sip of his milk.

"Hold it!" I said.

"What's up?" he said, confused.

I took the milk carton and carefully examined the picture of a missing child on the side. It said, "Have you seen this child?" All of the young boy's stats were there along with his real name. It said to call the Center for Missing and Exploited Children's toll free hotline number. The picture was of a much younger boy, but I was sure I knew who it was and he was sitting right beside me.

"Spunk, is that you?"

He hadn't even noticed it the whole time. At first for a split second, a look of shock came over his face. Then he replied with his ever-so-charming smile. "Yeah, that's me. They think I'm missing, but I know exactly where I am!" He laughed it off and changed the subject. "C'mon man, let's go." He tossed the milk carton in the dumpster and we never spoke of it again.

I wrestled with this in my mind for several weeks. It was all I could think about. Shouldn't I tell someone where he was? His family was looking for him so they must love him, right? Sadly, it was not always the case. Most kids ran from home to escape abuse. They ended up on the cruel streets and fell prey to all that awaited them. Some made it; others wouldn't get past the first forty-eight hours. If I told someone, that meant I had to break the code. Squat leader Spunky himself enforced that one. You talk about someone's real identity and you were out of the squat, if you were lucky. If you were not, you might be dead.

In a single second I had memorized all of the information on that milk carton. I knew where he had lived, his real age and his name.

Finally, I had made up my mind. I knew what I had to do. It was the right thing to do. I couldn't help but think that someone out there must love this guy enough to want to find him, not just to beat him up. So I decided to confront Spunky back at the squat. I was going to talk to him and see if I could get through to him somehow. I headed back to the squat and he was nowhere to be found. No one had seen him in a day. But that wasn't unusual. I checked around until I noticed that one item of his was missing. Only I knew where it was. It was his most prized possession and that was his Indian peace pipe that he used to smoke his pot. Spunky was gone. I never saw him again.

The milk carton had blown his cover. I went back to the same convenience store and found another carton with his picture on it. I called the toll-free hotline number and told them what I knew about Spunky. They thanked me and that was that. I figured that I could once again rest easy, knowing that I had done my part. I thought that the rest would fall into place.

A year or so later, I called the center back, to see if Spunky had been reunited with his family. They gave me his mom's number. She had left a message, should I ever contact them again. She wanted to speak with me. I called his mother collect.

Yes, she had been reunited with her son. I felt proud,

good and totally alive as if I had finally achieved something positive out of the horror of the streets. She went on to explain that since the reunion, unfortunately, he had passed away. He should not have been drinking when he drove and on New Year's Eve. Spunky, his three passengers, and the two people in the other car all died. Behind the wheel, he lost control, crossed the centerline, and hit another car head on. Spunky had never spoken of me to his mom.

She learned of me through the Center for Missing and Exploited Children. I had many conversations with his mother over the next few weeks. She wanted to know everything about the son who left home at thirteen and grew up on the streets. He was twenty-four when he died. I was the only person who knew him well enough. I had the answers that could help this poor lady to close the coffin and allow her son to rest in peace.

She begged me to tell her all I knew. She told me that she couldn't go on with her life until I did. She told me a little about his life before the street. His father, then in prison, used to beat him and his little brother. He would come home drunk and take his aggression out on his two boys. She said that many times she would come home only to find her son on the floor in a pool of his own blood. Her husband used to beat her, too. She had remarried and wanted to move on, but not until she finally knew the truth. I didn't want to tell her the truth. I told her that some things were better left unsaid, but she refused to accept that. I had actually decided not to tell her and make up some fantasy to protect her from knowing the reality her son lived every day until I asked where his younger brother was. She told me he was missing, too. He had disappeared at the age of fourteen and was never heard from again. That got me. I knew I had to tell her. I had to help this lady any way I could, even if the truth hurt. I told her his street name only to discover that he had a dog at home named "Spunky." I told her everything. His drug abuse, his prostitution, his pimping of the girls, his expertise as one of the greatest scammers I had ever met. I told her about the squat and about the house rules. I told her all about it over many collect calls that she gratefully accepted. She could begin to heal now. She knew the truth. She sounded so relieved. At least it was over for her son. She gave me all the information that she had about Spunky's brother. However, she felt he was somewhere in Florida in a warm place with a beach. She mailed a picture of him, which I carried around with me for years, always looking for that face I hoped to someday see. I never did.

There was a kid in the squat who called himself "Mike." Twenty years old physically. Emotionally, he had one foot in the grave. He was obsessed with what he could have been. Instead, he was dealing with a serious group of Vegas drug lords. He thought he was an insider, a big-time drug dealer. He couldn't have been more wrong. Mike was a really nice guy. Lost in the blur of reality that was the street, he struggled every day, trying to find himself.

What was his true purpose in life? We often talked about such things. One night Mike and I were walking across an empty lot, heading back to the squat.

I found out he was a former gang member of the other side. Some of his fellow gang-bangers confronted us in the empty lot close to where we lived. They didn't need to tell me to stay the hell out of it. I backed away as they gathered aggressively around him. Their beef was with him, not me, and they knew I would spread the impending message to the rest of the gang. The argument got loud. I was off to one side and behind Mike. He was facing the leader, and they surrounded him. I moved to get a better view, but kept my distance. Without warning and in the middle of a sentence, he pulled out a gun. BANG! Mike's back exploded. Another street life freshly over. One of the gang members tossed the warm body over his shoulder and they left. They didn't have to kill me. They knew I knew the code. I couldn't call the cops. Another pinnacle point in my street career had just passed.

I sagged and fell to the ground as if the bullet through Mike's heart was ripping through mine, new fodder to join other images of horror my head can't stop replaying. A life was gone. I would never see him or any of the other gang members again. I lay in the field and stared up at the stars of the dark night sky, not really thinking about any thing at all. I was numb. I couldn't move. It was as if my body had come to a full stop. I experienced an overwhelming desire not to think. To stop my brain. To shut it up. Too powerful, too strong, it was a force well beyond my control. It was the first time I actually thought about ending it all myself. Dying didn't seem like a bad option. The more I thought about it, the more peace I seemed to feel as if the only way out was the open door my friend had stepped through so effortlessly. It was the perfect way, the only way, to stop my brain from killing me ever so slowly, one day at a time.

I felt good for Mike, knowing that he was in a better place and wasn't suffering any more. It was quick, painless and easy. I thought and thought and thought about it for hours. Death officially became an option.

I was almost angry that they had not shot me as well. The pain I endured was far greater then what Mike had felt. I asked myself, "How much longer can I live like this?" and "What are the real chances of me ever becoming a famous entertainer?" I thought about the tens of thousands of actors in Hollywood, New York and Las Vegas struggling for a dream they would never achieve. I questioned my own talents. "I'm not really that talented and I know so many more magicians far better then I and who were much better-looking. They are the ones who will make it."

I figured that I would grow old chasing the mirage of a career I would never fully enjoy. Vegas had taught me a lot about show business. It wasn't about your skills as an entertainer. It was all about who you knew, who you were willing to sleep with, what was in it for them, and how you looked. I knew a female magician who was sleeping with a top casino executive, and not just her, but another member of her family as well, all to keep her show in the main showroom. I didn't want to go down that road. I knew I wouldn't be good enough at playing those games. I knew that I wasn't close to being an attractive Hollywood stud. I didn't have fake boobs, either.

I knew that in this business, it was all about looks and great hair. Neither of which I had. I thought about the odds and knew the truth. For the first time, it was clear to me how high the odds were stacked against me and how hard it would be to change that. I did not have the effort in me. I was too tired. Tired of struggling, tired of the daily search for food. Tired of living underground and constantly afraid of being found out by the people I knew in Vegas that really mattered. Carefully balancing my two lives (my struggle to gain access to that illusive inner circle that can make or break a career in Vegas and my struggle to stay alive on the street) was too tough. In the blink of an eye, all desire to live had faded away. I was at peace. I felt good. I was in control. I was making a clear decision, and I knew I could make it happen. I knew that I would be in control and not my brain. I had grown to hate my own mind with every fiber of my own being. I couldn't stand the never-ending loop that played in my head continuously.

I remembered the murder of my friend's mother in that red-soaked apartment, and the rape, and the drug O.D.'s I saw around me all the time and everywhere I went. People were slowly killing themselves with the demon of their own choice. It was painful to see and be around everyday.

Bang! Mike's back exploded. Bang! Mike's back exploded. Mike's back.

For those of you with OCD who have not been homeless, the situation you are in may not be nearly as dire. Even so, there is much more to your life that you could be doing than wasting your time on your obsessive compulsions. A line from the theme song of the hit television sitcom "Friends" comes to mind: "…seems like you're always stuck in second gear." A car can function and go forward in second gear, but the engine will wear out a lot faster. A human can function to some degree with OCD, but the person will wear out a lot faster, too. So will the patience of the people around you. I urge you to seek help immediately if suicide seems like a way out to you. Even the brief, fleeting thought of suicide as being an option is very serious.

You are not in control of these thoughts as you might like to think.

Right now, stop reading this book and call somebody you trust this very minute and tell them about your situation. This is not a game. It's your life! I promise you that you do want to live. You may not think you can go on any more; it is a temporary state of mind and it can be fixed. Suicide is not an option.

The images wouldn't stop and I didn't want to live like this anymore. I don't really know how long I lay there that night. The stars were so very beautiful that I felt at peace, having finally realized that the end of my insanity was close at hand. I felt it was time to admit my defeat and the reality of what would be my final days. The day to die was upon me. It was time to prepare for the ultimate disappearance.

The dawning day's heat awoke me, shining through the roof of the moon room. I didn't know how I got there or what time it was, but I knew the sun didn't usually shine through that room in the squat until later in the day. My pants were unbuckled and my belt was gone. So were my shoes. Once again, I had been robbed. The few dollars I had in my pants pocket were missing along with the security badge from the Flamingo Hilton, where I ate nearly every day, so often that hotel security had grown to believe that I worked there. Indeed, I would have to get new shoes and swipe another badge. That wasn't going to be very easy. My head felt like a frozen pineapple. I had never had a hangover before, but I imagined this must be what one felt like.

Bang! Mike's back exploded once again.

Finally, a lucid moment arrived and I thought to myself, "Time to dig up some dough." I went to my secret spot, making sure that I wasn't seen or followed. I dug up my cash stash and peeled off a few bucks, enough for a pair of Payless shoes - if they were on sale. With new shoes on my feet, my next stop was the Flamingo Hilton. I called my friend George, the show's producer, and asked him if he had dinner yet. He agreed to meet me at the showroom. We watched the show and had a really good meal. We talked and I guess that he noticed that something was very wrong with me. He began to pry and asked me some serious questions. "Steven, you have got to tell me what is going on, honey. I can help you." The way he said it got to me, and I began to break down. I told George everything. Everything, including the fact I was living on the street. It was no surprise to him. He had figured things out for himself. George was an old queen, admittedly, but a very street smart one indeed.

George looked at me and smiled. He told me that he had a friend who lived by himself and did work on the show's wardrobe from time to time. George offered to give him a call and see if he had room for me just until I was able to get back on my feet. Then, he arranged for a security badge to be made with my name and picture.

Now, I could eat any time I wanted. Maybe my days weren't numbered. Maybe I could hang around for a little while longer. After all, it wasn't as if I had anything more to lose.

I moved into my new friend's tiny house. He was of American Indian descent and had lots of Indian style art and décor around his home. It was perfect. I was very thankful I was no longer on the street. Though I thought a lot about my friends on the street and back at the squat, I knew I could never go back there or tell them where I was. It was better if they thought I was dead.

BANG! In my mind Mike's back exploded.

On the street, you have no address, no phone number, no ID and usually grimy street clothes. Trying to find a job is nearly impossible. Even the burger flipping joints don't want to hire a kid without identification. This new temporary home changed everything. Now, I actually had a chance to find a job. I could watch TV, something I hadn't done in a year. This was temporary and that was clear from the beginning.

I had to find something. George called me one day and told me that he knew of a convenience store near the airport that had begun construction. He suggested that I go there and find out if they were hiring. I did.

The next morning I put on my least grungy clothes, cleaned up as best I could, and headed over to the store. Out front a sign said they were accepting applications. As luck would have it, the owners happened to be there, inspecting the latest round of changes. I talked to them and began to tell them a bit of my story. I explained to them that I was a magician who came to Vegas and had fallen on hard times. Pete and Kim Desantis, the owners, were a very young couple and had worked very hard to realize their dream. Kim immediately related to my story. They hired me on the spot as a store clerk. The store was a month away from opening. They asked me to call them in about three weeks so I could begin training. George was happy. He gave me a few bucks for some clothes and shoes.

In Vegas, there are what seemed to be a hundred different cards or permits you must have to work in any establishment with gaming machines and/or that sells alcohol. In Las Vegas, nearly every convenience store does. It was going to take some time to get these permits and go to all the classes as I learned. First, I needed a sheriff's card. Next, I had to attend a class and be tested on the do's and don'ts of selling liquor. That class came with a card, too. Before long, I found myself at the health department taking a class on food handling and preparation.

That class came with another card. I found the whole thing rather disgusting actually. It made me never want to eat fast food again. It took almost the entire three weeks and over one hundred dollars of borrowed money for the honor of working in the city of my dreams and nightmares. I was happy to do it, though. I was excited to have a job although it wasn't what I truly wanted to be doing. Money was money and I was in debt once again. The thought actually occurred to me, "Wow, it costs a lot of money to live in the real world." Living on the street is free of charge, but not without a price to pay. I figured that I was going to make a slow recovery.

Pete talked to me about my living situation and came up with a plan to help get me my very own apartment down the road at a place called "Harbor Island".

A few weeks later, I moved into my own place. I was very proud. Pete knew the folks down there and made a few calls for me. You know, sometimes, you meet real saints. They don't have halos or wings, but they will. Most of them walk among us masked as ordinary working folks. That described Kim and Pete. Faith in other human beings is a rare gift that God gives to special people. The miracles of these real-life saints' faith is that it makes the human beings they help believe in themselves.

Moments In Time

Marty Allen and Me sailing the high seas

My very first publicity photo AGE 11

My favorite kitty and me in the pool on a hot summer day

King Arthur Rex and Me

One of the biggest Cats I had in my show weighing in at about 750 pounds

They are so cute when they are small...but they grow up fast
(Sorry about the 80's hair)

Same Cat 10 years later

My teddy bear was real!

I really can talk to the animals

Learning to fly. David Who?

One of my early tour pictures

Me and the co-host of Nubeluz- Lima Peru

Me and my famous performing Parakeets

My world famous duck and co-star Aflack

Aflack feeling a little flat!

The art of creating wonder

Arriving in Style

Leviting Cars

Me, the step monster and my father

My dear mother

My best friend in the entire world to this day... Punky

Today 2007

CHAPTER NINE
Leaving Lost Vegas

Las Vegas was a beautiful place. Thanks to Pete and Kim, I had a one-room studio apartment at Harbor Island. There was a beautiful tropical motif throughout the property. I couldn't believe that it had a huge swimming pool, a hot tub, laundry room as well as a clubhouse and gym. I couldn't have been happier. Finally, I was moving up in the world. My very own apartment. Small though it might be, it was my own private palace. It had a locking door to which I had the key. After paying the weekly rent, I had $67.50 left over from my paycheck to live on, and that was more than enough for me. My street skills had taught me how to survive on nothing for long periods of time. I wasn't worried. I knew that I was going to be okay, especially since I had a new badge at the Flamingo Hilton and all the free food I could eat. Life was good.

Call me crazy, but I couldn't help but think about all the kids on the street. Everywhere I went I would see new ones that had just arrived. The teenage homeless population lived on the streets of Vegas in vast numbers, being a few hours from Hollywood, another massive stomping ground for homeless teens. Vegas and Hollywood shared a lot of the same kids who would go back and forth at will. Greyhound was usually the main mode of transportation. That was the reason that the bus terminal downtown was always filled with the most undesirable characters. Pimps looked for young girls and guys as new recruits. Child molesters preyed on whomever they chose. The Mexicans became mules for the drug trade. Traveling young people formed a constant and never-ending supply of fresh, warm bodies to prey on. I wanted to do something. I thought about Spunky and all that he did for me, and I wanted to continue the tradition. I was in a position to help someone as he had helped me. I have often wondered what would have happened to me had I not crossed his path that fateful night in front of the Barbary Coast. I wondered who was out there like me.

It wasn't long before my little studio apartment gained a reputation as a safe haven for kids new to the street. I never allowed jaded, street-smart kids in the door. That was only asking for trouble. I knew that some of them were so slick, they could swim without wetting their clothes. However, I did allow the ones who were terrified and new to street life in so I could lead them in the right direction. Some of them I found a job for, and they eventually got their own apartment at Harbor Island. I was proud of that. It was very important to me to try and give something back. I had survived. I felt it was the least that I could do. As long as I lived at Harbor Island, a steady stream of troubled kids flowed through. I told them my story and what I experienced. If they were runaways, I would try hard to convince them to reunite with their families except where abuse at home was the case.

Many times, these kids were running from molestation and/or drug abuse, sometimes by a parent, a brother, cousin, or even family friends within their own home. Others were the products of parents who were more interested in their next drug fix, than they were in their own children. A couple of teens I knew ran because they were being sold to family friends for sex in order to support their parents' drug habit.

I knew one guy who had been raped by his father since he was ten years old. He was seventeen, tired of the abuse and beat his father, nearly killing him, before running away. His father was home schooling him to hide the crime and to limit his contact with other kids. This guy was one of the saddest cases I ever ran across. His emotional scars ran deep. His self-confidence was almost non-existent. I became a sort of counselor, friend and therapist to most of these kids, the only person some of them had trusted in their lives. At some point, they all left. It was always hard for me. I put my heart and soul into them. I wanted the kids who ran away because of stupid family arguments to return home. I often became their mediator with the parents by phone. The parents always wanted them back home. I was careful to figure out which side was lying. Usually, one or both sides were. I became quite good at finding the truth and making decisions as to what the truth of the situation really was.

Some of them I would determine were too close to call or that it wasn't safe to return the kids to their parents. Many times the parents were violent and would begin conversations with threats of possible action if the child didn't return home. Those were the ones I chose to ignore. I felt that if there were any love for the child, a loving parent would be relieved to know where their missing offspring was. For some parents, it was as if someone had cut off an appendage of their own and it was missing. I thought, that was the way it should have been, but it wasn't the case most of the time.

When I had no other option, no place else to turn and the street kids began to cost me money to support them, I would suggest that they turn to Dr. Louis Lee for help. While I was on the street, I learned about an amazing organization out of Los Angeles called Children of the Night. A wonderful woman named Dr. Louis Lee, herself a veteran of the street, created it. Children of the Night is a street-smart, grass roots level outreach program aimed at getting those who want help off the street. I had the honor of meeting and later having long phone conversations with Dr. Lee over the years. I sent many kids her way. Her program survives solely on the donations of caring people across the country. It's one of the only street programs I really trust. What I like so much about them is that a lot of their staff are former and reformed street folks themselves. They never force anyone to do anything. They simply provide many great options, including medical and psychological help, all at no charge, but only if the person really wants it. It takes a lot of effort on the kid's part. They don't hand anything to you. The kid has to prove that he or she wants assistance and only then they will truly help.

Everyone on the street in Vegas knows about Children of the Night. Word spreads through the kids coming from the L.A. area. They are a tough, very savvy group to con. They have seen it all and a lot of the kids that go there never accept the help they have to offer. Although it's free of charge, there is a price to pay. Tons of street kids are lazy. They feel the street is much easier than going through the tough love programs Children of the Night offers.

They won't help you until you are committed to helping

yourself. And for many, they aren't there yet. Getting high every day seems far more important to these kids than getting help.

I believe this wonderful organization should be a model for every city in the world. I never went through the program myself, but I knew many who did, and Dr. Lee became my hero. She is a tough lady! Anyone who knows her personally will tell you just how tough she can be, but that's what it takes on the street. Otherwise you won't make it very long. I wanted to make a difference like she did. Children of the Night are still up and running strong, but they need your help. I challenge you to give if you can.

Some of the kids listened to me, some of them didn't. I still remember many of their faces. All of them remain in my prayers. I have often wondered how many of those I met had OCD themselves. I'll never know. How could I? I didn't know that the disorder existed then. Helping the few I could validated my time on the street. I really did it in honor of my friend Spunky. He was the first to care for whatever reason he did. Though he had many issues both good and bad, I found him to be a wonderful human being with a caring heart, if you were willing to look past his tattooed, tough, and colorful outer shell. He didn't deserve to die. He needed help he never found at home where he lived. It's a real shame. For every Spunky I met, there are thousands more we will never hear about out there today. How many have to die before they find help? It kills me to think about this. So few are willing to help or do anything to make a difference in this it's-all-about-me world we live in. Of course, for those of you with OCD who have never been homeless, the situation is not nearly as dire. I will never be able to impress upon you how life changing and utterly gratifying helping just one other beside yourself can be. You'll never know, unless you stop thinking of yourself and use whatever you have to help someone else. It might be only a single meal a week for someone who doesn't even have that. I have been there and I know what being hungry is like. Try it for a few days, and you will become a true believer.

I worked at the San Tropez convenience store on Harmon Ave for almost two years, saving money, buying new tricks with the overtime money I earned and keeping my eyes open for any new opportunities in magic. I felt truly empowered after all I had survived on the street. I felt that I had graduated from Street Crime U at the top of my class. I was ready for whatever life had to offer with a "Bring it on!" attitude.

Around this time, I met, through some of my new casino contacts, an agent and businessman by the name of Alex. I had heard good things about him around town and I got to know him a bit. I found out that he owned several popular sub-sandwich shops around town and was a very clever businessman who didn't put all of his eggs into the same show business basket, so to speak. He booked acts all over the world and seemed to be one of the very few agents (and believe me, it's a very short list) that people spoke kindly about. Naturally, he found out that I was a magician. I was not sure what it was, but he saw something in me, and let me know that he would be glad to represent me if he ever ran across a good deal.

I quickly called my dad to have him send me my old brochures and videos, which I gave to Alex right away. Meanwhile,

I began looking at the acts around town, using the contacts I had developed to get me free tickets to some of the biggest shows. I had to know what I was up against if I was going to be the Comeback Kid. I wasn't just looking at potential competition; I was also searching for agents and potential investors in town who were seeking for the next big thing. Magic is a serious business. Within show business (I learned that *show business* is two different words because they are very separate divisions in the entertainment field, a fact most magicians fail to realize.) everybody is money hungry. Especially the agents, and even more, the investors in this high-risk biz. Investors usually are really looking for a good tax write-off.

One night I found myself at a seedy and dark little casino called the Marina on the corner of Tropicana and Las Vegas Boulevard. It has long since been torn down to make way for the MGM Grand that sits there now.

In the main showroom, or the main closet cabaret as I called it, they were featuring a certain female magician known in Vegas as " The First Lady of Magic." I'll call her Linda. Linda came up the hard way. Her mother, an ex-showgirl, was her manager and used to pop valiums in her mouth like they were M&M's candy. Linda worked hard, but never was able to get over that show business hump that takes you from a glorified lounge act to a national star. She often got a bad rap in Vegas. Her shows and her magic were usually disappointing, in my opinion. The rumors that swirled around town about how she kept getting booked were certainly no help and endless. I attribute most of that to poor management and having a basket case for a manager. Linda was beautiful, sexy and could have been really big had the right people surrounded her. There was a running joke in town that she was on tour in Las Vegas, having moved so often from one casino to another.

    This particular night, I sat at a table with my friend Harry Blackstone, whom I first met as a child when Harry pulled me up on stage and gave me a live bunny rabbit. Linda's new boyfriend, television's famous presidential impersonator, funny man Rich Little, was sitting with us. We sat in a booth at the back, which was really only about fifty feet from the stage if that tells you anything. It wasn't very hard to overhear any conversation in the room, if you were good. We all watched the show and afterwards, she joined her mother in a booth next to us along with some Japanese and Korean businessmen. They looked like money. They were also within earshot of where I was sitting. While I continued to talk with Harry and Rich at my table, I also had one ear trained on the conversation Linda and her mother were having with the investors.

    It didn't take very long for me to figure out that they were looking at Linda because they wanted her to do a much larger version of her show at a big resort complex in Korea. My ears perked up as they discussed the money. Linda's mother was asking for one hundred thousand U.S. dollars a week. Although she would have to produce the show and pay all of the people involved with that money, they wanted to think about it and left. Of course, I followed them closely. Outside, the businessmen got into a Caesar's Palace limo. I knew the short cuts and took off sprinting on foot. I didn't have enough money for a cab. I took my chances that they were going back to the hotel. I soon arrived at Caesar's, completely out of breath and waited for them to arrive. Not too long after, the white Caesar's limo pulled up to the main entrance. Soon they were heading inside. I reached in my pocket and asked the limo driver to find out what room the leader was staying in. I pulled out eight bucks and gave it to him. Luckily, he knew the valuable information I needed.

He told me not only which suite they were all staying in, but when they were leaving, because they had made arrangements with him to be picked up for the trip to the airport. Money talks.

So do your friends. I had a friend who worked in the entertainment department at Caesar's Palace. I went to her for help. I knew that she would know someone who could give me an idea of their plans for the next day. She did. She knew not only their room attendant, but she had close friends among the concierges at the front desk. A few calls later I learned of their reservations at a restaurant within the hotel the next evening.

Mission accomplished. By this time, I had my portfolio back in order and a stack of my videos to back it all up. Dressed in a suit borrowed from a friend, the next evening I showed up promptly at five-thirty p.m. and knocked on their door. I figured if they weren't in the room, I knew where to find them at six p.m. The door opened. I introduced myself and they invited me in. It was a huge, palatial penthouse looking out over the Las Vegas strip, not unlike the one in the movie "Rainman" which was filmed at Caesar's in one of these same suites.

It was December of 1990, and I was dealing with the big boys now; I knew it. It was show time! I had my chance. I knew if I wasn't good and very solid, I would be quickly shown the door. These men were in their fifties and sixties. They seemed very serious and knew exactly what they were looking for. I knew I had to put the heavy artillery up front and went straight for the videos. The first one I showed them was a home video shot by my friend Lou Cipher. It showed me swimming in his pool with some real tigers and real wolves running around the pool and jumping in. It was very clear that I had a solid, loving relationship with these huge, exotic beasts. I had one of the tigers wrapped around my shoulders, and I was kissing him on the nose. They had been talking to Linda about using wild animals in her show for them, and I knew this tape would be of the most interest. I was right. It blew them away. They were completely fascinated, and had a hundred questions about the big cats and me. I showed them my magic videos and the next thing I knew, we were off to dinner.

"Gentlemen, I can give you the exact show you are looking for at a fraction of what Linda's mother wants to charge you! I have something she doesn't. White tigers! White tigers had never been to Korea before and when I showed them this video later on, it was perhaps what sealed the deal. They were originally interested in Linda because she was a female magician and they felt that it would be very successful in the Asian market. I didn't have her beautiful looks or fake boobies, but I had white tigers. Even trade.

White tigers impressed them. The videos worked. If I could put exotic animals and a bunch of blonde-headed, big-breasted women as dancers on their stage, it looked like we had a deal. But there were issues. First, they wanted the show to open in less than six months. They also wanted really big illusions. In addition to that, I would have to perform three shows a day, seven days a week for a year. They could have told me that I needed to provide my own transportation to the moon and I would have agreed. I didn't care. I was going to get this deal if it was the last thing I did. It nearly was. They understood that the show was going to be custom-produced with the standard advance deposit and asked me to prepare a complete presentation, including storyboards and wardrobe designs, for them to review in only two weeks. They also wanted to see the animals. They were going to return to Las Vegas. At this point, we had agreed on all the major points and on the money. Now, it was time to figure out how I was going to pull all of this off. I knew I could; though I had not a penny to my name to spare and I was working full time at the store. Call it blind innocence, but I knew that somehow, someway, with a signed deal, I would make it happen.

The next morning I called my friend Lou who owned the animals. He didn't believe me. He thought I was kidding him. Realizing that I wasn't going to get through to his hard head, I hung up and called my new agent, Alex. Alex was impressed and agreed to help me put the presentation together. We had a lot to do, and it wasn't going to be cheap. Not only that, but he had some very strong contacts in Korea himself. Suddenly things began to look more positive.

The Koreans had given me some really impressive brochures of the billion-dollar resort hotel and theme park that my show would go into. The massive indoor water park and a full amusement park with all the rides surrounded the Bugok Hawaii Hotel in Korea. This was it. This was my chance to show people what I could do.

One day Alex got a call from the Koreans saying that they

were not going to be able to come back to Vegas. They wanted us to travel there. Two first class airfares were waiting for us at the airport. We had not yet finished the presentation and needed a few more days, so we delayed the trip. I couldn't believe this was happening. It couldn't be real. Before I knew it, Alex and I were on a plane and heading toward a distant land in what would be the longest journey I had ever taken in my life. I believe it was the first time I grasped the concept of how big the world actually was.

After about the twentieth-hour mark, I was more than ready to get there already, if you know what I mean. Once we arrived in Seoul Korea, the driver who would take us to the hotel picked us up, and we began the journey. The hotel was another six hours from where we stood. We drove through the Korean countryside. It was very different from everything that I knew as normal. This might have been Earth, but it was like another planet to me. Riding through the vast network of rice paddies, I saw hundreds of laborers in the fields up to their knees in muddy water, tending to the plants by hand. I didn't see a single machine helping out. Not a single worker looked young. I begin to realize that in an agrarian economy, peasants are born looking old for their days. What shocked me most was that I kept thinking this was a genuine democracy. Why, Seoul was a bustling cosmopolitan megalopolis! Here in the countryside was nothing but peasants. Old thin people, toiling by hand. I shuddered to think what life in Communist North Korea must have been like. I suddenly began to believe the rumors about there being no more dogs or cats in the North. As I looked out over the passing sights, I couldn't imagine that the road we were traveling would lead us to a massive billion-dollar resort.

Sometime in the wee hours in the morning, we arrived at the famous Bugok Hawaii Hotel; I couldn't have cared less. I wanted to find a bed and sleep.

Mrs. Kim, my inept, but well-meaning interpreter, showed me to my room and proudly told me my suite had a luxury bathroom. I needed to use the bathroom after the long trip. I went in. I came back out. I tried to explain to Mrs. Kim that someone had stolen my toilet. There was nothing in the bathroom but a big hole in the floor where the toilet should have been.

Koreans smile a lot. When they are embarrassed, they laugh, too. I finally figured out that Mrs. Kim was not cracking up with merriment over a practical joke my hosts had played on me by swiping my toilet. She was smiling and laughing because she was embarrassed that whoever assigned my room forgot to include the phrase "western style luxury bathroom" on my reservations.

A standard Korean hotel bathroom has a hole in the floor. A luxury Korean hotel bathroom has a large hole in the floor. I couldn't figure it out and had to be shown how they used that thing. Talk about mysteries. In moments, Mrs. Kim got me a new room with a western-style flush toilet. It was as devoid of moisture as the Sahara Desert at noon. I used it anyway. I appreciated all the efforts to make us comfortable; however, I felt that neither Mrs. Kim nor the hotel really grasped the concept of American indoor plumbing. And why would they?

Mrs. Kim duly informed me of the dinner that evening, where I would meet all the people involved, including the hotel's owner. I thanked her again, closed the door and collapsed on my bed. I slept dreamlessly until a few hours before the big meeting.

When I called Alex that first day and asked him if he wanted in on a really big deal, I remember him asking me, "Define big." To which I replied, "A four thousand seat arena with a massive one hundred twenty-five foot stage in the middle of a billion dollar resort with an owner willing to pay me tens of thousands of dollars a week to perform there." Nothing further was required. Alex was sold and wanted to know more. However, when Alex and I finally awoke the next morning, neither of us was prepared for what was before us. It was all far bigger than I had pictured.

Suddenly fear was beginning to settle in once again. Ah yes, my old friend, always there when you least needed him. I was afraid of not being able to pull this off once I began to realize the scale and true size of this deal. Maybe Linda's mother had it right. It was going to take a couple hundred thousand or more U.S. dollars to produce a show big enough to fill that stage. One person, or even a group of twenty, would look like a few peanuts on an empty shopping mall parking lot on that stage. I knew I was in trouble. The advance I had asked for wasn't going to cut it at all. I needed a lot more. A whole lot more. More money than I had ever dreamed of before. We were going to have to go home and find some financing and all that came with it. The problem was, I didn't know what that meant.

Later that day, Mrs. Kim met us and escorted me to the big event. I must say, although she couldn't interpret her way out of a paper bag, she was at least genuinely nice. She neglected to inform me of Korean etiquette and protocol in such an untimely manner, that I managed to single-handedly look like the biggest fool since the establishment of Korean-American diplomatic relations. The resort's owner greeted us and handed me his business card. Without really thinking about it, I slipped it into my back pocket, effectively putting his face right between my cheeks. The room got very quiet and I was then informed of the innocent error and asked to remove the card.

We were led into a beautiful Korean-style banquet hall that looked like it could easily hold the White House. It made the Palace of Versailles seem tacky by comparison. I began to think that I was at a "Men in Black" convention. Every male there was dressed in a very expensive-looking jet-black business suit. As I was being presented to my potential employers for the first time, they all looked important, and they all smoked a lot, too. My next big protocol blunder was speaking to the first person I saw in the line. Giggling and smiling again, Mrs. Kim explained that it was disrespectful to speak to someone of a lesser position before speaking to the main man. Once again, her timing was perfect. Which one was the boss? They all looked the same to me. Thinking like the American I was, I figured he must be the tallest one in the room. Right? Wrong!

Well, I muddled through as best I could, apologizing to the vice president of the hotel, Mr. Chung. Fortunately, Chung had a sense of humor and made me feel right at home. I was told that if this group of men liked my new presentation, we would meet the hotel's owner, Mr. Bae, and do it all over again for him.

This dinner became my first lesson on how Korean businessmen actually thought. Getting a straight answer out of them was like pulling teeth. I began to understand that Korean culture works by indirection. If Koreans drove the way they negotiated, they'd signal for a left turn whenever they wanted to turn right, while looking straight ahead. I had trouble trying to figure out whom I needed to suck up to first. It was a difficult dinner, but I managed to get through it alive.

Alex and I made the presentation, and it worked. They liked it. Now, I needed to figure out how to levitate a car in the show like I was promising everybody I would. I knew I was in big trouble, but I didn't let them see me sweat. After a year of being homeless and hungry, after two more, struggling to refocus on my career, I was finally on my way back. I wasn't going to allow the small details to stop me!

The next morning I made a collect call to my animal friend, Lou. I called him collect so that he would believe me this time. I knew that it was going to take his animals to pull this gig off. This time he believed me. There were many other places that I could have rented tigers from. I knew lots of magicians, freaks and other trainers who had them. It was pretty expensive for an individual performer to care for a large show animal like a white tiger around the clock, so a lot of the magician's in Las Vegas and elsewhere simply rented. In my opinion, Lou was the best at what he did. I knew him very well and was extremely comfortable in performing with his animals. I had never seen or worked with animals better trained. The trainers you use are very important when working closely with several thousand pounds of carnivorous animals.

You see, if an animal in my show gets grumpy and doesn't want to perform, let's say my famous duck for example, it's not such a big deal. Grumpy ducks tend to quack four letter words at you and flap about a lot. Grumpy tigers tend to eat you.

For some reason, this is perceived as bad for business. Nibbling on the star of the show must be avoided at all costs.

After only four days in Korea, Alex and I were heading home with a signed contract and a deposit check of fifty thousand U.S. dollars. That sounds like a lot until you realize that sometimes a single Las Vegas style showgirl's costume can cost upwards of twenty thousand dollars. I was in trouble, and it scared the hell out of me.

Psychiatric research so far has not really made it clear whether or not OCD can spontaneously disappear without treatment. In the majority of cases, patients do not get better without therapy and medication. However, there are instances where my own OCD seemingly appeared to vanish completely.

Sitting in that plane with a huge check and a signed contract totaling more then a million U.S. dollars, it would have been an understatement to say that I was exhilarated. In my case, I believe that what happened to me was that the flood of endorphins from having accomplished what I never thought possible only a few months before, was likely masking the OCD symptoms, creating the illusion they had all but vanished. All I know is, for about the next three months, I wasn't aware of being obsessed. I didn't feel the doom and gloom or dread that terrible things would soon happen if I didn't feed my OCD cycle. Remember, I had no clue what OCD was at the time. I only knew what the feelings I had would make me do. I was far too busy putting my ideas down on paper, meeting with people who could build my illusions, putting together the members of the team that would put on the best magic show in the world. This was my chance and I was obsessively focused on what I had to do next.

OCD sufferers ask yourself: Has your OCD cycle ever stopped on its own? If it has, what were you doing that made it stop, or appear to have stopped? If your obsession had a practical application in the real world, maybe you fed it so much that it took a nap. If it started up again, what were you doing that made it so hungry?

I was very glad to have Alex next to me, willing to help me make this happen, although, it was my name, and my name alone, on the contract. Alex felt with the signed contract we would be able to find an investor somehow. All I could think of the entire way home was, "From his lips to God's ears." Over and over and over. A day later, we arrived back home. Exhausted, I noticed that the Vegas Lights were once again shining brightly in my eyes.

CHAPTER TEN
Mission Impossible

Constructing world-class illusions is a very expensive and time-consuming process. It's not as if you can go into a magic shop with a shopping list. The big stuff must be custom made by expert magical craftsman. I knew the best illusion designers and builders in the world. That's a really short list, by the way. I showed them all what I wanted and they put in their bid. The cheapest bid isn't always the one to go with because in this business, you really do get what you pay for. There was one builder, however, who, for some unknown reason, gained the reputation as the number one in the world. All the magic freaks wanted him to build their equipment because they thought it would make them better magicians. He was over-priced by more than three hundred percent most of the time. He loved to see magical suckers with rich daddies walking through his door. The funny thing is, although he produces some of the coolest looking illusions in the business, they rarely ever work right! I knew better than to allow him to put in a bid, but I did it anyway. Finally, I went with a little-known West Coast builder, one of the best-kept secrets in the business. This guy was a class act and really knew how to make props that lasted on the long haul. He had built for David Copperfield and the great Doug Henning -- a beautiful spirit who is no longer with us anymore -- for many years. I only had enough money for him to build a couple of big illusions for me.

As we returned, Alex and I decided that we would have to pull in at least one investor to finance the remainder of the pre-production process. Alex had a number of contacts we felt might come through for us. Times were tough then. We tried them all, but none of them were able to participate for one reason or another. Now we had a really serious problem.

Somehow we came across a real show-biz fruit-loop I'll call Paul. He was a big time wanna-be producer who owned a construction company and used the profits from that company to fund his show-biz adventures, mostly, because he found it much easier to pick up girls if he was the producer instead of a part of the audience. Paul was a tall, overweight, and a balding sex maniac of a bear, with an ego that would make Donald Trump's look tame. He once told me that the only real way to cure baldness was to drive a Porsche!

Alex was able to make a deal with him to fund the rest of the production to the tune of over one hundred and fifty thousand dollars. However, there was a catch. He wanted me to sign the million-dollar contract over to him. This meant he would be the one in control and have all of the power. I was very young; I had no money. I wanted this gig to happen more then anything in the world. So I did what he requested. Stupid! Stupid! Stupid!

My mother loves telling everyone she meets my story. She always prides herself on saying, "When Steven moved to Las Vegas, he didn't have a clue and about as much sense as a bed bug!" in her best Southern Baptist country accent. I was beginning to believe her. Through all of my effort to make my dream come true, although I suffered hard to get to where I was, I gave it all away with the stroke of a pen. I knew it and there was nothing I could do, or so I thought. Suddenly Paul had a million-dollar contract in his hands and I became a puppet on a string, nothing more than an employee. Alex could only look at me with sad eyes. Alex knew he was going to be sitting pretty. You see, as the agent for the deal, he would be making fifteen percent of every payday, no matter who was producing the show. I trusted Alex, and I still do. He's not like most producers in Vegas. He does have a heart and knows how to use it. He is a very good person. I can't blame him for being a good businessman as well.

    Paul, however, should have been a heart donor, since his was hardly ever used. He was a smooth criminal who did everything he could to make the deal one-sided. His side. Signing over the contract was only my first mistake. The second was using my old friend Lou and his animals. Lou and Paul got along really well. Too well, in fact. That should have been my first clue. As my mother used to tell me, I guess I didn't have a clue. Somehow, everyone decided that I was going to be working for Lou. He was going to pay my salary out of the money he would be getting for the animals and illusions that went with them, which he would be putting into the deal. Having been officially lost in the shuffle among all the greedy adults, I knew I wasn't going to make a single dime from the deal I found, sold to a group of billionaire Korean and Japanese businessmen, and lived on the street to realize. There was too much money to be made. I wasn't going to be making any of it. Lou knew that I wanted this show to happen more than anything on earth. He knew that I would do every single show (three per day, seven days a week) even if I weren't being paid. An ego can kill you.

He was right. I was completely blind, thanks to my OCD. That show and every detail of it were all I could breathe every second of my day. Lou convinced me that I owed him for all that he had done for me. The truth was, I never made a penny while working with him. That was far from the case for Lou. I would get the shows and other gigs, but he would make the money and he always had a handy excuse why I couldn't be paid that time. But the next time I was going to cash in big. I was another revenue stream to him. A driving force and unwilling to accept anything but success, he found it very convenient to have me around. Those animals eat a lot and the cast of slaving characters he used to help care for them did as well. Lou was a powerful manipulator the likes of which I have never seen since. He routinely made anyone believe anything he chose. His underground operation and the apprentice contracts he made his followers sign, created a very comfortable little cult for him. They did all the work and he reaped all the benefits, not unlike the cult that committed mass suicide in Waco Texas by setting their own house on fire, a few years back. But Lou is another book in itself. One I would never care to write for fear of what might happen to me if I did. Let's just say that Lou makes the devil himself more than a little nervous.

OCD robs you of much in your life. It steals not only the time wasted doing repetitious rituals over and over, but it clouds your ability to think clearly, and to see the reality of situations around you. Instead, it fills your mind with the illusions you want so badly to be reality. Sometimes, as in my case here, it gave me tunnel vision only allowing me to think about being up on that stage and nothing more. I was going to be a star, no matter what it took. Those around me without the honor of being an OCD sufferer saw me as an easy mark and jumped at the chance to take full advantage of the financial opportunity that I had created.

No one would listen to me. I was fighting hard to produce an award-winning show. Not Lou, not Paul. No one cared to listen. I knew what I was doing. I knew how to produce that show the right way. I had created the perfect show. It was amazing, impressive and unlike anything that had been seen in Korea before. That is what sold the hotel so easily in the first place, but no one cared except me. Paul and Lou began cutting corners everywhere. They claimed that what I wanted to produce was too expensive, and the Koreans wouldn't notice the difference anyway.

I knew they were wrong. These businessmen were far from stupid. They didn't achieve all they had without being clever and very smart businessmen. Not to mention the fact they had spent months traveling the world seeing every major production they could, searching for the right show. No one listened to me. By the time the backers' version of what I had sold the hotel had been produced, I was ashamed to stand on that stage. My name was on the marquee, not theirs.

The costumes were poorly designed and second rate. The illusions were mostly second hand and very worn. The soundtrack was a complete joke. Not a single person involved knew what they were doing, except for Alex, but his hands were tied. He was just the show's agent. The dancers they hired were the cheapest they could find. They got what they paid for, too. To get the kind of dancers the hotel wanted, you needed to pay top dollar. It's hard to get young, hot, talented kids to live in the middle of Korean rice paddies for a year. Even if you are in a billion dollar resort hotel.

Greed was destroying my dream, and I couldn't do a thing about it. Had it been me, I would have been content making less on the over-all deal, and walking away with a happy client who would use me again, than I would be to produce a horrible show, screwing the hotel and getting fired after only six months. That was exactly what happened. Of course, it was all my fault. I blamed myself right along with everyone else.

I did three shows a day, seven days a week with eighteen costume changes per show inside a four-thousand-seat arena with no air-conditioning, and an indoor average temperature of ninety degrees, not to mention the hundreds of stage lights and thick, hot costumes I wore. All of that combined, brought me to the brink of death. I collapsed on stage three times, but no one cared.

No one except for my production manager, Jim E. Meadows. Jim ran on stage, picked up my nearly lifeless body in his arms and carried me to a hospital. He was more like a Mash 4-0-7-7 unit by himself. They put a glucose IV in my arm. An hour or so later, I got up, went back to the theater and finished the final show of the day. One time I had to be dragged off stage by one of my legs. The show never stopped. I woke up in my dressing room as Jim patched up a cut above my left eye. Unable to really understand what had happened, I realized that my cue was coming up and ran back on stage.

I remember Jim looking at me closely and saying, "Steven, you are not superman, and I don't want you to end up like Elvis, either. You have to stop. You are dying man." I wish I had listened to him, but I didn't. He could see what I wouldn't let myself believe.

Bythe time the show was finally cancelled, I weighed slightly over one hundred pounds. My knees were completely shot. In severe pain from no rest and the abuse of performing so hard, I could hardly walk on my own. I was sick. I began to realize that Jim had indeed been correct. When we begin to die, something inside gently urges us to get things in order. I guess that you could say I was listening to a very strong voice in my head, and it wasn't mine. This inner voice prepares you for your final curtain call, and you begin to review your life. I was at peace, though. Still in great physical pain, I knew the end was near. I had felt that kind of peace before. I began to think about all I had been through and survived to end up in the physical condition in which I found myself. I was so disappointed that this was how I was finally going to leave this world. I was too tired to fight any more. Life wasn't going to work out for me, and I was okay with that.

Exhausted to the brink of death itself, I felt as if I had survived a life sentence without parole. I had crippled knees, an emaciated body, and a broken spirit. I opened my briefcase on the plane ride home and counted my fortune. Five thousand twenty-four dollars and thirty-nine cents. Most of that, I had received from the hotel directly in a secret deal I made with them soon after I had arrived in Korea and explained what was going to happen. I knew that if anyone knew I had that money, it would disappear. In constant pain, after surviving more than five hundred shows in six months, I asked myself if it was really worth it.

Since it's virtually impossible to treat OCD if there are overlying conditions which may mask a correct diagnosis, conditions such as manic depression, post-traumatic stress disorder, among others, may also be present in an OCD sufferer. These problems need to be treated before the underlying problem can be attacked.

I know that I am repeating myself, but this is so important that I want you to fully grasp this idea and hang on to it tightly.

People have told me that schizophrenia occurs when you hear voices in your head that aren't yours. The voice in my head that I was hearing was definitely not mine. Does that mean I was schizophrenic? Of course not! I have never been diagnosed with schizophrenia, so whose voice was it? Was it truly the voice of a higher power? An angel sent to protect me? There's a cynical aphorism, which goes something like this: "In Biblical times, people who heard voices in their heads were called prophets. Today, we call them insane."

I do not agree. I think the voice in my head was a gift from a higher power; a warning meant to break through my self-destructive OCD behavior and save my life. After all I have survived, I have come to believe that faith is an essential asset in overcoming OCD. I don't care what faith you practice or what higher power works for you. As long as faith, prayer and daily silence are a part of your life, you will always make it through the rain.

One of the greatest tools for controlling your OCD until

you are able to get the help you need through medication and therapy is silence. By that, I mean making a commitment within yourself to spend a few minutes a day to simply be.

Silence and daily meditation give your mind a break from the spinning and destructive internal dialogue that makes OCD sufferers so crazy inside. It doesn't come easy, either. It takes practice. Even spending as little as fifteen minutes a day, trying as hard as you can to clear your mind, to relax and stop the chatter in your brain will produce amazing results in the first few weeks. Nothing worth achieving is easy and at first you will find it nearly impossible. The OCD mind wastes so much of the sufferer's own energy that it's exhausting. A "normal" (whatever that means) person's brain uses about twenty percent of the body's over- all energy for the day. I would venture to say that the OCD brain uses double that or more. I know it sure felt that way to me. I found that by spending some time with nature, I was able to access great abilities long since repressed.

Things like my creativity became much stronger. It took a long time before my creative juices were rejuvenated, but I found them more profound. This enriched the quality of my life. I felt I had lost my creativity forever. It was always there, however. OCD hides our abilities from us and fills that space with useless mind chatter. I discovered that my memory improved. I suddenly had a greater command over what was going through my head.

To experience true silence requires the self-taught ability to periodically withdraw from the world, from your familiar surroundings and from the activity of speaking itself. For me, finding a peaceful place like a forest, a grassy hill in the sun or a quiet spot near the ocean is perfect. I find that being there relaxes me, especially when I focus on breathing deep, slow, lung-filling breaths of fresh air. By denying yourself a regular opportunity to free your mind, you are creating more turbulence in your brain, and the internal dialogue becomes more destructive within.

I promise you that in the beginning your internal dialogue will become more turbulent. Your OCD will fight you for control every step of the way. Don't listen to it. Refuse. You might begin to feel an overwhelming sense of urgency and anxiety to speak. But do not. Just refuse. Eventually, the mind will give up and your internal dialogue will stop the useless mind chatter. At that point, the silence you experience will become very profound indeed. Silence is a beautiful thing. A retreat you will long for every day thereafter.

Experiencing silence will open up a world of potentiality you never knew existed in your life. You will think much more clearly; you will begin to see that your creativity has improved far beyond what you thought possible. You will notice that you feel more in control of your mind and your life. You will have much more energy to make it through the day. It's a shame that I never understood such things until I was about twenty-nine years old. I could have suffered so much less than I did. In the Bible is the expression: "Be still and know that I am God." I finally understood this profound concept and came to realize that it could only be accomplished through silence. I urge you to become a seeker of silence, as I am. Tap into that inner peace that exists within you.

Find it and embrace all that it has to offer you. Try it;

make the effort. I know you are tired and worn out both physically and mentally. I was, too. I wanted to die. I felt there was no further reason to live. I had given it my all and failed yet again, so why continue? Why suffer a single day longer? What I didn't realize was that it wasn't me talking. It was my OCD, the demon living within my mind. Convincing me of a reality that was, in fact, an illusion. OCD is a powerful force that can convince you of anything it chooses, even that death is the only way out. I assure you that's it's not.

Give silence a chance. Pay attention to that inner voice telling you to stop your destructive OCD behavior because you might literally find yourself being touched by an angel, and they don't like to be ignored!

CHAPTER ELEVEN
Viva Las Vengeance

After some serious healing time spent with my sister Shelia who had since moved to Wendell, NC, I finally made the clear decision that I was not a quitter. I was going to make it or die trying, whichever came first. I had not come this far surviving everything I had, to quit. I believed in myself. I believed that there was something inside of me worth sharing. Every day I felt the urge getting stronger to try it all again. My best magic friend, Bill Robinson, was the only one who never called me crazy. He always believed in me and told me that if anyone could make it, it was going to be me. I could only pray that Bill was indeed right.

I was totally obsessed with proving myself. OCD has a really mean way of messing with your logic circuits. As long as I've had OCD, the main theme of my cycle has been, "Everything would be better if I worked harder." It was a never-ending mantra in my head. Day in and day out, the same repetitive mind loop played over and over. I would think in circles, until exhausted, I passed. My daily ritual was rehearsing, non-stop for days and weeks on end. I did it in many forms. I felt that if I were the most professional at my craft, there would be no way that I could fail. What I failed at was in realizing that not everything was under my control, and a control freak I was.

I was armed with knowledge and experience this time, which I felt would serve me well, if my knees would hold up. I could hardly walk. Especially up-stairs. Vegas hadn't been all bad. I remembered some fun times and silly things that happened.

For example, I remembered one day while working in the convenience store, about the time the Hard Rock Cafe had opened, this guy came into the store to buy something. I looked him over and said, "Has anyone ever told you that you look like Steven Spielberg?" He smirked and replied, "Isn't he a short little Jew?"

Laughing and good-natured, he paid for his mints and left the store. As he was walking out, I caught a glimpse of the jacket he was wearing. It read "Amblin Entertainment" on the back. It displayed a big picture logo of that famous scene of the moon with ET in silhouette flying through on the bike. Pure magic! Wait a minute! That *was* Steven Spielberg! Without thinking, I leaped over the counter and ran into the parking lot to say hi. Graciously, he stopped and had a brief conversation with me. He encouraged me to keep the faith and continue my journey toward my dream, as he had. Before he left, he shook my hand and told me that he would bet our paths would cross again someday. It was a pinnacle moment in my life. It gave me hope that all was not lost.

Returning to Vegas was going to be the ultimate challenge and I knew it. I slipped quietly back into town, not because I was modest, but because I was wary. My goal was to play hardball. If I got burned again, it would be my own fault. This time, I knew the game. I was not innocent any more. Now I felt angry, cold-hearted and fearless. The worst that could happen already had, and I had survived. What did I have to lose? It was tough. Tough was exactly what I knew I would have to be in order to survive. What had begun as a labor of love for me as a little child, had now become a tool for vengeance. This time I intended to succeed in spite of the odds. My rational mind demanded that I stay focused on being a street-wary guy. After all the backstabbing I'd been subjected to, I knew that maintaining my focus was essential for me to survive this time around in Las Vegas. It was really difficult to do that, what with the OCD telling me that the reason I'd been screwed over was because I hadn't been careful enough, hadn't worked hard enough, and allowed myself to be an easy target. Guilt plays a major part in the day-to-day life of any sufferer. I always had a difficult time trying to understand what made some people so bad. I mean, I believe that when we are born we enter this world with the very same good, basic human qualities. Things like honesty in its purest form, the basic need to give and receive human affection, the ability to love without judgment of any kind and only the most innocent of thoughts.

These aren't things that are taught to us later in life; we are born with them pre-installed in our hard drives. We are good people from the very first day. At what point do we learn to back-stab and to hate and to judge people from a simple glance? I became totally obsessed with proving myself to the world. I don't think I ever again was as focused as I became during this time. It was as if I had tunnel vision. I could think of nothing more than succeeding and proving to the world that I wasn't the wannabe I was so afraid I had become. It was all I could eat, sleep and do, day in and day out. I had taken the art of obsession to an even greater height.

In Las Vegas, as in so much of the entertainment industry, no matter how talented you are, it all comes down to who you know. Then, they have to like you and that's the hard part. Although you are one of the best in the business, if the powers that be don't like you for whatever reason, you ain't got a chance. I planned my strategy as if my life were an undercover military operation. I needed to infiltrate the innermost upper echelons of power, to discover the enemy's secret weapons, where they were, and who had them. In this campaign, my battlefield was the party scene. I knew that the most well connected people in town were, without question, the casino hosts. A casino host is usually a stressed-out, nail-biting, heavy-smoking, cell-phone obsessed, guy or girl the casino puts in charge of the most serious of gamblers and finding new ones.

These gamblers or "high rollers" as they are sometimes called, can regularly drop hundreds of thousands of dollars, millions in some cases, in a single weekend or a single hour, without blinking an eye. The casino host's main job is to keep that client very happy and in a gambling mood, although they may be losing. Keeping such a demanding person happy can be a very stressful task. Nonetheless, these casino hosts must have major contacts in town and the ability to pick up a cell phone and make every wish of each client come true immediately. Hosts were often hired based on who they knew and the relationships they have developed in town alone, making them very powerful people in their own right.

Entertainment is a huge part of a host's world. They often

have to find at the very last minute several tickets for a concert, show or fight that has been sold out for months. These guys know all the major entertainment players in town. If they don't, they don't last very long. I knew that winning the confidence of a few important casino hosts would be key in my plan and the fastest way to gain entry into that upper circle who signed all the deals.

The Las Vegas party scene infiltrator requires great camouflage, and the fine art of acting can be useful as camouflage, too. It's all an acting job in this town. Smiling in the face of evil and becoming "friends" with some of the lowest human elements this world has ever seen is a great skill to develop, because they often are the most powerful people in town. Everything about Vegas is an illusion. Over time it becomes difficult to distinguish fact from fiction. There are often several layers of crap to muddle through before actually discovering the facts. This is done by design. You see, everything in Las Vegas is a secret. No one wants anyone to know what is really going on at any given time for fear of having to block someone else's chess move.

Plans, projects and dinner engagements are all kept under wraps. It's the competitive nature of such a high risk, high stakes, twenty-four hour town. This was one of my greatest skills. I knew well how to play the game of secrets and had a few tricks of my own for gaining the secret knowledge of others for my own personal use.

The parties in town were where the powers that be mingled, mixed and made deals. Think of it as sort of a glamorous fishpond teeming with very expensive golden carp. Getting invited to the best parties was never difficult in those days, as long as I agreed to bring some magic and entertain along the way. If you take a closer look at that pond of fish swimming around in the sparkling water, you might notice that the pond actually is a cesspool, not to mention that most of those carp were really leeches. Talk about illusions! This pretty pond was a breeding ground for carp wannabes, too. If you asked my opinion and even if you didn't, there it was. The thing was, some of those leeches did manage to make it big.

    This meant you couldn't blow off every wannabe you found. Developing a rapport and winning them all as friends can be a great asset because you never know which wannabe's today, will be tomorrow's most important carp. Once you grasp the concept that every big fish in town and even a few of the little ones are out for themselves and are really nothing more then a leech in disguise, you will begin to play the game on a higher level. Trusting people you know in Vegas is like sending a box of mud to help hurricane victims. It's stupid.

    Playing this game is multi-leveled. If you look like a nobody, you'll certainly be treated like one. You have to act the part, look the part, and talk it, too. Now I'm not referring to the gold dripping, white suit wearing pimp-daddy style you see the all over the strip. We call those tourists. They are also called flashers, losers, and wannabes. You know the type I mean. They work really hard at being something they are not. Usually they have way too much product in their hair, while driving a leased car they couldn't afford to buy. I learned quickly that most fish have to keep their mouth open to breathe and that is usually what gets them caught. Sound like someone you know?

Business is serious in Vegas, and to be trusted among the decision-makers in town, you have to be smart about every move you make, including the clothes you wear, the places you are seen and with whom you are seen. I became very successful at infiltrating the party scene and making alliances along the way. The key was having something these people wanted. For me, it was my sleight of hand and charming southern personality. I entertained thousands. I would perform for one person at a time or groups of any size. It didn't matter. Casino host, hotel concierge, and a casino president or two all used me to entertain their most important guests in exchange for favors and whatever tips I gained. I performed in the back of limos on the way to the airport, in the most glamorous casino high roller suites and in the private VIP rooms of nearly every casino in town.

I always kept in mind that every ally was a potential adversary and continued to collect business cards, phone numbers, useful information and great contacts along the way. I would network with all I came into contact with, promoting myself and my magical services discreetly at every opportunity. It was a high risk, dangerous game, knowing all the while, that if I were caught doing such a thing by the powers that be, I would never work again. Trust was everything in Vegas behind the closed doors of this secret world. The ironic thing however, was that in Vegas, trust was fake, an illusion of the highest order because you could actually trust no one, not even your best friend. I used to say, "If it can talk, it will betray" because it was only a matter of time. People were easily swayed in Vegas. Temptation was everywhere and almost everyone was looking for a fast buck. The only thing keeping your best friend from turning into your worst foe was the amount it would take for him or her to betray you. Damn! I loved that town.

Las Vegas was a chess game with thousands of players constantly analyzing every other player's last move. They thought about every other player's next move, while trying to figure out which next move of their own was the best move they could make. It could be exhausting, but it could also be exhilarating. During every game, each player was naturally out to get a piece of the pie, and each player tried to be aware of the strengths and weaknesses of the other players in the game. Figuring out early on which players were pawns, which ones were kings, and which ones were the evil and dangerous queens was the key to survival in this game.

When other players thought that you were out for the same piece of the pie that they were after, especially players with the same amount of power as you, they were going to try to take you out any way that they could, by getting some dirt on you, or creating gossip and spreading rumors that could destroy you instantly. They formed alliances with other players, any way they could. They were as hungry as you, but not powerful enough to take out the stronger pieces. The more powerful players tended to watch you with a detached and somewhat bemused eye. They knew you were hungry; they knew you wanted what they had. They realized you were not strong enough to affect them -- yet.

The powerful players waited to see which of the lesser players were clever enough to outmaneuver other lesser players. Intrigues amused them. They knew what you were doing, because they had been there, done that, themselves.

They were older, more experienced, and I want to say

wiser; however, wisdom denotes kindness and benevolence which they did not possess. Cunning might be a better word. Once you started to move up and became a potential threat to the big dog's own power, they started paying attention to you like never before, drawing you closer into their inner circle. It was usually at this point in the game that they decided whether they could continue to use you for their own purposes or whether they needed to crush you like an eggshell. I learned quickly that the trick to staying in this game would be to create the illusion of being harmless and a threat to no one.

The best players are the ones who fit in with the other players and look like players but are not perceived to be a serious player by the others in the game. Another thing which I found very helpful was Sun-Tzu. This Chinese, Fourth Century BC warrior / philosopher's classic book of strategy, *The Art Of War* is the handbook for survival in Vegas. It taught you how to use your enemy to achieve total victory, among other things. Chairman Mao studied it to defeat the Japanese and Chiang Kai-shek. Now it became a tool for having my way with the predator capitalists I would be up against. Who would have imagined this?

In the midst of all of this, my goal was to position myself so that I become an indispensable interface of information. I knew that getting in through the front door of show business wasn't going to work for me, since I had tried that one in the past. So, the backdoor it was going to be.

I took copious notes and guarded them wisely. It didn't take very long for me to figure things out. After a while, I could tell you who knew who, and how who knew who, and who knew what about when and where.

I began selling information to some of the casino hosts in town. Because a big part of their business is creating new gambling clients and /or stealing clients from other casinos, I knew who was at what casino at any given time for the most part. I usually performed for them at some function they attended or got my information from the limo drivers who picked them up. I had a fleet of limo drivers all over town on my payroll. They were paid for every juicy piece of information they got for me, which I would turn around and sell to my clients, the casino hosts.

Hotel suite room numbers and dinner plans cost extra. If I knew exactly when and where a whale was going to be at any given time, especially if it was off of the property they were staying and gambling at, that information could be worth as much as a grand. I have sold many phone numbers over the years to some of the world's wealthiest gamblers for major bucks. If a casino host could lure a big gambling fish to their casino, it could mean cash in his pocket, which also meant some pretty nice bucks in mine, too. It was simple economics. Supply and demand. I had to be meticulous in every detail, obsessively so in fact, and very clever in the way information was exchanged. I couldn't allow myself to be known as the source of this info. In fact, more than a few casino hosts only knew me by my voice. It was not unlike being a spy.

My skills as a magician were very meticulous, to say the least. I was good at figuring things out and finding the best solution for each problem that arose. I was making great money, more than enough to purchase my own custom-built illusions and buy the right clothes I needed to match the attitude I had to portray. Image is everything in Sin City. Projecting the right image

-- not too much, not too little -- is the secret.

For a normal person, being nice, doing favors and getting favors in return is heir to the everyday stress and strain of living and interacting while at home or work. For someone like me, suffering with OCD, doing those things while having to deal with my daily rituals of non-stop rehearsing and a host of other obsessions was like trying to type while wearing really thick, stiff, mittens. It was more than just difficult.

Here I was trying to be cunning and clever without being able to think straight. How do you out-think your opponents when you can't finish a thought of your own? It was pure insanity. What I was attempting to do would be challenging for anyone with a normal brain. For me, having a dysfunctional mind and all that went with it, at times, it became too much.

I would crash for days on end. Sometimes I would have massive panic attacks alone, in a bathroom somewhere, leaving me without the strength to breathe. My chest would lock up in my desperate attempt to fill my lungs with air. It felt to me like drowning. I could always tell when one was about to hit and I knew that I had about thirty seconds to find a private place to suffer. If anyone saw me in such a state, I knew I would be ruined. I was deathly afraid of someone finding out and thinking I was a drug addict or something. I had taught myself a ritual to help me get through the attacks. I would quietly sing, "When You Wish upon a Star" in the corners of my mind over and over until I could finally once again breathe. I don't know why I picked that song. It chose me, I think. I remember one day at the Hard Rock Hotel, during a bad attack, it popped into my mind. It stayed there, and to this day, whenever fear comes my way, I mentally sing that song.

When you have OCD and you don't know you have it, you feel schizophrenic, but you are not. You don't really perceive OCD as a separate entity, but you know something's there. You realize that it is a part of your mind that does the constant worrying, rituals and all that goes along with this disorder. The other part of your brain tells you how crazy you are for doing the things you do. It's a never-ending battle between the two for complete control and that is what exhausts you. Trust me on this one. The fear, the worry and the exhausting rituals that keep you from living your life are much more difficult to handle than any therapy and medications you will take. Don't be afraid of the medications, either. I was terrified of taking the medications because I had silly visions of walking around like a zombie without a clue. That is not the case. Not even close. We will talk more in depth about the use of medications in a later chapter.

Another part of the seedy underworld of the power game in Vegas is that young, strong, blond-haired, blue-eyed boys were always in big demand by a select few of the most powerful fish in town. I decided to use my DNA as leverage among this secret ruling class of psychosexuals. The real trick was going to be getting continually reinvented to their parties without having to reveal my magic wand. I had not forgotten my past encounters with the sexual predators who crossed my path years earlier. However, this time I was much stronger, wiser, and in far greater control over what was happening to me. I felt that getting access to the select few members of the "Velvet Mafia" as we called them, would be yet another step toward achieving my goals.

I had been invited to a celebrity-filled, power-packing

party at the Riviera Hotel and Casino. The gay owner of a large radio broadcasting company was looking for company, and I was his pick of the litter. This party was a who's who of the entertainment scene. A new show was opening and after the premier of "Splash" there would be a massive invite-only party where anybody who was anybody would arrive in style. I had to be there although it meant accepting the invitation from someone who wanted to show me a little sleight of hand of his own. And just what was it that some of these exclusive male entertainment directors, lawyers, casino executives, executive secretaries, executive assistants, and public relation directors wanted? Well, most of it is better if it remains unspoken. But believe me, through subtle gestures and body language, code language and innuendo, they made their every wish known. If you could read their minds, you'd need brain plugs because sometimes it's too much to handle. I had taught myself how to walk a very fine line between using the powerful and being used by them.

The secret lay in filling them with expectations, while extracting what information I could and moving on before they could accomplish what was really on their agenda. Call it the art of misdirection. It was not an easy game to play and if it became at all obvious to them that you were indeed playing a game they dropped you like yesterday's news. Playing mind games with people with a lust for power, money and success is one thing. Throw in a healthy libido and a lust for something they couldn't have, and you were playing with fire. It would be like having sex while holding a pin-less grenade. At some point you were bound to drop it if your partner was any good.

These guys didn't like to play games they couldn't win or

be rejected. They didn't like games which made them feel as though someone else had won and they had lost. More than a few in Vegas have never been seen again because they knew someone's most intimate sexual secrets. In Las Vegas, that knowledge alone could earn you a free one-way trip to the desert. That's not a joke, either.

Overall, I became a pretty good facilitator. Because of my skills at taking mental notes and storing information and not being perceived as a threat to any of the major game players, I managed to become a vast clearinghouse of useful information for all kinds of players over the years. Not only on my level, but on upper levels as well. For example: Let's say that some hopeful had a project he wanted placed on a certain casino president's desk. Through insiders he heard of my reputation for getting people together, so he came to me. Through my connections, I knew this president's golf caddy. This caddy was a person this president trusted after so many pleasant hours spent on the golf course. So this president was in a mellow mood with his guard down when the caddy happened to slip him this certain project proposal that has now bypassed the usual phalanx of functionaries, and well, there you were. Another favor done. I was very careful about what projects and proposals I passed using this method. It had to be something that the president was going to be interested in seeing and of the level such a person would expect. Such favors would cost big money and/or big favors in return. The trick was in being very genteel and pleasant to all concerned. A lot of times, the people who were helping me never knew they were helping me.

The old godfatherish cliché, "I-do-you-a-favor now--

someday-I-may-ask-you-to-do-me-a-favor" routine didn't always work. You had to be flexible and creative in your approach each and every time. Soon, favors I had not been calling in started coming to me unbidden. I had a steady stream of corporate gigs. I was making good money again. I was a bit puzzled at my own behavior, though. Here I was, the innocent burned by experience. I had returned to Las Vegas cold-hearted, out-for-vengeance, trusting nobody, playing the game. And what happened? I ended up getting favors because I appeared to be a nice guy. I never felt so wrong. I realized that my greatest skill was one I despised most in others. I had the strong ability to get what I wanted, whenever I wanted it from anyone. I grew scared at how good at this I was.

It was through one of my strongest contacts that I was introduced to a producer who was looking for a highly visual act to be featured in his next production heading for South America. "The Farfan's Present Circo Las Vegas!" A six-month tour of several countries was at hand. I jumped at the opportunity to be a part of it. I wanted to escape the Vegas lifestyle and return to what I really wanted to do. My first love always was performing. It's where my heart is and always will be. As I prepared to leave for South America, I noticed that Las Vegas was changing. The old Mafioso pinky-ring-style of cigar-smoking, show-biz agent was being replaced by the new and often very young, clean-cut-looking corporate guy. Family values seemed to be taking over The Family in Vegas. It's still as cutthroat as ever, but now it's a corporate, clean-cut kind of cutthroat.

I guess that in the mob's heyday in Vegas things were a bit easier. You could eat dinner and see shows for free, since what you lost at the gaming tables and in the slots covered the cost of paying for things in a roundabout way. After all, the mob always was very good at creative accounting. They still do those things today, but believe me, it comes with a heavy price these days. It isn't free anymore. In most cases, it's cheaper to pay for things yourself. Now, the corporate types have realized that not only can they suck your wallet dry at the tables, they can also nail you at the box office as well. Entire families flocked to the new, wholesome Las Vegas although tickets to the average Broadway show now cost less than tickets to the average Las Vegas production, as insane as that may be.

Hey mafia! If you're reading this, "Nothin' personal." It was better back then. Today, it is big business, megabucks corporate business.

CHAPTER TWELVE
Bienvenidos a Lima!

The tour of South America kicked off in Lima, Peru. After some intense rehearsals at Mr. Farfan's training compound in Vegas, we headed to Miami where we would be catching a direct flight. It was fun getting back into the performing game again. The producer's sons, Tato and Gino Farfan, were world famous, record-breaking flying trapeze artists, The Flying Farfans. The best in the business. They had been the star flying attraction for Ringling Brothers Circus for nearly ten years. I learned a lot hanging around these guys. I felt, for the very first time, that I had met some people who could actually understand me. The Farfans had not always had it so easy. Long before the big Vegas house, the fancy cars and all that went with success, they had it pretty rough. They were immigrants who came to this country in search of a peaceful existence and a little of the American dream. Show business had been in their blood for more than seven generations. Tato and Gino were basically raised on the famous Ringling Brothers Circus train while traveling around the country.

Their father was a relentless rehearsal dictator, often making them rehearse for ten hours a day whether or not their hands were bleeding from gripping a steel trapeze bar. Then, they would have a couple of live shows to do that night. Let's just say they didn't have an easy childhood.

So there we were, about thirty or forty of us from all across the country, in Miami International Airport awaiting our flight when I suddenly caught a glimpse of that day's newspaper headline. I can't remember the exact title now, but it said something like: "Lima Blacked Out by Terrorist Bombings." Wonnnderful. That was just what we all needed to see before getting on the plane. Mr. Farfan reassured us that he knew about the uprising and had been in contact with the tour promoters in Lima. "The media is making a big deal out of nothing.

"The show is going on and our opening week is sold-out already." For most of us, that was reason enough to get on the plane. Me, as excited as I was, being the first to board. I couldn't wait to get there.

It was another one of those brilliant moments in my life when I didn't have a clue. Thanks to a higher power that I didn't, too! I believe that sometimes, following your heart with wild abandon is good for the soul. It makes us stronger humans from the inside out.

The Farfans had developed a very smart deal by combining our production with a hit children's syndicated television show produced in Lima called *"Nubeluz,"* which in Spanish loosely translates to Cloud Light. The show was seen live each Saturday and Sunday morning from nine a.m. to twelve noon in more than twenty countries by eighty million viewers every week. This was a powerful marketing tool that would announce to every Spanish-speaking country that we were coming their way soon. The hosts of the show were two very talented and strikingly beautiful girls, Monica and Almendra, both of them young girls themselves in their early twenties. They, along with their backup singers and dancers, would be performing in the middle of the show, which gave all of us the extra-long intermission, we were for which we were thankful.

I don't think that I was ever before as excited as I was the night we finally landed in Lima, Peru, but that quickly disappeared. On the Farfan party plane, I scanned bits and pieces of the article over somebody's shoulder as we flew across the ocean. It didn't look good. "Power plant bombed...Lima water supply disrupted... car bombs rock the city... President Alberto Fujimori declares emergency.... peasant uprising...fanatic Marxist terrorist group *Sendero Luminoso* (Shining Path) claims responsibility." The captain announced, "We are on final approach into Peru's capital city." This meant we had to stop throwing our food and crawling over the tops of the seats, watching porno on lap top computers and playing tag up and down the aisle. The circus people and I all had to be put back into our cages and strapped down for landing.

I think we gave those poor flight attendants a nervous breakdown on that trip. I couldn't tell where we were from the air, since the power outage had blacked out the city. In the distance we could see a few dimly lit runway lights getting closer and closer. We landed safely. I assumed we must be in Lima.

I felt a strange and eerie sensation as I walked off the plane and into the airport. Everything was deathly quiet, as if time was about to stop and the earth was slowing down. I saw few people in the terminal itself. The ones we did see, all had machine guns and wore battle fatigues. I had a new respect for Dorothy in the "Wizard of Oz" movie I watched as a child. It became all too clear, really quickly, that we weren't in Kansas anymore.

Ka-boooom!

The loudest, most earth-shaking noise I had heard in my life, instantly created a force that rocked the bus we were all in as we sat in the airport parking lot awaiting our departure. I came to my senses on the floor of the bus with about ten of my now closest friends. Glass lay everywhere. Apparently, we were traveling with a South American dignitary the Shining Path wasn't too fond of so they blew up the American Airlines luggage terminal right in front of our bus. Yes, we got all of our luggage and none of us were really injured. At the speed of light, the bus took off, flying as fast as it could go into the Peruvian darkness in search of safety. As we all began to crawl off the floor and clean our pants, someone noticed that a team of serious, machine-gun toting military guys on motorcycles surrounded our bus. They freaked us out, and some of the girls began to scream and cry. Mr. Farfan shouted with clear authority, "EVERYBODY! SHUT UP! THEY ARE WITH US. THE PROMOTERS HAVE SENT THEM TO PROTECT US JUST IN CASE!"

As the bus flew down the road, I felt relieved. WAIT A COTTON-PICK'N' MINUTE HERE! IN CASE OF WHAT? I begin to think to myself.

Down one street and up the next in total darkness. We begin to realize that we had landed in the middle of an active civil war. This time, it was the poor people who were pissed. That fact didn't make me feel any better. I could feel a huge anxiety attack heading right for my chest. It was time to drown again. In the distance, we could hear gunfire. It was hard to remain calm, but most of us were able to manage, mainly because we were too busy trying to hang on and stay in our seats.

Without warning the bus came to a full stop. We were at a safe house for the time being. Hidden deep within some unknown neighborhood we could not see, we unloaded the bus and found our way, in the dark, without a single source of light. We climbed up the stairs of the big house we would call home until daylight came. We were told that only two places in the city had power and running water. Neither of which we were going to be staying at. One place with electricity was the airport. NOPE! Not going back there. The other was the Hyatt Regency, which was sold out, and protected by military lock-down. No one could get in or out.

I guess it could go without saying, that none of us were able to sleep that night, especially having made such a spectacular entrance. So we did what any other traveling troop of talented, show business, globe-trotting kids would do. We sat in the dark in a big room by a moonlit window and played Truth or Dare and the ever popular spin the bottle. To be honest, I think that unconsciously our brains were seeking some form of comforting comic relief and someone happened to find a bottle.

Lima was a city of nearly five million people living in a mixture of Spanish colonial architecture, modern buildings, beautiful old mansions and more than a few hideous slums. In Lima, you were either very rich or very poor. The middle class hardly existed at all. The poor people of Peru had finally endured enough of the wealthy class getting richer and more powerful while draining their country's resources dry. It was a sad thing that was happening, but as the days passed we learned of the poor and how badly they had been suffering. I actually began to side with them. I felt sorry for their plight and their suffering. Quietly, of course. With machine guns everywhere and not knowing who was on whose side, I didn't think it too wise to let my feelings be known. I was happy to see that they were taking charge and fighting for what was rightly theirs in the first place.

As time wore on, I grew closer and closer to Tato and Gino. I eventually became one of the Farfan cheerleaders in helping to keep everyone in the show calm and focused on the real task at hand, that task being the grand opening of this massive production in the middle of a war zone.

New to everything in sight, we were pretty much clueless that this show, *Nubeluz*, that we had never heard of, was actually the most popular kids' TV show in the entire Spanish-speaking world. It was so huge that Pan American Television Corporation had purchased a twelve-thousand-seat concert arena to produce the show in. This was the only venue in the entire country big enough to hold the sets and massive television production paraphernalia involved in the live TV broadcast itself. Not until we walked into that arena for the very first time did we fully understand how important this kids' show truly was.

The Farfans were not ones to wait around, so we were unloading in the venue that very day with whatever workers we could find. A great deal of hard work had to be done prior to the first rehearsal. It would take about a week of solid eighteen-hour days to rig the show for the first time in such a massive showroom. Since we had traveled to Lima with only the entertainers in the show, we first had to hire a local work crew to help with the heavy task of unloading and rigging our production. It didn't take long, either. Word got around quickly. The next morning a line of job hopefuls wrapped around the venue. Everything from young thugs to very old men were in the running. Work was in short supply in Lima and the prospect of a job was an exciting and very welcomed opportunity for most. Although we were still living in that big house with no power or running water, things had calmed down for us and were getting back to normal. Well, as normal as one could be under the circumstances at hand.

My mind was reeling uncontrollably. I begin to be very excited about the opening of the show. In the awesome atmosphere I saw all of the other acts spread around the huge venue rehearsing on their own while the work crew continued rigging in the middle. I was happy, yet scared to death at the same time. For many of us, it was the first time we actually saw each other perform. I was very impressed, too. All of the acts hired for this show were really good. The Farfans clearly knew what they were doing and had hired the best of the best. I couldn't figure out why I was among them. I had never been in a performing arts circus before.

Never had I worked with such amazingly talented and daring people in all my life. I was a simple magician with a few illusions, a two-hundred-pound mountain lion, several white ducks and a twelve-foot python named Snappy who didn't really like me very much. No one had ever heard of me, and I didn't speak a single word of Spanish. Most of these folk spoke at least three languages. Mrs. Farfan alone spoke more then five languages clearly and another five or so in bits and pieces. No matter what language you spoke, she was always able to communicate and get her point across.

So, who was I to be in the middle of such show business royalty? These people had more talent and skills than they realized in most cases. They had been born with it in their blood. Years and years of pain, broken limbs and endless training had made them what they were, and they were far from what I was. I wondered if they would like me. Would I get out there and fail in front of thousands? Was I going to get fired when they saw my act?

I was starting to become overwhelmed with fear. I thought, I am not as good as these people! Oh, my gosh! I can't do anything like THAT, as I watched some amazingly crazy stunt being rehearsed by the life-long professionals among the cast. Not only couldn't I do what they did, but why would anyone in his right mind possibly want to?

I was among a group of people who were clearly not my peers. All I envisioned was totally wrapped in self-doubt and insecurity. I began to panic quietly as I had done in secret throughout my life. I would find a hidden spot, suffer alone and sometimes even vomit my fears out of my body until I was able to get back out there and try to look as if I knew what I was doing. Playing the role of a successful entertainer was a part I had trained myself well for. I decided that I was going to take "Fake it until you make it" to a whole new level.

And then, there was Stephanie, the queen diva of all divas. She was an aerialist power act. I had never seen the likes of her before. What a body that babe had! Muscle on muscles, but in the most feminine way. Sexy was too tame a word for this girl. She was so hot, that Gino Farfan went straight for the take down the second he laid eyes on this one. You see, Gino was an internationally famous ladies' man since the age of about ten years old. Bagging show business babes of any age was one of his many endearing talents. We all loved Gino. We had to, because nothing was going to stop him. Stephanie and Gino were so alike in personality and ego that Tato and I looked at one another and said, "Somebody's going to get hurt."

I began my rehearsals with a couple of female assistants that the Farfans had selected for me. Renatta was a natural. Her beauty, grace and sex appeal on stage made her one of the best assistants I had ever worked with. The other assistant named Tania was a different story altogether. After a short time, I began to call her Princess Tatiana. Never in all my years in show business had I seen such an amazingly beautiful girl. With fiery red-dyed hair, she was a complete knockout. She often wanted to go back to her natural color, but she honestly couldn't remember what it was. I likened her personality to the famed character, Jessica Rabbit, in the movie "Who Framed Roger Rabbit?" She had sex appeal oozing out of her skintight clothing and knew how to handle herself. Poised and elegant as long as people (especially male people) were watching, she instantly transformed into a bumbling klutz, barely able to stand up in her own spiked heals the second they were not. She was high maintenance, too, which earned her the royal title of princess. Back in New York City where she grew up, she got to be well known at all the top salons. When Tania went to the beauty parlor, she used the emergency entrances to set off the alarms, so everyone was aware that she had arrived. "Oops, was that me?" Think Anna Nicole Smith with a really hot body. Oh, and there was one more thing... she was screwing up my act.

Yeah she was sexy all right, but I tried hard for the first three days to get rid of her fast. At one point I had her in tears because she couldn't understand the physical mechanics of what I needed to be done. I had endured enough and time was running out. I was tired of wasting my efforts with her and wanted another girl. At this point I didn't care what she looked like, but the producers refused, saying, "Steven, she is so hot that no one will even notice that you are out there. She stays!" Well to me, that was all the more reason to get rid of her. Granted, she did make me look good, and I must admit that she knew how to work that body on stage. She could give the strippers in Vegas a lesson or two as well. I was not sure that she hadn't. I had to work with her, regardless of whether I liked it or not. So back to the drawing board I went, knowing full well that she hated me. The experience was amazingly stressful. I had nothing against her personally, in fact, I actually loved her as a person. We got along well and were pretty close to each other so long as we weren't in rehearsals, but she wasn't what I wanted for an assistant.

Tania's strongest talent was manipulating the drooling male masses that did her bidding. She never lifted a finger. She had guys fighting each other over who got to take her whatever she was asking for. She once met a guy at a bar in Lima one night and actually convinced him to give her his car! Keys and all. She had only one problem. Tania didn't know how to drive, but she did that night. We were all in the new, and oh-so-lovely hotel we had moved into, hanging out the windows and watching all the hookers on the corner, when we heard this car honking its horn loudly as it came up the street. It was Tania in her brand new car!

All this was accomplished with grace and a great amount of poise. There was simply no man in South America with the skills to handle the likes of the bombshell princess. She had broken hearts in every country she visited and had them all smiling and blinking their tear-filled eyes when she left.

Opening day came and went to a completely sold out arena on a Friday night. Of course, Tania screwed up the big finish where I transformed her into a mountain lion, but I don't think anyone really noticed. When that big cat leaped across that stage, the audience went wild.

I had never in my life performed before such a large, incredibly excited and cheering crowd. This was one of the most exhilarating feelings I had ever felt. I couldn't help but think that this must be what all the rock stars talked about. It was a massive head rush, a high, all-hitting you the second you ran out on stage. I couldn't believe that I was on that stage. There I stood in front of thousands of screaming fans having the time of their lives. I couldn't have felt any better than I did right then. I had finally found my own utopia. I did my twelve-minute act and ran off stage to the biggest response I ever got in my life. I knew I had done well. Running down the hall, heading for the men's dressing room, I passed Tato running toward the stage, and he said, "WOW! Listen to them! They loved you!" When I got to the dressing room, I was alone since everyone else was on stage. I sat down and silently cried my eyes out. This time, the tears were from great joy.

This was the dream I had always wanted to live. I had wanted my entire life to perform my craft and be accepted by my audience. In South America, they rarely got to see such massive productions. I was thrilled to be a part of this one. Crying was the release of my bottled-up emotions, which I had kept neatly locked away inside. I could hold them in no more. The floodgates were open, and tears began to pour out.

I felt as if I had finally proven what I had always known was in me. On that day, all of my obsessive rehearsing rituals had finally paid off. No more was I having the uncontrollable urge to hide and practice under the false illusion that it would make me what I had envisioned that I needed to be in order to succeed. For the first time, I felt confident on stage. Secure. I knew that I had given the audience exactly what they wanted to see. It was the first true "Oh, my God!" moment in my life.

I suddenly got it. I understood. These people liked me for me, just the way I was, not some vision or silly image that I thought the world had to see me as. No amount of practice, no amount of obsession over the details would change that fact. It didn't matter what I looked like. It didn't matter that I wasn't perfect. The audience loved what I did because of the way I did it. Trying so hard to be what I thought the world wanted to see, I had forgotten who I wanted to be. I think that what it all boiled down to was a young boy searching for the love and approval he had never gotten at home.

When you have OCD, simple things are often not so simple. Some people are afraid to go to sleep at night without checking the door lock exactly forty-seven times or whatever number their own personal obsession tells them to check it. As I have stated before, the ritual performed is irrelevant. It's the fact that something is controlling you using fear. OCD is fear-based.

It makes you feel that if you don't perform that ritual, no matter what that ritual is, something bad will happen. Over the past few years I have met and talked with many young people suffering with OCD. One young guy from Chicago told me that he was actually afraid to leave his room. It took his parents and teams of experts more than a year to get him to walk outside. Another guy I interviewed was what most people commonly refer to as a germ freak. I was a bit of that way myself. This twenty-seven-year old man was obsessed with cleaning and not getting dirty. He couldn't shake your hand or use a phone you or anyone else had used without going through his own special cleaning process many times. Handrails were simply out of the question. Door knobs, too. He had very special systems for doing everything that would make every task he did ten times more complex then it needed to be, slowing down his life, wasting time, and causing him to worry about getting sick. He would clean twelve hours at a time and wash his hands more then thirty times a day, so many times that they often bled. It was too painful for him to live in that prison of his own creation until he finally got help. To the average person, that may sound silly, but it wasn't silly to him. It was very real. OCD controls you and everything you do. Every decision, every thought, every action taken or not taken. I sometimes refer to my OCD as my pimp because it does the very same thing a pimp does to his working girls on the street. OCD completely controls your life. I became obsessed with magic out of my fear of not understanding what was happening in the real world around me. The only good and positive thing in my life at that time was magic. So that's exactly where I retreated to. My experiences in the real world were less than heartwarming. Yet, when I performed magic, everyone gathered around. We move closer to that which gives us good results or comfort in our lives and away from what gives us bad results or pain. For a long time in my life, my magic was the only good thing. It gave me something to focus on and a way of blocking out all that I didn't understand.

The Farfans let me be myself and do my thing. It worked. They liked me the way I was. It wasn't long before I knew the guys would be coming back into the dressing room, so I cleaned up and got ready for my next appearance. This time out, I was going to have the time of my life showing the world what I could really do.

The next day, I appeared along with Tato and Gino on the live children's TV show *Nubeluz*. It was fun. I really enjoyed being on TV and having a live studio audience of about three hundred children there to watch me. It was one of many shows that we did the week before opening to promote the show. I had no idea how my life was about to change. I didn't realize what had taken place until the next day.

Having accomplished a major task, I woke up late as did most of the performers. We were all exhausted. It was a bright Sunday morning, and I awoke pretty hungry. I got dressed and decided to hunt for some food. As I was walking down the street, I noticed that people in cars were honking their horns a lot. I kept trying to figure out what they were honking at. I looked around but never saw a thing out of the ordinary. Then, a car stopped and out plunged a car-load of kids all screaming, "*Mago! Mago!*" which I quickly learned was the Spanish word for magician. Everyone, including the adults, was talking so fast that it would have been impossible for me to understand had I spoken Spanish. I had kids hugging my legs. Mom was taking pictures and the rest of the kids were jumping up and down, screaming at the top of their lungs. I couldn't understand a word. It was very clear to me that these strange people I didn't know, knew me. They were acting as if I were Michael Jackson or something. It blew my mind. Another car stopped and the same thing happened. In a matter of about two minutes, I had stopped traffic. A mob was growing. I signed whatever they handed me. They took at least fifty pictures and then kindly bowed out and said good-bye. By this time, some kids on bikes had arrived and they were following me, talking to me as if I understood every word. I began to walk a little faster and they followed. I finally entered a store and bought a few things when suddenly I was surrounded again. It was the same response, but this time there were many more people. People were touching me, pulling me their way so they could get a picture with me and fighting over who went next. I thought I must be dreaming. This could not be happening to me. Who was I? Why, all of a sudden, did people care? What were they thinking? They must believe I was one of the Flying Farfans. Yeah, that was it. It had to be a fluke! The store manager was asking me to leave his store and step out-side because of the scene that was getting out of control. "But before you go," he began in broken English. He wanted an autograph.

I realized that there was no way I would be able to walk back home, so I jumped into a cab. Confused and dazed, I didn't believe that these people could be reacting like this because of me. They had to think I was somebody else. But who? A few days later the producers of *Nubeluz* asked the Farfans if I could make another appearance on their TV show. Realizing what a great opportunity to gain some additional exposure for the show this was, they readily agreed and came to talk to me. The second appearance was better than the first. I began to enjoy this TV stuff. I was getting the hang of it all as well. It was fun being on television so often. I was out there having fun. They let me play in some of the games with the kids on the show. That was a bonus to me. I loved it. Whatever I wanted to do or be a part of, was fine with them. So I basically took over.

 A few more days went by and the producers of *Nubeluz* were asking for another appearance. I could tell that Mr. Farfan was beginning to smell something fishy. I, however, was excited that they kept inviting me back. I loved doing the show. The two co-hosts spoke decent English. They were a lot of fun to work with. They would climb in my boxes and do whatever I wanted them to for the sake of the show. It was great. I felt as if I belonged there. Little did I know, but the TV producers had a plan. These appearances I was doing weren't a casual guest spot. They were a screen test. They liked what they saw and came to me with an idea. "Steven, do you have a lawyer? A manager? We would like to make you an offer and take you to dinner tonight." I told them that I would be happy to go under one circumstance. That we go alone. None of the Farfans or anyone else associated with the show could be invited. That was exactly what they had in mind. Making some silly excuse, I slipped out of our new hotel and past the hookers who by now knew my name because of my new found fame. A driver in a black van with tinted windows picked me up. He drove me to the agreed-upon location. The stage was set for a life-changing, mind-blowing dinner. It seemed that the viewers of *Nubeluz* had spoken. They had responded in large numbers to my appearances on the show. The show had received a huge number of fan letters addressed to me. The kids that watched the show had found something they could really relate to: magic! Though I spoke not a word of Spanish, my illusions were a visual art that anyone could understand.

I was also a rather crazy character on the show as well, and it struck a chord among the masses. Never in the seven-year history of the show, had a single guest created such a stir, not even the very young Ricky Martin. Magic was more than a song or a dance for the young viewer of this show. It was something tangible they could grasp on any level. The show's producers and the network all agreed that I could breathe some new life into an otherwise stale, formatted show. It was time to put the magic back into the live show, so to speak, and I was the man for the job.

I barely ate a single bite of my food, listening to what was being said. These people wanted me to be a part of one of Latin America's most popular hit television shows? Me? I was confused but oh soooo happy at what I was hearing. There was only one problem. The Farfans and the contract I had signed with them. My brain was screaming at me to sign the deal and forget the Farfans, but I had grown close to the group. I had begun to love them quite a lot. I was happy with them and in my heart I knew that I couldn't leave them.

So I turned *Nubeluz* down, explaining that if they wanted to sign a deal after my contract with the Farfans expired, I would be more than happy, but I wasn't willing to leave the family who had given me the chance of a lifetime.

I got out of the van up the street from the entrance to the hotel so as not to be seen and went to bed, knowing that I had passed up an even bigger and more important chance of a lifetime. And I couldn't tell a soul.

The Farfan tour finally ended in Santiago in the most charming of beautiful South American countries, Chile. It was the Farfan's original birthplace and they had come home to show their own people what they had accomplished.

It was a wild success story that the press loved to cover. I was ready for the show to end. *Nubeluz* was on my mind.

Almost to the day my contract with the Farfans ended, I received a message from the producers in Lima. They were thinking of doing a tour and wanted me to help with its creation and also come along as a guest star of the show. It took me less than a second to say, "Yes!" I was ready to get back to what I really wanted to do. After all, fame and fortune awaited. Or so I thought.

When you actually become a public figure on a large scale, there isn't an easy way to describe what happens to you and your life. Everything you do is news. You learn things like: if they don't get a picture of your face, the photo can't be sold. In South America the press can be vicious and evil at times. The last thing you want is to be caught in public looking like a bum. I didn't like to dress up when I didn't have to. In my free time, I wanted to dress comfortably like I used to when I lived among the cows.

People chasing you down was a common thing. People followed you anywhere you went, taking pictures from afar, as well. Things you bought in any store could make it into gossip columns and could be analyzed as to why you bought the things you did. Simple things like going to a movie or trying to buy some of your favorite music in a store could be a stressful experience. The strange thing was, that although you felt as if you had lost every bit of your private life, the attention could be very addictive. I would be lying if I said I didn't enjoy it, because I did. Well, for a while anyway. By this time, I was doing every TV show in the Spanish-speaking world. My Spanish was improving. I was now able to speak, or at least get my point across, to the fans on the streets. I had never been one to sit around and do nothing. I would get out and explore everywhere I went. I developed a very approachable relationship with the public, which always seemed to work in my favor. Within a year, I was an American, non-Spanish speaking wild man on *Nubeluz* and living the life I had never dreamed would someday be my own reality.

    Magic combined with laughter and a warm smile is a universal language that communicates with all. You only need a heart to understand. The days were long, but that was okay because I was a workaholic anyway. Thanks to my dad, of course. Most were eighteen and twenty-hour days. It only took about two years to become somewhat fluent in Spanish. Before then, my poor business partner, Bruno, went through hell as my twenty-four-hour translator. It nearly drove him insane. I guess you could say that I learned Spanish on live TV with millions watching. People thought that it was funny that I was trying so hard to speak and never failed to murder the Spanish language every time. It became one of my many trademarks on TV.

Sometimes I did it on purpose, a feat I learned from the great show business legend, Charo! I think the only thing I wasn't fluent in was fame. I had no clue what it did to you, your life, and those around you that you cared about. I had friends who no longer wanted to hang around me because it slowed them down and was an event everywhere we went. Fame changed everything and not always in a positive way. Yet, millions spend their entire lives hopelessly in search of it. I began to ask myself why. I quickly learned the fame game. Fame is easy to get, but difficult to keep. Sometimes people think they're famous when actually it has been a slow news day for the real stuff. Those who keep fame, learn how the game is played. They learn how to use the system to their own advantage. Sometimes that comes with a very heavy price. However, I was not prepared for it emotionally, physically, or mentally. It takes a very strong person to handle a public life. You have to have a do-whatever-it-takes mentality to stay famous, and I was never really that kind of a guy. By nature I was not a cutthroat or vicious person. In this business, sometimes you have to be. Vegas had prepared me well. It was exhausting work, and very expensive!

The money was rolling in, thousands of dollars at a time, and I was on top of my game. But, I had this entire staff of people working around the clock for me. Managers, producers, publicists, agents, stylists, lawyers, among a whole host of others, including magic consultants and illusion engineers, which you need when you are a magician constantly creating new illusions to perform on TV. All of these people have to be paid. It was non-stop and expensive, exhausting, but very necessary to staying on top.

Bienvenidos a Lima

You could perform and do interviews and promotional shows in several different countries in a single day and conduct press interviews on the plane on route to the next location. You must do whatever it takes to stay on top. You hire people to worry about the details, contracts and legal stuff for you. Your only job becomes being yourself and performing when they tell you, where they tell you. You keep smiling and looking good while doing it. Life becomes a big blur. Time didn't exist. You lose track of what day it is, what country you are in and who is the president of your own country. World news is impossible to keep track of, so you don't. All hotels begin to look alike. People always seem to ask you the same twenty questions, no matter where you go. You develop standard answers and learn how to repeat them as if it's the first time anyone has ever asked you that. You become a master in the art of avoiding the questions you don't want to answer. As far as the pubic and my crew knew, I was completely up to speed. Smiling, performing, always being "on," delighting the kids along the way, touring, and always being grateful and humble to the public that made you is very hard work. "You think you know, but you don't" to borrow a line from the MTV documentary show "Diary." Inside I was disintegrating. Physically, it was as punishing as Korea at times. Mentally, fame took a serious toll. Financially, I had no clue how much I had in the bank. I really didn't care. There was always more to make. Money was like water. It kept flowing in until one day a few years later.

Kapow! Silence.

Blood splattered the wall. She fell to the bedroom floor, her face a mangled mess from a single gunshot blast to the head.

Suicide.

RING, RING….

"Hello…Steven, it's Lucho. Monica is dead! She killed herself last night after a fight with her boyfriend!"

With that single sentence, millions of fans would be heartbroken, millions more in disbelief. The press would grow angry and three hundred very special people lost their livelihoods. Three hundred families were now left to fend for themselves. When she pulled that trigger, Monica had successfully cancelled the show we all had put so much into over the years. It was devastating to all and a wound that would never fully heal in my soul. *Nubeluz* was over and the worst was yet to come.

CHAPTER THIRTEEN
Seventeen Days

Flash forward, eighteen months or so later…

I heard the excited crowd in the nearly sold-out theater as I made my way from my dressing room onto the stage for my next performance, which was about to begin in one minute. It was the second performance that night. I was getting into my secret spot so that I could magically appear, when one of my guys came running up to me in the dark and said, "Steven, one of your sisters is trying to get in touch with you. She says it's very urgent!" I asked, "Which one?" He replied, "Shelia. Do you want to hold the show and call her?" Time stopped yet again in my life. This time, it was really going to hurt.

My heart sank like watching an NFL playback in slow-motion. It was the middle of the night where Shelia lived. I knew in my heart what had happened. If I called her, I would never make it through the show so I decided to block it out, something I had become very proficient at over the years. It was my answer for everything I didn't want to deal with.

"No. Let's rock and roll now!" I yelled, and the curtain went up. I magically appeared and did the show as if nothing had happened. As the performance wore on, I grew completely numb, emotionally void, on automatic pilot, going through the motions the best I could. It was like an out-of-body experience.

I was there, yet I was detached somehow, looking at things from a different perspective, watching myself perform.

Still in costume, I walked offstage to a cheering crowd, and ran out the back door. During the show I had arranged for the van to rush me back to my hotel.

Once in my room, I asked everyone to leave, except for my close friend and most trusted advisor, Jim Meadows. We both knew what was about to be revealed. Dialing the numbers on the phone, I began to shake.

"Shelia? What's wrong?"

Instantly she began to cry. "Stevie... it's Daddy."

"Shelia, is he dead?" I said with a cracking voice.

"Yes, he's gone."

The rest was a blur. The only other thing I can remember clearly was calling my step-monster and having her hang up on me.

She said, "Are you happy now? You killed him with all the stress you have put him through!" Click.

In the blink of an eye, my world crashed on top of me. It was too much. I couldn't handle that in the middle of a tour. I knew that there was no way in hell I was going to be able to return to the States right then. There were contracts, massive obligations and surely major legal battles to come if I took off. What was I going to do? How was I going to be able to get through this one? The light of my life, the man who taught me how to dream, the one who built my first puppet stage and helped me learn my very first trick was no longer alive. How could this be? Was it true? Was he really gone? Was it April 1st? This had to be a joke!

Seventeen Days

It was March 21, 1995. The day my father died.

He had been a very sick man. Seven heart attacks, two triple bypass open-heart surgeries and awaiting a new heart for a pending transplant, he simply stopped breathing in his sleep. His time had run out. I'm sure having a wife that was working at the only bank in town and sleeping with a married bank employee in that little town of Phenix wasn't helpful either. Yet, she blamed me. I put down the phone. Jim came over and hugged me tight. Only he could really understand what was going on inside of me. He had lost his mother only a few years earlier. He knew what my father meant to me in my life. Had Jim not been there, I might have thought about doing something crazy.

For me that night was a torturous time of rage in the fetal position in a hotel room in some foreign country, somewhere far from where I wanted to be. I cried until no more tears came. Then I screamed. I longed to be with my father.

The thought of being alone in this world without my hero was not an option I cared to explore . I was tired and did not have the skills to cope with my loss.

Anger and hatred became two of my closest friends. Actually, they had been long-time friends of mine. Since the days my mother used to kick me as I lay on the floor, I had always been angry. But now, I was full of rage! I hated Nancy! I hated my biological mother . In fact, I had stopped speaking to her for several years at this point. I hated the world we lived in, the superficial people in it, and what I had become. I was angry at my higher power for taking away my only source of guidance, my best friend, my father.

How dare this happen to me at that moment! I couldn't

stop thinking.

My mind began a fast-paced spiral downward toward OCD, my old friend that had in large part been suppressed for a short while, but who now returned in full force, stronger than ever. I could do nothing but hide, cry, shake and fear.

Guilt consumed me. Especially since I realized why my father had the specific conversation he had with me seventeen days earlier. I had been so busy that I hadn't picked up the phone to call him in seventeen days. I had actually lost track of the most important thing in my life and the only thing that really mattered to me, which was my relationship with my dad. He was gone, and I would never again hear him say, "Son, don't ever let them get you down. You just hang in there and you'll make it." I would never get to tell him just once more how thankful I was that he had been my father, how I appreciated what he had done for me, and how I knew that he had done the best he could. I would never hear him laugh again, or see him quietly smile when I did some trick he couldn't figure out.

I would never again have the honor of hugging him, and saying, "Good-night Dad," as I went to bed. I would never see him out in the field tending to his best friends that most other people called cows, rabbits and goats. I couldn't go to his funeral. My two sisters were actually telling me that it might be a good thing if I wasn't there. They knew full well that Virginia wasn't big enough for both Nancy and me. Never in my life had I been such an evil-thinking and enraged human being. To end her life, making it a very slow and painful death, would have been what might have taken place had I attended my father's service. Why was I having such violent feelings? I had never thought about harming anyone before. Well, except for "Jeff – not his real name" and "Lynn the Bully" and maybe another one or two in there somewhere.

    I remembered something that my dad had told me during that now-famous conversation. He specifically said to me that he didn't want me to come home should anything happen to him. He said that he wasn't going to be there anyway and that funerals were for the living and not the dead. I remembered discussing this in great detail with my father. He hadn't wanted me to stop working and come home. He had wanted me to keep entertaining as any workaholic would. I can still hear him telling me to keep doing what I did and get better at it every day. So I made the decision to stay and work although I was on a downhill course of self-destruction, poverty and deep despair.

    Later that summer, I had a beautiful twenty-sixth story apartment overlooking the Andes Mountains in Santiago, Chile. The touring was long over. The TV appearances had stopped, and the economy had taken a turn for the worse. I couldn't have cared less. I needed some time to think. I decided to hide for a while and just think. I was running out of money, and my business partner, Bruno had decided to leave me to direct his own feature films and start his own production company. My company folded. Soon, I was no longer able to afford the extravagant lifestyle I had grown so accustomed to.

    Many upon many friends came to my aid. Rudolpho, Leon, Adrian, Billy, Jim, and Veronica, to name a few. Try as they might, nothing really worked. I began to fall into a deep depression. I felt like a failure and was embarrassed to show my face.

I didn't know why, either. Anger had become my breakfast when I awoke each morning. Hate kept me full throughout the day. I couldn't see a way out. I had lost my will. I became lazy, stopped eating regular meals and answering the phone. I would sit in a dark room covered up on a couch for days at a time watching TV in the dark. In show business, people forget about you quickly and you can become yesterday's news in the blink of an eye. As months passed, fewer and fewer people recognized me. The crowds were gone. Finally, no one cared. My life alone became deafening silence.

Fame. So quickly it came, only to disappear faster than I expected. I thought I had cured myself of wanting to be famous. The experience taught me some very valuable lessons. Fame, money, and power are temporary. True friends, love and relationships are all that really matter when the chips are down. A trusted and true friend once explained it to me like this: Material things and status are desires based on the desires our ego, not what we truly need.

For example, if you were the CEO of a major corporation, you had a fancy title, a fancy salary, took fancy vacations and had a certain amount of power that went along with being a person in that position. You enjoyed those things and might have worked very hard for them, but I can assure you of one thing, they only last as long as the job.

Your true friends, the love around you and that of your own family that you share, and the relationships you have developed will always be there. Ask hurricane victims who have lost everything they owned. Standing in front of a pile of rubble they spent a lifetime obtaining, they will tell you what truly matters in life. Hurricane victims no longer have fancy houses or cars. The material things they so worshiped are no longer objects of their desire and they now value the very basics of human existence. You are alive, the lives of those around you have an entirely new meaning. The dog who faithfully loves you without a reason, comes waddling out from under the wreck of what used to be your home. Suddenly, you understand. You finally get it. Life is so much more than anger, hate and material things. It's bigger and better than the most important thing anyone owns.

For me, I got it in a big way. I realized that happiness, love and all the things that we truly need, we all have within. None of those ego-based objects of desire will truly enrich your life. Only the things that money, fame and power can't buy help you to find your way to the happiness that already lives inside of you. Seek and ye shall find. My anger, my hate and all of the negative feelings that consumed me every second of every day, were about things I no longer had that my ego desired. I don't care how much money you have or don't have. If you can't be happy with the contents of your heart, no amount of money, fame or power will ever change that. Think about it.

My one true passion was still magic, but I continued to play in my room alone at times. It was if I had reverted back to the little boy I used to be, the only comfortable place my mind had ever known. I had no clue what I wanted to do with myself or with my life now that my father was gone. I couldn't sleep. Nightmares usually filled my head. I had no energy, no desire, no will, no emotions, no cares, no love, no social life, no business, no money and no peace. Years passed as I struggled harder and harder to make it through each day. Several times I nearly became homeless once again. I felt it was only a matter of time before I ended back where I began, yet I couldn't force myself to leave my room. Depression had become a way of life. The inner reaches of hell were at my door every time I opened it, until the day came when I could no longer afford to eat.

Funny, but when the food supply ran dry, I suddenly had the energy to move and get out there. "Hey, aren't you that magic guy?" I used to hear that a lot whenever I did venture out, sending me deeper and deeper into the silence of the darkest place I knew. When people recognized me, it only served as a painful reminder of someone I used to be, and of the horror of the being I had become. I found it much too painful to deal with. So I didn't. I hid myself however I had to whenever I went out. Strangely enough, when I was on TV, I had done everything I could to be noticed when out in the streets. The more people who spotted me, the happier I thought I was. Hell, I remember times when I would go out in public just to sign autographs, because I was so addicted to the attention. These days, the only thing I was addicted to were sleeping pills.

I swear that I slept through entire months at a time without ever seeing the light of day. Daylight was something I avoided at all costs. Through it all, my good friend, Jim, never left my side. He fed me, made me shower when I hadn't for days, prayed for me, talked to me, got medicine for me when I was sick and never gave up believing in my dream. I remember days when Jim would drive me insane until I gave up and went out doors with him. We would sit on a bench in a popular section of trendy Santiago and watch the people I used to entertain walk by.

We used to sit there looking like bums and laughing at all

the fashion faux pas that passed our way. We studied people and the things that were so important to them and discussed the reasons why. Jim was there for me when no one else cared. It never mattered to him whether I had money or not. He never cared about anything much except keeping me alive and well, and his missing daughter that he never forgot for a single moment. Jim was divorced and his former wife disappeared with their only child, never to be seen again. Every attempt to find her had failed, but he never forgot a single birthday. He bought her a card every year and wrote her a letter as proof, knowing that someday, she would cross his path again. Jim had a heart of gold, even when life got him down.

    I am ashamed to realize that I never took the time to notice all he did for me back then. He defended me when people in the industry or anyone, for that matter, would laugh at me or call me a has-been. The children who once loved me were older now and had moved on to bigger and better things. This was very hard to take. Too much, too quick, too young. You get yourself so caught up in how great you think you are that your feet begin to lose their connection with gravity and the real world below. Jim finally convinced me to give my career another try. After years of the worst hell you could imagine, deeply in debt and feeling sorry for myself, it was time to get back out there and give it one more shot, for better or worse.

    Through the grapevine in Santiago I heard of a guy who wanted to get in touch with me but didn't know where I was. His name was Cookie. No kidding. Of East Indian decent, he had been born in Chile and came running up to me as I came out of a tiny little Chilean stage show one day. Cookie explained to me that he knew of a group of investors who wanted to produce a show, and he felt that I was exactly what they were looking for. One of them owned a restaurant called The Broadway on the outskirts of Santiago. He wanted to arrange a meeting with the owner, who also owned several other businesses around town. I agreed. A few days later, Jim and I were picked up and driven to a tiny back-alley printing company and shuffled into a very cluttered and nasty old office. Behind the desk sat the boss himself, a short, fat, smiling Chilean version of "The Godfather." He was exactly what you are picturing right now. It was like having been in a scene from the "Twilight Zone." I was afraid to sit down before he did. Everywhere people were running around doing his bidding. They even called him the Chilean word for boss.

His name was William in English and I actually found him to be quite charming. It wasn't long before we had discussed his plans for building a theater or music hall as he called it on his property near the restaurant. The idea being to eventually build a hotel and make it into a full-fledged weekend resort complex for families traveling on the highway to Vina del Mar, the most popular beach resort in Chile. He felt that a magic show was exactly what he needed to attract families to his complex. He had a freestanding building on his property that he currently rented out for large weddings that we thought could become a great venue for a theater expansion. It would cost big money. He had it; he was willing to invest it, and that wasn't all. He owned a construction company and could have any theater I designed built at cost.

Then there were the issues of producing the show, which was also going to cost big money, since what William really wanted was a massive million-dollar Las Vegas showgirl-infested review.

I did everything I could to convince him otherwise. I knew that wasn't going to go over among the good, Pope-fearing Catholics in Chile. He didn't know that. In fact, he knew nothing about show business, never having seen a real Las Vegas show.

This was going to be my advantage, or so I thought. He gathered a group of his friends and the next thing I knew we had the money to build the theater and produce the show. His lawyers handled the contract. I agreed to produce and star in the production itself. The show was called "The Power of Dreams" and was designed with a Broadway theatrical flare that told the story of a young boy who only dreamed of magic. What else? So with funding and contracting in place, I began designing every single inch of the theater, from ceiling to floor, including the stage, the backstage and all that went with that. I worked with his engineers and helped them create what would eventually become the Broadway Theater. At the same time, I was designing every single aspect of the show from the illusions, to the wardrobe, the sets and the soundtrack. The auditioning of several hundred of the most talented dancers, actors and young kids Santiago had to offer was only one of the many phases in the production process.

This was my baby and my chance to show people that I was not just a children's magician. I was a serious performer with talent, knowledge, experience and know-how. I felt alive again! I was climbing out of my hole and I could actually see the sky.

It was a very long and extremely difficult birth. "The Power of Dreams" was not without massive production problems, to say the least. The main one being that William and his friends were very slow in coughing up the production money, but isn't that always the case? Let's say that it was one of the top ten most stressful experiences of my entire life. The longer it took to get the money, the closer it got to opening night, and no one but me seemed to care. Wardrobe was in full swing and it required more then two hundred costumes, forty wigs, and a host of other unusual props to bring the production to life. A new lighting system with more than eighty programmable, moving lights and another twenty special effects, including liquid nitrogen low lying foggers all needed to be installed. Most of the lighting and sound system was purchased in Italy and had to be shipped over. That didn't come cheap either. All the illusions, the people involved and so much more had to be handled on a daily basis. The producer's job in any show is not only to create and produce. I would say his main job is as a problem solver. What a producer does all day is put out those production fires that pop up unexpectedly. That happens to be one of my strongest skills. How I was able to pull myself together well enough to handle this production, I will never really know. But I did, and I did it well.

Maybe even too well, because little did I know of the subplot unfolding in the background, behind closed doors when I wasn't around.

The show opened to rave reviews. It was a very successful production, the likes of which had never been seen in Chile before. Beautiful girls flew around the theater, I appeared inside of a giant six foot tall crystal diamond, was shot from a huge cannon over the audience, sawed myself in half and, of course, there was the grand finale where I levitated a real car on stage and made it disappear into thin air. It was a truly heart-warming show for the entire family.

The show's phenomenal success was mind-blowing to the Chilean investors, and strangely enough, that was the problem. Not for me, but for the investors! Trouble was brewing in the background, in the shadows beyond my circle, and I didn't have a clue. Months later, after the opening excitement slowed down, I realized that the audience was getting smaller and smaller and so was the show's marketing. In fact, I had been so busy with the show that I had failed to notice that there was no longer any marketing at all. What was going on? I began to complain. Loudly.

I sent Jim to investigate and investigate he did. It didn't take us long to uncover the truth. One of the first things we discovered was that the cell phone I had been given to use was bugged. They were listening to every word. Second, the Chilean investment partnership which included a very high-ranking supreme court judge, were really some of the major players in the Chilean Mafia everyone claims doesn't exist. I assure you that it does. I saw it first hand.

You see, "The Power of Dreams" was a front for the mob's latest money-laundering operation. They never wanted the show to succeed. They thought I was going to produce a disaster. When they saw the show opening night, among the sold-out crowd and massive standing ovation at the end, their teeth nearly hit the floor. They knew they were in trouble.

They wanted the show to fail for the tax write-off. They

had planned to use its slow death to clean a lot of dirty money in the process. Here is how it worked. In Chile, the government requires you to pay a tax on every ticket sold. They ensure you do this by requiring you to pre-print your tickets and have them individually stamped and numbered by the government itself. You pay these taxes up front. The rest of the money is yours. So, if you stop promoting your show, people stop buying tickets. Tickets you, as the promoter have already paid taxes on. The Chilean government doesn't care if people actually come to your show or not. That is your problem. You have paid the required tax on each ticket to be sold and have followed the law. So the government is quite happy.

If no one comes to your show in a three-thousand seat venue and the taxes are paid, you can now do some creative accounting with your books (called cooking the books) and show that every performance was sold out although it wasn't. All of those empty seats were there for a reason: This was to justify dirty drug money that they couldn't deposit in a bank. It was a big problem for the mob. You couldn't hide such large sums just anywhere. We're talking tens of millions of US dollars. You had to own printing shops, construction companies, nightclubs and restaurants to help you hide it all. Keeping the money moving was the key.

The mob took the proof (paid government tax receipts) of where all of this money came from and deposited the clean money in the mob's bank account. Instantly, previously unjustified money had legal proof of how it was made. A brilliant illusion, don't you think?

The South American mob and a few corrupt government

officials were making money hand over fist, which wasn't the case for me. I was getting a percentage of the ticket sales. If no tickets sold, I made nothing. Deeper and deeper I went into that scary dark place called depression once again.

I complained to what I assumed were honest government officials. They told me to take my backers to court, but actually suggested that it might not be good for my health to do so, upon learning the names of all involved. It was the first time I actually understood how powerful these men really were. Their names alone caused people to flinch. I had some of the best and most expensive lawyers in town telling me the same. These folks weren't talking about my emotional and physical health during the stress of a public trial, either. They were talking about me losing my life. I got the message clearly. The official legal advice was to pack up quietly and leave the country without saying a word, losing everything I had built, but saving my life in the process.

Sometime later that year, I quit performing and decided to take legal action. It closed the show and therefore the entire operation.

They tried hard to force me to continue performing, but I realized that I was in a losing proposition no matter what I did. So I didn't show up one day. It wasn't long before I found myself trying hard to make ends meet. Once again couldn't afford my staff and I let everyone go. They thought I was crazy because they knew what I was going to try and do. I wanted to sue the mob, but with a Supreme Court judge in their pocket, it would be like nailing gelatin to the wall. I had spent what money I had made on legal fees pursuing justice. Justice wasn't going to happen, not to mention that none of the top lawyers in town wanted to be involved. I decided to make a deal with the mob. I decided to confront the partners face to face and show them copies of my evidence. My plan was to leave the country quietly and not go to the press with my story so long as I could leave with all of my equipment and illusions.

Note to self: Don't threaten the mob. They were not amused. In fact, I was politely informed that if I tried to sue them or go to the press, the only thing to disappear would be me. That night I called my good friend Bill Robinson in Knightdale, North Carolina, for some serious advice.

Billy had been kept abreast on the latest news which we used to call the "Diamond Up Date" throughout the hundreds of hours of phone conversations over the course of pre-production.

Billy was very straightforward that night, and anyone who knows him, knows what I mean. This is what he said. "Steven, you get on the next plane out of Chile and come to my house, right now. They know you can go to the press and that means you have to be dealt with. If you don't get out now, you may not live to see tomorrow, and I am very serious!"

I had never heard Bill Robinson talk like that before. He was dead serious, which was a very unusual thing for one of the funniest people I know. I hung up the phone and began packing my bags. I called Jim to come over and informed him that I was getting the hell out of Dodge. I was going to leave Jim behind to pack up my things and deal with my apartment. He understood and also felt it best that I leave.

We feared the apartment could have been bugged and that someone might have heard my conversation with Bill. That would tip them off and allow them time to cut me off at the pass. Bill and I had talked about some crazy stuff, including taping interviews telling my story before mailing copies to every reporter in the country. Once at the airport I was seriously afraid for my life. I didn't know what was going to happen. Suddenly, we spotted someone we knew and he was not a good guy.

I feared that they would have me stopped by blocking my passport and prevent me from boarding a plane, fearing that I had given them up to the press already. After all, what did I have to lose? I was angry, broke, and out millions, thanks to them. One of my very best Chilean friends was a well known journalist for the most popular national network with his own TV news magazine program. They knew that. Such a task as ensuring I didn't talk was simple work for these guys. Anything was possible. If they spotted Jim, it was like spotting me, knowing that he never left my side. Jim insisted on going. It was one of the most intense and crazy nights I have experienced in my life. I finally got my plane ticket and went to customs for inspection when the agent at the window suddenly yelled, "Hey, look who I have! It's Steven Diamond, the magician on TV."

Every single head within earshot of his insanely loud voice was instantly looking at me. He wanted an autograph, but I was terrified that it was some sort of a signal. I felt as if a plan was going down and I had a big red target painted on my ass. William was after me. If he wanted me dead there was no doubt in my mind that his bidding would be done. Once I passed through security, I was on my own. Jim could only stand there and watch me get farther away. I asked some security people who approached me for an autograph to escort me to my plane and they were happy to do so. The entire time my heart was pounding so hard, I felt as if I was about to pass out. I was sweating profusely and felt as if I was going to have a heart attack right there. I jumped every time someone spoke to me. I had never experienced true terror before, and I wasn't sure I would be around to experience it again, either. I viewed everyone I saw as a potential threat, including the Chilean Airport Security personnel who were at my side. One of them asked me why I was so nervous, and I replied, "Because today could be the day I die."

It was time to board and I was escorted on the plane first. Security called for the plane to be secured as long as it was on the ground and in minutes it was. Once on the plane I began to calm down a bit. I could breathe again, and I was given something to drink. Every person that boarded wanted to shake my hand, but I was the one doing all the shaking for sure. I could barely sign my name. I was a total mess and completely convinced that until the plane landed on American soil, anything was possible. Throughout my many TV appearances over the years, I had performed many live televised escapes. Once, I hung myself from a burning rope while tightly confined in a regulation straight jacket under a helicopter more than three hundred feet above the world below. That's higher than the Statue of Liberty in New York Harbor. However, if I arrived in America alive, I was going to consider this one my greatest escape ever.

I remember looking out my window as we took off and thinking to myself, I came to South America in fear and it is in terror that I am leaving. It was a profound moment in my life, one that made me realize maybe it was time to get out of magic, stop chasing the dream, get a real job, live a normal life, be a real person and just be me, Steven Scott Mosley, that person inside, I had never gotten to know.

CHAPTER FOURTEEN
The End's Beginning

Vancouver, British Columbia, is a beautiful place to be, any time of the year. I had often been there before to perform at corporate conventions and other occasions, but never really spent much time looking around or getting to know the town. When I am working, I am usually in and out pretty quickly. Vancouver is a booming Canadian version of Hollywood, having some of the greatest production craftsmen in the world. The craftsmen there produce some of the biggest budget films and TV shows, and lately have been giving Hollywood a run for its money. The cost of producing such productions can at times be half the price of those in California. Vancouver is a very clean and friendly town, full of creative juices flowing everywhere you go. Artisans gather at the local coffee shops and brainstorm new projects in a most refreshing atmosphere of modern-day thinking. It's a quiet and peaceful town, where people of every kind exist in harmony and generally care about those they meet.

When my former employee turned Vancouver Film School student offered me the opportunity to come and stay with him for a while, I decided to take him up on the offer. Matthew was my all-around technical director for the "Power of Dreams" show in Chile. It was no small task, either. He was young, just eighteen years old, but one of the smartest and most eager people

I had met. His unbroken and innocent spirit won me over and beat out many other applicants with impressive credentials. He turned out to be the show's greatest production asset. When the show ended, Matt took off to study his real love at one of the best film schools in Canada, but we kept in touch.

When I arrived, Matthew gave me a warm welcome and made me feel right at home, which is a lot more then I can say for the Canadian Customs Officials at the Vancouver Airport. Everywhere I go, I travel with a little case of magic gimmicks, props and tricks. I always have. There is nothing really valuable in it, just silly things I use to make people smile and giggle from time to time. You never know when some sleight of hand may come in handy, and so this case goes wherever I do. Admittedly, it's a very strange and unusual collection of secret toys that to the untrained eye could warrant a closer look.

I have traveled throughout more than thirty countries around the globe with this little case of magic. Yet, every time I go through customs in Vancouver, some official, who wants to entertain himself and his coworkers in my magic case for several hours, holds me up. EVERY TIME! I can explain that I am a magician all day long. I can show them my full-color promotional brochures, to no avail. They don't care. You would think that I was carrying a case of explosives or firearms with all the commotion these guys like to cause. Once they grab the radios and call their buddies, I know it's going to be a while. The outcome is always the same, however. They eventually give me my belongings and allow me to enter the country like everyone else. I guess they feel more important this way and since that's the case, well, then, what can I do?

Having finally made it through customs more then three hours late, I met Matthew who was sitting there waiting for me on the outside of the building. He could see me through the windows, but the custom officials wouldn't allow us to communicate at all. It's the worst boarder-crossing point in the world if you're a magician.

Living alone in a beautiful high-rise apartment on Beach Avenue in the heart of the West End, I was able to fit in comfortably without getting too much in Matthew's way. I was an emotional mess, and to be honest, I didn't need to be around anyone in such an unstable condition, especially Matthew. I should have been in a hospital somewhere. I was broken, in every sense of the word. My spirit, my pride, my self-esteem, my bankroll were all shot. I couldn't collect my thoughts. I could hardly carry on a decent conversation with Matt as it was.

I had failed yet again, and for the first time in my life, I had decided to quit performing and leave magic behind. It wasn't working although I had given it my best shot. I had somehow convinced myself that if I had been born a better-looking guy, maybe I would have made it. I was thin, and my eyes were dark and sunken into my head. I was losing my hair and refused to end up like my dad, combing about fifteen hairs, believing it was actually covering something. My brain could do nothing but continue to repeat over and over that I was a failure and would never achieve my show business dreams. I had never felt so low and so unimportant in all my life.

I didn't want to see people, talk to people or have anything to do with anyone at all. I used to get angry at Matthew for introducing me to people and telling them that I was a magician.

They would expect me to do a trick, and I have always had a difficult time saying no. I hated that and I wanted nothing more than to forget my past and look for something new in life. Something safe, without risk, something I was sure to succeed at was what my brain kept telling me. I wasn't going to put myself out on a limb any more. For what? Why go through all of that stress and work so hard to end up with nothing? I couldn't figure out why. The payoff was no longer there. I would often spend days in the apartment shaking and nervous when awake, followed by a deep, sleeping pill induced coma until my body decided it was time to get up, whatever time or day that might be.

     With a high school education, what would I be qualified for? What would I do? I didn't know. I didn't want to think about it either. I wanted to sleep my life away. Sleep became my drug. It was my only escape from the real world, and I had stockpiled enough sleeping pills while in South America to keep peace in the Middle East for several years.

     Life can sometimes be too much for one person to handle, especially if that person doesn't have a strong network of supportive people around him. We all have our melting points. I had finally reached mine. I was beginning to feel dizzy when I stood. I couldn't do much without having the overwhelming feeling that I was about to pass out. This would happen several times a day. Blackouts were not uncommon for me. I did everything I could to hide them from Matthew. I had always been strong around him, and I didn't want him to see me like that. The outside world was a blur. I couldn't remember things I wanted to, only the bad things. They would play over and over in my mind like an endless loop. I was very angry. Angry at the world, at myself, at everyone and everything I knew. I began to lose track of certain events and when they happened and in what order. My body was tense all the time, growing weaker, and I ached from head to toe. At times I couldn't breathe while sitting quietly in a chair, trying to watch TV. I was terrified to meet new people and got very nervous whenever Matt would invite his friends over. I sweated all day long. At times I felt as if I was going to vomit for no reason at all.

I would cry for hours on end while Matt was at school. Staring out a window, I wondered why I should keep going, thinking that this was my punishment for having lived such a horrible life and treating so many people the way I did for so long, Matt included.

I felt as if my body was slowly shutting down. I felt as if I was dying. So this is what it feels like? I used to think. I remembered my dad and all that he went through prior to his final day. I couldn't help but wonder if this was what he felt like before he died. My sisters had told me that the day my father died, he awoke early that morning and got out of bed, full of energy and feeling better than ever. Nancy was shocked, but let him do whatever he wanted. I was told that he went down to the barn and helped to deliver some baby goats, as if nothing had ever happened. He walked back to the house without any help and continued his day. They said it was the most perfect day he had lived in years. He was happy and alert and feeling fine. I felt that when my perfect day came, I would know the end had arrived for me as well. Was this the feeling that made him call me and talk to me so seriously? Should I be doing the same? Should I call my family and my friends and say good-bye without saying the actual words?

This was no way to live. There was nothing in my life I wanted to do that I hadn't done already. At this point, what did I have to lose? I had been a famous magician. Made, spent and lost more money then most people would in several lifetimes and traveled the world while doing it. I grew up playing with lions and tigers and became best friends with a black panther named Shadow. Boy, what I wouldn't have given for one more warm lick on the nose from him. I began to relive my life through remembering the past. Over and over, my past would relive itself. This used to happen so often that Matthew used to tell me to move on and get over it nearly every day, but I couldn't stop, no matter what I did.

In my few moments of coherency, I was able to flash back to certain times in my life that made me smile. Though rare, it did happen at times. I watched some old videos of myself and realized that I had indeed lived a truly adventurous and full life. There wasn't much left for me to do, and I was looking for a way out in case my perfect day never came. Suicide was never far from my mind. I didn't want to grow old and go through all that comes with that.

I had worked many cruise ships over the years and had heard enough blue-hairs complain about how much getting old really sucks to know that it wasn't something I was going to enjoy. So why look forward to that misery? I searched hard for answers. I came up with a plan, too.

In case I didn't find a peaceful solution, and finally called it quits, I convinced Matthew to make a video of me walking and talking along the beach. I floated out over the ocean in that tape.

In almost a Jesus-like pose you could see me floating just above the water's surface in what was my own way of saying that I was ready to go. It showed me laughing, happy, sad, doing some close-up magic in the street and playing around with some of my street-performing friends. It turned out really well. Matthew didn't know it, but that video was made to say good-bye. I wasn't sure if I was going to pull through yet again. I didn't have the strength. I wasn't feeling well and didn't care if I lived or not. So I wanted to have a video for people to remember me, that would show me as I really was, a difficult thing to do without creating suspicion in Matt's mind, but I got it done. I think Matt knew that something was going on, but because he trusted me, he didn't push the issue. I knew that out of all the people that I called friends, Matt was the only one strong enough to handle my sudden disappearance. I wasn't going to do anything gross, though I felt like soaring out of the twenty-seventh floor of the high-rise and gracefully flying to my final destination. I always dreamed of flying. The only thing that stopped me was the thought of Matt having to see the mess left behind. Out of respect for a great friend, I felt as if I should just disappear, vanish one day, never to be seen again. Then Matt would find a document I had written to him explaining what to do and who to call and so forth. I had finally figured things out and found a way to achieve a painless end that would create the least amount of stress on all involved. The letter I wrote was thirty-eight pages long and took more than a month to write. I thought it was important to answer nearly every possible question anyone could have, even after the fact. I didn't want to leave my family hanging and wondering why. I also didn't want Matthew to get in any trouble. I was most afraid of someone trying to pin my suicide on him as a murder. I was going to be careful and very smart in the way I did things in order to protect him. So I had my letter notarized. It seemed like the perfect plan. Once the video was done, I felt a lot better and actually more in control of things for the first time in a long time.

I couldn't allow myself to go crazy and end up committed into some mental ward somewhere. I wasn't going to go out like that. I was going on my terms and with dignity. My mind wouldn't shut up. Nothing I did or could do would stop the useless chatter. I didn't want to live if that was what I had to look forward to.

After many weeks in an emotional rock-bottom haze, I decided to call the one person in my life I trusted more then anyone else, now that my father was gone, the man who had taken me under his wing many years before and always gave me the right advice, Burton Brown. He was the President of the Stardust Hotel and Casino in Las Vegas and for whatever reason, was never more than a phone call away no matter what time of the day or night and no matter where I was, anywhere in the world. Burton was my mentor and never failed to tell it like it was whenever I would call him with some crazy situation, uncertain of what to do. He never offered me any money throughout all the years. I knew him well. He never said no to my calls and gave all the business advice I wanted for free. He used to tell me that I had what it took to really make it in this world, and he wasn't talking about magic. He taught me about what you need inside and upstairs to stay alive in this game and keep yourself on the right path. I didn't always listen to Burton's advice and learned the hard way that he was rarely wrong. He and his live-in girlfriend of more than ten years had become like family to me. I was ashamed to call Burton with the news of my latest failure in South America. I didn't want him to know the condition I was in, but I knew that he would know anyway as soon as he answered the phone. We were that close. I always felt that Burton saw something in me that reminded him of himself and was grooming me to be a successor of some sort.

    I knew that I needed to pull myself out of this hell if there was any hope of my making it to my thirtieth birthday, which was only a few years away. Something somewhere inside of me wasn't ready to go although I felt like dying. There was still a spark in there somewhere, trying hard to find the light of day. I knew that Burton would help me find the right path. He always did. I picked up the phone and made the call to Lompoc, California.

    Burton was completely rejuvenating. He told me that he was proud of me for having made it this far so young. He told me that my father was proud, too. He only asked me one thing, which was to take a while and just be. Forget about everything and exist. Walk by the river, sit in a field, listen to quiet music and let my spirit come back to life. What Burton was telling me was to let my inner silence speak. Let whatever was inside of me have a chance to air its voice, whatever that might entail. Talking to Burton again was like watching the calming of the seas.

    I can't explain it, yet I went from an evil, deep and very dark pit to feeling as if I still had something left in me, all within a single three-hour conversation. Burton was never without the right words to say.

Having struggled hard throughout his life, Burton had great experience from which to draw. He would not end a conversation without ensuring that I felt as if I could never say no, never quit and never give up, no matter what I did in my life. "Life goes in cycles, Steven. You might be down now, but up is on the way. You can give in and you can give out, but you can NEVER give up!" he would tell me. I believed him, too.

Before I hung up the phone, he said to me, "Steven, pick yourself up; start over like you always have. Don't stop until you finally get what you want. It's out there! You have more persistence than anybody else I've ever met and you're going to win eventually because of it. I'll talk to you soon."

I felt like I knew I would. I felt as if I still had something to share with this world. My mission here was far from over. I knew that if I spent some time by the river, in the field and listening to the music Burton spoke of, that the answer would reveal itself when the time was right, as he said. He was never wrong. But, what if this time he was?

What if? can be a serious mental disorder itself. I certainly had that one among my list of disorders. We must live in what is and not what if because you can what-if yourself to death.

One Sunday morning about ten, only a month after Burton became newly- married to his beautiful partner in life, the phone rang. It was Burton's wife. Burton Brown had died after a severe asthma attack. Years of cigar smoking had finally stopped the clock. I reached for my sleeping pills, crawled in bed and left the world behind.

It was late spring and I had become fascinated with the vast network of the Internet. I spent thousands of hours on-line exploring all it had to offer. I found it fascinating because of the wealth of information, but also for the ability to talk with other people far away, and living differently. When you were chatting on line, you were anonymous in every way. It was a lot of fun for me. No expectations, no questions I didn't want to answer for the millionth time. Just people talking to people about anything that came up. Which was mostly sex.

I will never forget the day I met this guy like me on line. I was talking with a strange guy somewhere in the USA about depression when he began to tell me his story over the course of many long conversations across the Internet. His name was Jason and he was a twenty-three-year-old body builder recovering from a horrible past of self-abuse, drugs, and other addictions. His story was not unlike many I had heard before while living on the streets. I had seen the end of that movie already. But Jason's story had a twist in the form of a man he had never met that he called Brother Charlie. The first time I heard him say that, I felt as if someone with a *Watchtower* magazine was going to be sending someone to knock on my door pretty soon, so I was careful from the start. Jason told me about how Charlie had saved his life and how he had never met anyone more mysterious or just in all of his life. He wanted me to talk to Brother Charlie. I received an email the very next day.

Now my first thought was that this guy Charlie had to be either a Mormon who wanted to save me or an Amway salesman who was going to try and save me with some Amway soap, shampoo or something.

The odds were fifty-fifty I was going to be right. Either way, they both wanted the very same thing from you, a donation as they so pleasantly enjoyed calling it. Jason wouldn't tell me much about Charlie, only about what he had done for him in his darkest hour. At the time, I was far from in a mood to listen to some salesman make his pitch about the latest product or the latest news on Jesus for that matter. I reluctantly opened the email and read what it said.

Brother Charlie is a monk, the director of an orphanage in Greece. His mission is to rescue kids from war-ravaged countries, educate them, and find them homes. I was more than suspicious. I decided to get rid of this creep quickly by telling him that the last thing I wanted to hear about was God and all the wonderful things He does for other people. Furthermore, it wasn't going to work no matter what, so he was wasting his time and should move on. Except I wasn't actually that polite.

I was angry, and I gave Charlie my own special brand of hell on line. I was determined to make this Jesus freak hate me, and I did and said everything I could to do that. I even sent him a picture of my -- well, let's call it my buttocks, on which I had placed a sign telling him where he could kiss. Charlie never budged. It simply didn't faze him. This guy was going to play the game the hard way. He wasn't giving up. Day after day we would chat on line at great length. I was often very abusive to him and to what he believed in, and then it hit me.

Charlie had never really told me what he believed in. He never really talked about his religion unless I asked about something specific. In fact, he never really talked about himself much. He wouldn't trade a picture with me, and he wouldn't talk to me about Jason. He only wanted to talk about my situation and what was going on inside of my head. The more I talked with Charlie, the more angry I grew at this goof-ball who wouldn't give up. He wasn't a sexual pervert like so many others I had come across on line, and his manner of speaking to me on line was calming to the point of being freaky. It was unlike any conversation I had ever had with anyone else in the world. Over the course of a year, I finally gave in and began to open up to Charlie. In fact, I became addicted to our daily conversations.

    Charlie was the most intriguing mystery I had ever uncovered. He wasn't pushy, he didn't judge me and had heard it all before. The funny thing was he never seemed to talk in deep, theological terms. Religious dogma didn't interest him. He was very constant, stable and pure in his words of wisdom. Earthy and simple, uncomplicated and extremely peaceful, he won my confidence through his many wise words. All the while I was keeping in mind that at any moment this guy could turn out to be a super freak, the likes of which even Rick James couldn't imagine.

    One day, Charlie asked for a mailing address because he wanted to send me something. He told me that any address where I would receive the mail would do. He made it clear that he was not trying to locate me or discover my home address. Cautiously, I gave him an address that would be forwarded to me by way of a private post office mailbox. It would take longer, but I wasn't taking any chances. A few weeks later a package arrived. It was a beautiful wooden religious artifact his children made by hand at the orphanage. It was post marked Ormylia, Greece. He also sent me a cassette tape of the monks where he lived, chanting as monks often do as well as some printed information about the cause he lives for. I finally believed him. He had to be real. If he wasn't, this guy was going to great lengths to fool me for no reason. I could see no opportunity for self-gain. He would call me every once in a while and talk to me for a minute or two because of the expense of calling across the globe. He gave me the orphanage's phone number and I would call him sometimes as well.

Charlie never asked me for a single thing. He never wanted anything and seemed to be sent from Heaven to help me through the rain. With Burton now gone, I was completely alone, trying to survive for myself. Charlie knew that I was tired of living. We talked about it. We talked mostly about my depression and my will to leave this world. Brother Charlie told me that every human being has a higher purpose in life, and that each person must do something to make a difference. He told me that life was about sharing and caring and helping others along the way. He said that was where he was in his journey. He explained things in such a way I couldn't help but listen. Never once did he try to force his beliefs on me. He let me ask the questions. He let me decide what we talked about and what we didn't.

My long conversations over months and months and eventually years made me wonder. I wondered how such a loving and truly caring human being could exist. Throughout every conversation over the phone or on the Internet, he never wavered once. Charlie was real. But was he? I began to wonder. I had to know who this guy was. I had to meet him. I began planning a trip to visit his orphanage in Greece. He warned me what it would be like with only the barest of living conditions. He lived a very meager existence as most monks do. In a way, I was testing

Charlie. I wanted to see what he would do if the possibility existed that I might show up on his doorstep someday. He never wavered. He welcomed me as long as I understood what I was going to be getting myself into while there. I decided not to visit just yet. I valued our relationship so much that it had become the most important thing in my life. I didn't want that to change. I mean, I would get out of bed and go right to Matthew's computer to see what Charlie had to say that day. He was always there for me, always willing to talk. I almost became scared of him. I was getting the feeling this guy was much more than a simple monk in the hills of Greece somewhere. I began to wonder if he was real or perhaps was some divine presence on the Internet. How stupid! I would think. Yet, I couldn't describe the experience of my conversations with him to anyone else. Matthew would shake his head and go on about his business. He thought it was funny, actually. I was beginning to wonder if I was losing my mind yet again, but things seemed more clear than ever before. Charlie encouraged me not to worry any longer. He told me to have faith in whatever higher power I choose to believe (because they are all the same no matter what name is placed on it) and allow things to happen and find their niche in my life. How and why didn't matter right now, he used to say. Crazy as it sounded, it made perfect sense to me. He wanted me to focus on sharing my life with all of those I met. He encouraged me to keep performing and to keep my heart open so that the answers would come. It wasn't far from the message I had from Burton the last time we spoke. It gave me chills. It was as if I was receiving a message, yet it was one that I had heard before. Reverend Don Simpson was the first to tell me of my gift and how I could use it in a special way. It was as if it all came together in my mind. A clear theme repeated itself every time I felt the end was near. It was like a gentle nudge from a mother bird to encourage her baby to spread its wings and learn to fly.

I couldn't ignore it any longer. It felt right in my heart and there it was in front of me. It had been there all the time while many had tried to make me understand. The answer was simple. It was a case of not being able to see the forest because of the trees that were standing in the way. Charlie's overwhelming kindness and profound understanding of whatever we talked about humbled me. He had taught me a path of self-discovery that would lead me to a higher purpose in my life. We all have one, but we have to listen. Those who listen fulfill their lives with the most valuable of gifts which money can't buy. Those who don't will meet resistance every step along the way. That's the way it is, he would explain.

Brother Charlie leads people toward finding a way to understanding the importance of helping others by using their lives. By so doing, they will get what they need in the process. I was unsure of how or why, but he reminded me to open my heart and allow the answers to present themselves. I remember telling Brother Charlie that doing magic seemed stupid to me now and unimportant in the grand scheme of things, but it was the only thing I knew how to do. He simply said, "Then get out there and do it."

The comfort of Brother Charlie's advice to me was a natural fit for the relief portion of the obsession-anxiety-compulsion-relief cycle. This in turn fueled my need to hear what he had to say about what had happened in my life and what it meant to me in the obsession phase of the cycle. Though we never met in person, I doubt there is anyone on the planet who knows me better. Please understand that I am not suggesting that everyone you meet online will change your life or is inherently decent. We've all heard of the horrors about the predators lurking out there behind the keyboards. They do exist. Fortunately, it was Brother Charlie on the other end for me.

    To Charlie, love was a verb. He proved that every day by what he did, thought and less importantly, what he said. It was how he said it that meant so much to me. I wanted my inner spirit to be like his. I don't put much weight on the words I hear from most people anyway. Actions and body language are a far better judge to rule by. As for Jason, the young guy who introduced me to Charlie, he disappeared one day, and neither Charlie nor I was able to contact to him again.

    In the afternoons I would sit and stare at the water in front of our Vancouver building. There was water everywhere, be it Deep Cove, Burrard Sound or the Georgia Straits. I loved the water. It did something peaceful to me. Ducks would paddle by and always seemed to come over as if to say hello in their own way. With so much to think about, all I was good for was walking, sitting by the water and staring out there somewhere.

    Sometimes I would babble with bums if they stopped my way. They, at times, spoke more coherently than I. Gradually, the sea, the fresh air and the kind people who passed began to breathe new life into my tired lungs. I began to feel the numbness slowly recede. I started to observe things again. I saw the little things I had never noticed before. Wandering around town, I came upon a famous little spot called English Bay. It's a charming intersection where the roads meet by the ocean. Street performers gather large crowds and do their thing. Fire eaters, jugglers and a magician or two all entertain to the delight of everyone around until the police would run them off, of course. They always came back and so did the crowds. People want to laugh. People want to escape if only for a single moment in a walk by the sea. I would sit and observe every day as the performers did their best to give their audiences all they could. They did it all for whatever spare change the on-lookers would throw in the hat. It was simple, yet it made me see clearly. I could feel that burning desire that made me keep going begin to spark again. It was the faintest feeling, but I knew that I had to get back out there and try it yet again, one more time. I couldn't imagine how. I couldn't imagine where the strength or money would come from to begin again. I had no energy and my body felt as if it was at least a century old, but I knew I had to do it.

    I remembered all the people throughout my life who had always believed in me. I thought about what Charlie said about leaving the details to work themselves out. My heart told me to forge ahead, to search for the opportunity, and the answer would present itself. I had to believe. I had nothing to lose that I hadn't lost before. It was not a scary thing this time around for me.

    I was used to the unknown. Nothing ever went the way I planned. It occurred to me while walking along the beach one day, that we as humans are constantly seeking security in one form or another. I felt that security was a very illusive and ephemeral thing. I wasn't really sure that I would find security in my life, since I had never had any. I had learned to function in the unknown that is life itself. We do not know what is going to happen tomorrow. Despite your very best efforts to plan, life has its own plan for the day you will next live. I also realized, looking back over all that I have been through, that when we become secure in our lives, things stagnate. Things begin to settle and become comfortable for us. I could see where the uncertainty and unknown in our lives was there to nudge us, to keep us moving and ever evolving as people. I figured that was a good thing. I decided right then to stop worrying about tomorrow when it was nearly impossible to make it through today. I was going to relinquish my attachments to every expectation I had for the future. Every plan, every thing I wanted to achieve was too heavy for me right now. I felt that I couldn't carry that burden, that self-imposed pressure to be the image of what I felt I should be in order to compete out there in the market place. Furthermore, I was going to erase the words *should, could,* and *wished* from my own vocabulary. They were useless to me. Far too many people around were willing to tell me what I *should have* done to prevent all that was now the reality I was living. I got rid of those friends as well.

My own mind was driving me into the ground. I wanted to physically get a new brain. My mind would run in what if circles from dusk till dawn. Only the occasional rational thought slipped in. Some days I could think clearly, others I couldn't even answer the phone. It was a daily crap-shoot. I could only wake up to see what the day was going to offer. I knew that if I was going to succeed in this business, I had to get a handle on my brain. I didn't really know what exactly that would mean or entail, but I knew that getting a grip was going to be the first step. I wasn't going to try and achieve anything, or set goals I would never be able to reach, either. I was going to live life for today and let tomorrow take care of itself. I decided to make daily goals that were achievable today, not after a year of struggle. I wanted to release my soul from the pressures of having to achieve anything, of having to be what I wasn't or of having a certain amount of money in the bank. I think that this was the day I decided that I was no longer going to allow the amount in my bank account to define who I was as a person. I was still angry about how quickly all my friends disappeared when the cash stopped flowing so freely. Their desertion amazed me. The thought made me sick. I was angry at allowing myself to be used like that. I had friends coming out of the woodwork to be next to me because they cared. But where were they now? Gone! Just like the money.

I suppose that I was following Burton's advice: I was re-booting and doing a manual mental re-install. It took much longer with a brain that ran like an ever- crashing PC than it would have had my brain been developed by Macintosh! I had been watching a series of young street performers do their thing at English Bay for a while. Some of them I had become friends with. Especially this one weirdo named Tom Comet who was famous for riding a twelve foot unicycle that blew a twenty foot fire ball out of his -- shall we say -- backside. He never failed to draw the largest crowds and earn the biggest take of the day. Watching these guys brought back memories of the days when I earned my living that way. I started to care for these guys, some of them good, and some bad. Eventually, I revealed myself and began coaching a few of the bad ones. They were grateful for my tutelage. I appreciated them even more so because they reawakened the spark to perform within me once again.

I called Brother Charlie to tell him what I was thinking. I still had my doubts, because of how empty magic had made me feel in the recent past. My passion was gone, and I wasn't sure that it would come back. Brother Charlie asked me a very simple question: "If time and money were no object, what would I choose to be doing?" Without a single hesitation, I said, "Well, I'd be on stage performing my magic!" I had just discovered my higher purpose in life. We had a long conversation about how much good I could do for my fellow human beings using my magic skills as the vehicle to carry my message of hope. I must admit that it was a bit hard to swallow since I had so little hope myself. Yet that familiar urge in the pit of my stomach remained. I knew that if it killed me, I was going to get back on a stage, somehow, some way.

Late summer arrived and I was calling every agent who had given me a business card, several hundred of them from all over the world. More than a few had not heard from me in years. Some I had never spoken to before. Nonetheless my new website was up and it was all that I had. I had to spread the word to the world that I was coming back with an all-new show, a show that had as yet not been designed, but only I knew that. I had no money to produce anything with, and I knew well that it would take hundreds of thousands of dollars to achieve such a lofty goal. However, I also knew that money had never stopped me before. Somehow, as if by magic whenever I have put my mind to work on a project, the money always appeared. This time would be no different. I was a human beehive of activity, running up Matthew's phone bill in the process. He was actually happy to help out, and loaned me some money to keep me funded in the process. I was very grateful to him for believing in me when I wasn't sure that I believed in myself.

At the end of Burton's life, he had been a consultant and operational director for Lido International Inc., which was a division of the world famous Lido de Paris in Paris, France. Burton had wanted me to go to Australia to work on the possibility of building a second Lido production show in Sydney. His death prevented that from taking place at the time it had been planned. Several months later, Burton's widow called me and said that there was still interest in my going to Sydney, but it was through Burton's business partner who actually lived there. Before long I met David in Las Vegas and made a deal to help finish the project that Burton had started.

Now I can't say enough good things about Sydney or Australia, for that matter. Without question, it's my favorite place on our planet. I would be living there right now, if they weren't so strict with their immigration laws. I love the Australian people, the atmosphere and the great lifestyle they live. People enjoy their lives down under like no other people I have found on the globe. There was always something interesting to do. I was excited to be going back again. I thought that I was going to work on the Lido project, but the universe had much bigger plans for me.

It was New Years Eve, December 31, 1998, and I couldn't think of a more exciting place in the world to be! It was about four in the afternoon and I was strolling around Hyde Park among what seemed like several million others. I was supposed to meet some new friends at the big water fountain in the park, but they were involved in a minor auto accident and never showed. While waiting, I began talking with a young guy next to me who was also waiting for friends who never arrived. We had hours to talk and talk and that we did. His name was Javier, a very smart and extremely bright guy. He was from Barcelona, Spain; however, he lived and worked in London. I asked him what he did for a living. "Nothing," he said. "I manage a merchandising group just outside of Buckingham Palace in London." Having been to London many times myself, I realized that Buckingham Palace was also in a park called Hyde. We laughed about the silly trivia and moved on with the conversation. Now it was my turn. He asked me the one question I hated more then any other you could ask me. "So, what do you do for a living?" I paused for a second to think. "What should I say?" I thought to myself, when suddenly as if someone else was in control of my mouth, I blurted out, "I am a magician from Las Vegas." He lit up like a Christmas tree. "You are? Really?" This response usually means another two hours of questions at least.

  Over the next three weeks, Javier and I became friends, discussing ideas, business, life and everything else under the sun. It was time for him to return to London, and we agreed to keep in touch. I never really thought I would see or hear from him again. That is typical in my business. You meet millions of people along the way, and usually you leave town and never see them again. It's the way it is. "That's show-biz!" as the saying goes.

  A few weeks later Javier called me from London. "Hey, let's get together and talk. I have been doing some thinking, and I might be able to help you produce your show." I was on a plane the very next day heading to London. I had given Javier some of my promotional videos to take back with him in case he ran across the need for a magician. I hand them out to everyone I meet like they are M&M's candy. Networking with my videos has always been one of my strong points. My promos are legendary for being quite entertaining. I never have figured out if that is a good thing or not. I did know that Javier was a very clever businessman and had lots upstairs when it came to making things happen. So I took a leave and went to hear what Javier had in mind.

It was a lot more than what I had thought it would be. Javier had mapped out a five-year plan. He wanted to become my business partner and fund my project. I told him that we were looking at several million dollars over the course of those five years, and he didn't even flinch. I sure did. I was trying to scare him, but he didn't budge. We spent several weeks in London talking over the particulars of such a deal and how we would go about making this crazy idea of mine work.

I have always been a big fan of figuring things out on paper first. I always say that if it doesn't work on paper, it likely won't cut it in the real world, either. The numbers have to be right because any good businessman will tell you that it's all about the numbers. If the numbers don't work on paper, you shouldn't go any further. Over the next month, still in London, I began to write a business plan. It took a while and we discovered that it was going to cost a little more than we had planned, but it was possible, especially if we did it in a few well-thought-out phases. The deal was done. Now all that was left for me, was to return to Vegas, produce the show, and finally get back to doing what I felt I was here to do, perform, entertain and be the greatest showmen that I knew how to be. Shortly after returning to the States, I began to feel a little strange. I was dizzy every day. My head spun like a tornado and I swore I could see a cow flying outside my windows. Each time I had a moment, as I called these episodes, I would shake it off and keep going at a million miles a minute. Las Vegas was blistering hot outside, so I blamed the heat. There was a lot of work to do and Javier would be arriving in Vegas soon.

Not only did Javier arrive in Vegas, he brought everything he owned with him. He was moving to Vegas and was going to work with me on the show full-time. I was more than shocked. It was hard for me to believe. I met this guy in some park on the other side of the globe. He called me, wrote me a fat check and seemed to have unconditional faith in my abilities, yet had never seen me perform live. How could this be possible? Oops, there went another cow. The room began to spin, this time for a little longer than before. The feeling was harder to shake off this time. Something was wrong, but I didn't dare mention a word of it to Javier. No one must know, because if anyone did, he might yank back his money and I would be right at square number one, broke, without a penny to my name. Javier trusted me wholeheartedly. I wasn't about to let him down. I was going to produce this new show no matter what. Dizzy or not.

There was so much to do. I had all of the new marketing to design, create and have printed and produced. I had wardrobe and illusions to design and have built as well. All of that was the very tip of the iceberg. I had to get us booked somewhere and that was going to take some real magic. I had been out of the United States for nearly ten years. No one was going to remember me. I was starting all over again. Yet, if that was what I had to do, then so be it. I intended to make this work no matter what. A part of my vision while in Australia was to create a magic channel for the Internet. I had envisioned the Internet doing to television what television did to the radio many years ago. Thinking ahead, I wanted to be the first on the internet with my very own children's programming. After all, who was more qualified then I to produce such a program? I thought it would be a unique way to reach a mass audience. Since the Internet is by its very nature interactive, I felt that there were endless possibilities for using the Internet over the TV to broadcast.

I knew that the Internet broadcasting technologies were still not perfect and probably several more years out before my idea would become acceptable. I had spent thousands of hours on the Internet researching "Web Casting" as it is called. I knew what I was talking about. I knew that it would work and so did Javier. The possibilities were endless. Getting there was going to be a slow process. It wasn't going to be cheap to build a multi-million dollar web casting studio in the middle of the desert. We needed to develop a project proposal and pitch it anywhere we could. In the meantime, live performances would keep the money rolling in and allow us to stay focused on our ultimate goal.

CHAPTER FIFTEEN

Branson, Missouri

One day the phone rang. It was my agent, Sandy, telling me that the Osmond Brothers wanted to talk to me. "Sandy, you mean the Osmond Brothers?" I asked. I had grown up watching the Osmonds all my life on TV. When I was a kid, I had done a pre-show warm-up act for Marie at Harbor Fest at Waterside in Norfolk, Virginia. I couldn't imagine why they would be looking for me. Sandy arranged a phone conference for the next day. On the other end of the phone was little Jimmy Osmond, the youngest of the family. Only he wasn't so little anymore. He was all grown up at thirty-seven and quite the business mogul at that. He was very smart, and an excellent manager with a keen eye for talent. Strongly self-confident, but very tender hearted, he has an infectiously exuberant personality. He and his beautiful wife, Michelle, have four lovely, well-mannered, well-educated kids. As with all the Osmonds I have worked with, family values are foremost in the raising of their children and it really shows. The Osmonds were producing a special variety show that was going to tour throughout Asia. Many people don't know how popular the Osmonds are in Asia. Especially Jimmy, having recorded his first hit album in Japanese when he was a little boy. Jimmy was the show's producer and was looking for some magic, but specifically a magician who had some serious international touring experience behind him. I was the right man for the job and priced myself accordingly, so that Jimmy would make his deal with me. This was exactly what I had been looking for to get us off and running.

It wasn't to be, at least not the way Jimmy had originally planned. World politics were in flux at the time and the US and China were fighting over a spy plane that had landed in China's backyard or something like that. It kept pushing the deal farther and farther away. Jimmy was getting frustrated with the whole thing, and I knew how he felt as well.

Finally, it became clear that it wasn't going to happen before the end of that year, and Jimmy was faced with a decision. He needed to decide if he and his brothers were going to appear at their theater in Branson, Missouri, for the Christmas season as they had for so many years. Tickets would have to go on sale soon and a final decision needed to be made. It took weeks, but finally Jimmy called with the news. "Yes, we are going to do Branson this year, and we would like to invite you to do the show with us!" I couldn't have been more excited. I signed the contract and faxed it back to Jimmy's office and to his ever-present lawyer, John. Don't get me wrong; I liked John and I realized that John was looking out for Jimmy's vast interests as he was paid to do. I have always felt that most lawyers practice because it gives them a grand and glorious feeling. If you hand them a grand, they feel glorious! Believe me, I have spent more than my fair share in legal fees over the years. Jimmy and John flew to Las Vegas to meet me in person. We clicked instantly. I took Jimmy and the ever-present John to my warehouse and showed him all of my illusions.

Jimmy was like a kid in a candy store; he lit up and wanted to crawl inside of one of my props. I pretended to cut his head off and sit it on a wooden crate. Everyone cracked up. The illusion was perfect, and Jimmy was saying, "Take a picture. Somebody take a picture!" He was having a blast and so was I. It was a done deal. September fifteenth through December fifteenth I was going to be appearing with the world famous singing family, The Osmond Brothers.

Life was good.

Meanwhile, I had enough time to finish producing the new act and have it all shipped to Branson. More cows were flying outside my window again. I could hardly stand up this time. Things were getting worse for me. I was beginning to feel as if someone had put me on a carnival ride and turned the speed on high. I couldn't imagine why this would be happening to me now, when things were perfect. I don't think I could have been any more confused as I continued to run around town at the speed of light, trying to get everything done on time for shipping day. Before I shipped anything, I was going to need a very big truck to haul my new act. Hmmm... Now where might I find one of those? Oh I knew! Linda, "The First Lady of Magic," had one and her brother David and I were friends. I'd call him. I first called Linda's production manager, Thom, to run it by him. The only problem with Linda's forty-foot semi-trailer was her thirty-foot half-naked picture on the sides. Linda had just finished playing Branson herself and had been run out of town. David agreed to let me have the truck to haul my stuff because he thought it would be funny for the other magicians in town to see her truck again. He agreed so long as I agreed not to tell his sister, he said. It was a done deal. I had called my good friend Jim to come back to work and be my production manager once again. I had Javier, and Matthew had moved back to Vegas to help me work on the web casting project as well.

We were days away from a major pitch to some seriously wealthy men who were going to allow us to grab their imagination for a couple of hours. It had to be right. Matthew spent hundreds of hours at his portable editing suite, producing visuals I had designed. We were flying in experts from around the world for this meeting. One of the most talented people I knew, Bill Terezakis, the owner of a massive special effects house in Vancouver, Canada, was coming down with some of his latest creations to help businessmen with little imagination for anything except numbers, imagine exactly what I was talking about.

We were pulling out all of the stops for this one. The investors were from Chicago and owned a successful internet business. They were interested in seeing some of the technology that Matthew and I had created for our own specific purposes.

The investors came and went. Our pitch had impressed them greatly. So much so, they wanted to buy our technology and hire Matt and I as consultants in the development of what they were trying to accomplish. We took the deal and lost our asses. The dot com era was over, and Matthew and I had done one of those "a little cash up front, plus a massive chunk in stock" sort of a deal. Their Internet business went belly up and so did our money. We believed in these guys and after some serious investigation, it turned out that they were a clever group of scam artists who had scammed the ultimate of scammers – a magician! It was too little, too late. I had been burned and was going to have to eat the loss. My big-time lawyers told me that the cheapest thing to do was walk away. There was nothing that I could do. Bill and Michael had protected themselves well as any smart con-artist does. Looks like my karma had finally caught up with me for all the shiesty things I pulled while on the streets in Vegas. No debt ever goes unpaid in the universe. Never!

In the blink of an eye, we were in Branson rehearsing for "An Osmond Magical Christmas" and I wasn't feeling well at all. Panic attacks were becoming an everyday thing. I was as nervous as a one-armed rock climber. The cows followed me wherever I went, but I had to get through this gig somehow. To say that I was a little negative and crabby would be an understatement. I was downright nasty to everyone I met, and I had no clue as to why. I began to argue with Jimmy. What was I thinking? Here he was trying his best to help me, and I was giving him hell from day one. The more we rehearsed, the worse it got. Suddenly I noticed Jimmy avoiding me at all costs. He was sorry he had ever met me. I could tell by the look on his face every time I saw him. We had a signed contract and Jimmy was doing his best to get through it. His lawyer had hated me from day one and was advising Jimmy to get rid of me any way he could. Thankfully, Jimmy's not like that. He really cares about the people around him and has the patience of a saint.

Over the course of the next two months, I got to know the Osmond family pretty well. They were truly wonderful people who actually lived by their Mormon faith, both on stage and off. Their children were in the show as well, and I got to play with them backstage every night. We had a blast. Jay Osmond was the father figure of the group. Originally the drummer, he was now one of the singers. He was a take-charge kind of guy. If Wayne and Merrill got too goofy with their practical jokes, it was brother Jay who would straighten them out and quickly, too. Very intelligent, Jay advised the brothers on most legal matters and was without question, one of the nicest men I had ever met. Ol' Wayne Osmond was a marvelous comic and was as crazy offstage at times as he was on. He was the very first to suggest a practical joke he didn't think he could get away with himself, whenever he could. Wayne was surprisingly rather quiet and reserved most of the time. You could usually find Wayne in his dressing room reading good joke books, or doing crossword puzzles, constantly improving his mind. You see, Wayne had nearly died from a brain tumor several years earlier, and after surgery it was doubtful if he would make a full recovery. I think it was Wayne's offstage personality that I identified with the most. I somehow understood Wayne on a very deep, emotional level. We had some great conversations. I learned a great deal from him as well. Fortunately for us, Wayne was a true survivor and wasn't about to give up that easily. He fought hard to live. He wanted to sing and entertain again. He eventually made a full recovery. Today, Wayne is better than ever and back on stage where he loves to be. Wayne's love of life is why he's with us today. I deeply admire his faith and perseverance.

Merrill is the group's lead singer. He has a strong stage presence that drives his female fans insane. I'm not kidding, either. Merrill fans are unlike any others I have seen in my life. Grown women who act like screaming teenage girls follow him everywhere. They have shown up outside his hotel rooms wearing only a bathrobe, if that! One night at the Osmond Theater the curtain went up. In the front row was this woman dressed in a leather straps and chains and no underwear! She was from England and had nothing to hide. It was plain for all on stage to see. It was Christmas. I guess that she was trying to offer him a present. Merrill ignored that fact she was almost naked while the rest of us were in tears, laughing at this stupid lady. Merrill did the entire show without a flinch.

His fans came from around the world, too. His fan club in Europe came all the way from England. Jimmy's fan club came from Japan. It was amazing to watch this Osmond mania night after night. They had this one fan who cooked them each their favorite meals. Merrill loves his fans almost to a fault. He'll hang around after a concert and talk to them for hours on end until someone finally drags him away. One night about one in the morning, I got hungry and decided to go for a bite to eat. No one had told me that in Branson everything closes at nine. When I passed by the theater, there in the parking lot was Merrill Osmond, still surrounded by his fans in the exact spot he was standing in when I left the theater after the show. I stopped and rescued Merrill. I couldn't believe it when he told me that it was those fans who made the Osmonds and he wasn't going to disappoint them no matter what it took. Merrill was almost a paradox, because once he was backstage, he was quite shy, almost a loner in the mode of Johnny Carson, I think. Nevertheless, he was not above cooking up a good practical joke, especially if it was aimed at one of his brothers!

I had great fun performing with the Osmonds. Especially when my sister Shelia came to see the show. She brought her whole family. I got Wayne to pick her out of the audience and make a few jokes in good fun. "Shelia is Steven Diamond's sister! Hey Shelia, I understand it's your birthday today. (It wasn't.) How old are you?" The audience erupted in laughter. Realizing his mistake and without missing a beat, Wayne jumped back in with "Oh, I'm sorry. I can't ask a lady how old she is. So, how much do ya weigh?" With that, Wayne had the audience in stitches. Shelia knew I couldn't miss the opportunity to embarrass her in front of a thousand people and took it in stride. I was backstage in tears, laughing the entire time.

Although we would all have a blast doing the show each night, I would crash every night the second I walked off that stage. I was beginning to melt. I couldn't handle it; I couldn't stop my brain. I wasn't sleeping at all. Jimmy and I were not seeing eye to eye. It wasn't his fault either; it was all me. But Jimmy hung in there. At one point, Jimmy wanted to fire me and offered me some nice money to go away. He hung in there after a little begging from me. He had seen this before. He knew what I did not. One time after a horrible day, standing right in front of him, I started to cry. I was crying harder than I had cried in my life, and I had no idea why. Those cows were kicking my butt and it wasn't pretty. I was a mess. Suddenly, the call was made that the front doors in the theater were open and the audience was going to be coming in. Jimmy asked for the doors to be held for a few minutes so we could go backstage to talk. Jimmy called his brother, Merrill. Jimmy explained to Merrill that he wanted him to talk with me and help me. Jimmy had a theater full of people to deal with and went back to work. Merrill looked at me as if he had been there throughout my entire life. We went to his dressing room and Merrill, Jay, Wayne and myself sat around and talked for hours. I was amazed and touched at how much they cared. In fact, I don't really remember anyone before them that I had actually met, caring about me that much. Ever! They knew well what I was going through.

The Osmonds have experienced some tough personal times in their fifty years in show business. Each one of them began to share some of the most personal moments of their lives with me. Their stories sounded really familiar, too, because I had lived them. I had done some of these same things. Yup, I had thought about ending it all. The more they went on, the more I felt like these guys had lived my life along with me. They knew what they were speaking about. Depression, thoughts of suicide and darkness, being misdiagnosed time and time again, questioning their faith, God, and themselves, the mental torture and uncontrollable mind chatter, the daily rituals you have to do, the shaking, the numbness, the mental disorientation, the confusion, the endless worry, the anxiety you couldn't stop if you wanted to, the nightmares that kept you from sleeping for years on end, the unbearable pressure of having to be something you were not while living in the public eye, the negativity, the hate, the anger, the mental and physical exhaustion, the fear, the feeling that you couldn't trust anyone around you, and the flying cows. Every bit of what I had lived was nothing new to these boys. They had survived it all.

Over the years I had been hearing about former U.S. President Ronald Reagan's battle with Alzheimer's. For many years I had convinced myself that I, in fact, had Alzheimer's myself. I couldn't tell a soul. Everything I heard about Alzheimer's sounded very familiar to me. I became obsessively fearful that I was slowly losing my mind, as people with Alzheimer's did. I felt panic every time I heard the word. Every breath I took was full of fear of someday not remembering who I was and the life I had lived. For me, it was the closest I had come to putting a real name to what was happening to me. There was no question that I was surrounded by the right people to help me. It was time to do the show and our conversations would have to continue later. That night I felt weaker than I had in a long time.

My mind had picked the worst time of all to get sick on the Osmonds. Only a few days after our conversation in the dressing room that night before the show, their mother Olive Osmond, the mighty matriarch of the Osmond family, had fallen deathly ill. They had been informed that if they wanted to see her alive again, they needed to hurry back to Salt Lake City, Utah. Olive was very sick. The call came at three o'clock in the morning. Within minutes, they were all on a private plane heading back as fast as the plane could fly.

CHAPTER SIXTEEN

The Greekarican

Enter Tony Orlando, stage right.

The next day I was at the theater early to water and feed my animals. From the moment I walked in the door, I knew something was very wrong. You could feel it. I decided to peek in the Osmonds' production office and see what was going on. Maryann and "Momma Yvonne," Jimmy's personal assistants, informed me of the horrible news. They had called show business's own personal go-to man, Tony Orlando. He had recently been in Branson performing to sell-out crowds. He turned right around and hopped on the first flight back to Branson to fill in for the Osmonds for as long as they needed him. Tony is one of those incredible entertainers who will always be there for you when the chips are down. With that night's show being completely sold out, Tony was hurrying as fast as he could come. He had not a clue what he was going to do when he came running in the backstage door less than thirty minutes before show-time with his production manager that I lovingly called "Quasimodo." Tony's first words surprised me. "Guys, I am here to fill in not to take over. Tell me where and how you need me."

He was talking to the sad cast and crew of the show, minus the actual Osmonds themselves. The technical director and I took Tony to his dressing room for a quick conversation. Everyone else gathered around to find out what the plan was. Tony didn't want to do his show; however, the Osmond band was more than willing to make it happen for him. Out of respect to the fans out there who had come to see the Brothers, he was going to try and do the Osmond show exactly the way they would have done it. It was Christmastime so most of the songs in the show Tony knew by heart. Tony told the entire cast and crew to tell him in between each number when to sing and what song. I thought it was going to be suicide, because Tony had never heard the unique Osmond song arrangements they sang in the show. It was going to be one of those shows you know was going to be a very painful birth to get through. I could only feel sorry for the man out in front and thankful it was not me.

Before Tony had arrived at the theater, I was the lucky one chosen to go to the parking lot and get on every tour bus that pulled in, loaded with excited Osmond fans, to inform them that the Osmonds were not going to be performing that night and why. I also told them that we had a very special surprise guest star who had flown in to replace the Brothers during this difficult time. The audiences were more than supportive. Only a few old grumpy ladies complained and asked for their money back, but the vast majority of the audience was overwhelmingly supportive and was happy to see Tony Orlando.

It was hard to believe how well Tony made it through that show. He looked as if he had done it a million times. I had never seen a better showman than Tony Orlando that fateful night. He earned my total respect. I don't know how he managed to be so smooth. The next night we were all calm when

Tony turned on that Orlando magic and had the audience eating out of his hand. Even Javier got into the act. During the show's final number, Tony suddenly walks over to Javier and puts a microphone in his face to help him sing "White Christmas." We were all surprised because Javier was typically a very shy guy, not to mention the fact that he's from Spain and had no clue as to the words to "White Christmas." He sang whatever he knew with Tony, and the crowd went wild.

They loved Tony, and so did we.

I had worked with Tony once before in Branson, as a support act in his show, so I knew he was a powerful entertainer, but this time, Tony had kicked it up a few notches so the Osmond fans wouldn't be disappointed that the Osmonds were missing. There was no telling when the Brothers would return. Olive's health had been going up and down like a yo-yo and they were all afraid to leave. After all, she had been there for all of them for their entire lives, and everyone felt that was exactly where they needed to be. There went the cows again.

Tony was taking care of business in the theater and we told the Brothers that there was no reason for them to hurry back, but that's not the way the Osmonds saw it. They actually felt guilty that all those people had paid money to see them in Branson and they weren't there. Within a couple of weeks, they were all back except Jimmy. Jimmy stayed behind to take care of their Mom. Marie returned back to the doll company she had just bought while Donny left to continue his tour in Europe. The brothers had returned to Branson for their fans. I could not believe their dedication to their fans. That night they went back into the show as if nothing had happened. I was not well by this time. Cow sightings were everywhere I went. I felt as if I was going to vomit all the time. I was so out of it that I barely knew where I was the night it all came to an end.

I had completed the worst performance of my entire career. It was on video, too. My vision was blurred. As I walked off stage, my legs decided they no longer wanted to support me, and down with a loud thump I went. That's the last thing I remember.

When I came to, Merrill Osmond stood in front of me. We were in the Osmonds' dressing room. I don't really know how I got there. Merrill was saying something about getting help for me and was on the phone. I was taken back to my hotel room to rest. The next day, Merrill called. He had doctors waiting and was sending me to his doctors whom he trusted. Within minutes, a car was outside ready to take me to my appointment, an appointment that would change my life forever. The doctors gathered around me as if I were the President of the United States. They ordered an entire battery of tests to be performed and advised me not to think about doing the show that night. I was completely numb to whatever they were saying. I think that I was actually more worried about my animals at the theater than I was about what was happening to me.

It was going to take a day or so for the test results to come back and I was sent back to the hotel to rest. Rest? What was that? Right into the theater I went, just in time for the show. Feeling better than ever, having had what seemed like gallons of blood drained out of me, I said not a word to anyone about the day's events and entered my dressing room. I had only minutes to get ready, which included all of the daily rituals that I had yet to perform before my act could take place. I was nervous. I knew I wasn't well. I felt horrible at how badly my performances had been lately. I was flooded with emotions I couldn't explain. I wanted to throw up but couldn't. I had a show to do. I had to focus. "Focus, Steven. Damn it. Focus. You've got to redeem yourself!" was all my brain could say. I barely had a voice, much less the energy to get out on that stage in front of more then a thousand people. I could hardly walk, but Jim and Javier were there, helping me however they could. The lights were hot. My costume was hot. I felt weaker by the second.

The curtain went up, and there I stood, really unsure of what I was supposed to do. I stood there until Javier gave me a nudge in the right direction. He kicked me in my butt! I did make it through the show and through the next week or so as well. Finally the test results came in. It wasn't good news. I was going to have to see yet another doctor. This guy was a chemical imbalance specialist. Whatever in the hell that meant. All I knew was that I had to go see this guy, Dr. Cohen, in Springfield. Time was about to stop yet again. This time it was going to be for good.

The entire meeting with Dr. Cohen was a blur to me. The only thing I knew was that he told me I was going to live, and I would remember everything. It was at this meeting that I first heard the words *Obsessive Compulsive Disorder*. Dr. Cohen was very good at calming me down. In fact, it was the first time in recent memory that I actually had felt relaxed although I was crying my eyes out. He began to tell me that he suspected that I also was suffering from Post Traumatic Stress Disorder as well as Manic Depression. Later I was told that with therapy and medication, I was going to be good as new and perhaps even better. Sounded like a television sound bite to me. I wanted to believe what he was saying was true, but I was very skeptical.

However, I made the decision that he was the doctor and I had to listen and accept his word if for no other reason than because I had never heard this diagnosis before. Besides, this was Merrill Osmond's own personal physician. My OCD did not want to hear all of this, but this time, I did. This time, I knew what is wrong with me. It finally had a name, and all I could do was cry.

I cried hard for several days. People were calling my hotel room to check on me; fans were stopping by with food and flowers. Every time the door closed, I would cry for hours on end, and I didn't know why. I couldn't stop. I had always visualized my OCD (although I had not known its formal name) as a demon from another dimension within my brain. I was hoping that this therapy the good doctor was talking about would eventually allow me to look that demon in the eye, grab it by the throat, and make it realize that I wasn't going to take this lying down. I had finally hit my own personal rock bottom. Time was up. I wasn't going to allow this "thing" I didn't understand to control my life for another second. I was angry for all of the time it had stolen from my life, for all of the pain I had suffered and for picking me as its victim. Dr. Cohen told me that it wasn't my fault, and that was also something I hadn't heard before. I learned I wasn't in full control because this disorder was the result of a serious chemical balance that was affecting the way my brain functioned. He told me that was the simple answer and that the complete answer was going to take years of therapy to truly understand.

Over time I learned valuable lessons on how to handle my OCD. Cognitive Behavior Therapy or CBT as it is called taught me how to keep myself in control instead of being ruled by my disorder. I learned to recognize the intrusive OCD thoughts for what they really were, and how to work around them.

This CBT, along with the new medications they put me on, continue to the present day. Meanwhile, I was doing the show each and every night like nothing had happened. The show must go on the proverb says. I didn't plan to be the one to stop it.

Dr. Cohen put my OCD notion about having Alzheimer's to rest permanently. Finally my rational mind was ready to listen. He told me my response had been a classic example of OCD at work. He also discovered that I had a serious sleeping disorder as well. I had not been able to really rest during my sleep, which is why I awoke every day feeling exhausted. By depriving myself of deep natural sleep in my nightly rest cycle, I couldn't possibly wake up refreshed and ready for a full day, yet I felt that it was my fault that I wasn't sleeping. I was convinced that it was some form of universal punishment for all of the bad things I had done in my life. Some people call it karma. The doctor told me it was likely that I hadn't had truly relaxing shut-eye for a decade or more.

I also learned that I was a workaholic. Because my OCD was so severe, if I didn't stay focused on working, I couldn't focus on anything, and I was becoming catatonic. I learned that I was not the worthless piece of street trash that I felt I was. I was not the bad, hateful, and angry person I felt that I was. No, not at all. I hit the wall emotionally, because I was mentally exhausted from OCD kicking the crap out of me day in and day out during my entire life. I eventually had begun to see the physical manifestations and so did everyone around me.

What about all that anger inside of me? It's what often happens to many of my fellow sufferers. We get angry at OCD, but because we don't really know what it is, we end up lashing out, taking our frustrations and anger out on those around us. My doctors explained to me that I physically did not know how to relax. I was actually incapable of being relaxed and had most likely been hyper-tense for most of my life. It reminded me of my days in the squat where I learned to sleep lightly in case anyone tried to physically attack or rob me. Realizing that the road to recovery had to begin with a good night's sleep, I was given a prescription for a muscle relaxant and told to get some rest. No sleeping pills for me, having had an addiction to them in the past.

I remember a funny thing that happened my very last night in Branson. I had been given a prescription. I went to the local Walgreen's Pharmacy right next to the Osmonds' Theater. It was literally almost in their parking lot. It was also the closest to my hotel. I stopped in and was going to have it filled when I noticed a crowd gathering around me. Now, I was not in the mood for picture taking, but I remembered Merrill's example. I decided to sign whatever they wanted me to and do the picture thing. It suddenly occurred to me that I didn't want these people to see that I was on medications, which might be construed as indicating that my elevator didn't go all the way to the top, if you catch my drift. Although the truth was that it didn't.

I was able to make eye contact with the pharmacist using

subtle gestures that only he could see and understand. He put the meds discreetly in a bag and set it down.

I was in a mild panic, because I was so close to getting the help I needed but terrified that all of these nice people gathered around me might find out how loopy I really was. My heart raced, and I began to move away from the counter towards the front of the store. The nice people followed. My OCD, of course, was doing everything it could to seize the moment, scaring me away from the meds only to loop back into the magic-magic-magic cycle all over again. I was able to spot the trigger and control myself from getting out of hand. Completely amazing myself that this CBT stuff actually worked, I figured that without this medication and therapy I was about a month away from being Captain Wacko, the World Famous Strait jacket Tester!

In the nick of time, an angel arrived in the form of my good friend, Javier. I greeted Javier in Spanish and told him to go get the medication in the back and meet me at the hotel.

After what seemed like eternity, the last of the nice people loosened their grip on me. I slipped back into my hotel. In my room, I sat on the edge of the bed and rethought the medication thing. I was afraid of drugs period. I had never taken any and really didn't want to start. I felt that drugs might make me numb and zombie-like. I didn't want to walk around like that. I was afraid of drugs and what they might do to me. I thought for a long time, until I finally realized that it was my OCD trying to talk me out of taking them I grabbed my glass of water with a vengeance. After taking the medication, I sobbed myself to sleep. That was the end of OCD's power over me. That was one battle that I was going to win, no matter what came my way.

The next morning I awoke. It was a travel day for me, and I had a plane to catch. As I sat on the edge of the bed, I felt sort of strange.

I thought of Pink Floyd's famous song, "Comfortably Numb," and wondered if the way I felt were what they had been singing about. It was like having the worst hangover in the world without the headache. It didn't hurt at all. I experienced a very unique, comfortable feeling of numbness. I looked at myself in the mirror and asked myself out loud, "So how do you feel, Steven?" I didn't feel bad at all. In fact, I was feeling pretty damn good. I think it was the first time in my life that I was completely and totally relaxed. I wasn't sure, since I had never actually been so relaxed before. This must be what it feels like, I thought to myself. I returned to bed to lie down for a while. So much was running through my head, but it wasn't like before. This time I could actually think a thought completely through to the end. With every day that passed, I got better. I was amazed at the control I had over my thoughts. In moving around the room, packing up some last minute things, I realized that I felt flexible and supple like never before. It shocked me at how agile and catlike my body felt. I experienced the warm and welcoming sensation of being alive in my own skin. I had never felt that way before. I started laughing out loud, and tears filled my eyes in the joy of rediscovering deep inside the first glimpse of the person I had so longed to meet. I could physically feel the difference in my mind and body. I knew for the very first time in my life that I was truly going to be okay. I was going to live and furthermore, I really wanted to!

It felt like the first day of my life, as if I was whole again and had been blessed with an opportunity to start my life all over. I was alive! There was no longer a question in my mind of the existence of God. It was as if I had received my marching orders. I had found a new mission in my life.

Magic was going to have to take a back seat because I was going to spend the rest of my days spreading the word. Help is there. Believe what they say. Give in and get help because once you do, you will get your own life back as a reward and a testament to tell the world and help the others out there suffering just like you. I promised myself not to make my mission a religious crusade. I didn't want to shove religion down anyone's throat as had been done to me. Personally, I am very much against organized religion. What you believe and what works for you is ultimately up to you alone. The point is that it works for you and it gives you hope that something greater than you is rooting for us down here which is a beautiful thing to me.

I would never have believed in a million years the power of a simple little pill and how easy it was to regain all that I had lost and more. Forty milligrams was all that stood between wanting to end my life and wanting to live forever, a thought that to this day still brings tears to my eyes. I couldn't believe how simple it was to over come a lifetime of suffering. I will always practice what I learned from Cognitive Behavioral Therapy. It works! I don't think I will always be on the medication as the doctors tell me that my progress has been amazingly swift. It was so much easier to get the help I needed than it was to suffer as I did for thirty long years. Simple techniques have helped me control my OCD for many years now.

It's what good therapists call the Four R's. It works something like this: First you RELABEL This means you hear the OCD loop in your head and instead of blindly following it, you relabel it for what it truly is: an OCD loop playing over and over in your head. Second, you REATTRIBUTE. This means you don't give or attribute your OCD loop to some great unknowable power outside of yourself like I did. Instead, you must recognize that your own brain is jamming up because of a chemical imbalance in your brain, not because of anything outside. In so doing, you reattribute where it's coming from. It comes from OCD, which is the real source of it. Third, you REFOCUS. Instead of following the old pattern of letting your OCD loop tell you what to do, you refocus your energy and do something else. In my case, instead of practicing harder and longer, now I might take time out and go for a swim, see a movie, or surf the internet . I do something that brings me pleasure and relaxes me at the same time. Right now, I can hear you saying, "Easy for you to say." Well, it is easier. It was hard as hell at first. I won't lie to you. I stuck with it and I promise the more you do it, the easier it gets! Finally, the fourth technique. REVALUE. All along in this book, I've been telling you that OCD is worthless to you, although OCD tries to convince you that it knows what's best for you. I am living, surviving proof that OCD does not know what's best. OCD is a master liar. When you revalue, you see what OCD is worth. Which always was, always is, and forever will be, diddly-squat. Practice the Four R's and you'll win every time!

I have purposely been vague in describing the Four R's technique. I am not a doctor. Something this serious requires competent professional guidance. I like to think of my therapist as a tour guide. She leads me through the winding road that is my life and helps me find the answers to my questions along the way. A good therapist only leads you to your own self-discovery.

You have to discover the answers for yourself. They help guide you along when you start heading in the wrong direction or get stuck in the mud of life. Believe me, this works. Therapy is not easy at first. In fact, it was pretty painful having to relive some of the worst moments in my life and discuss them in great detail with a complete stranger. Eventually, you really look forward to going to your therapy because you can see what a difference it makes in your life.

You are no longer scared of therapy. It becomes very easy to talk with this stranger who isn't all that strange anymore. You begin to see and feel what it really does for you in your life and it becomes a very addictive hour that you'll crave all week. At least that was my experience. I'm not going to tell you which medication to take because every person is different and a unique case that requires some figuring out by the pros. Your physician will tell you soon enough about the Serotonin Reuptake Inhibitors or SRI's that have changed the lives of millions all over the world. That's not my job, or the purpose and reason that I wrote this book. I wrote this book to spread the word. Help is available although you have no money. That's the word! There is no reason at all that you can't be treated successfully and regain your life so that you can live it the way it was meant to be. You can! You only need the desire to finally stop the madness in your mind.

I would have never believed the very words I myself am writing a few short years ago, but I took the chance. I risked everything I had, my career, my life, and my soul. What is the worst that could happen? Ask yourself that question. The very worst that can happen is that you will regain your life. Put that in your head and let it spin around a few times. Help is there. You only have to want it. Those who don't or don't believe or think that nothing is wrong with them, that it's the way they are. They aren't at their own personal rock bottom yet.

For those who want to help someone else with OCD, remember, forcing them to get help will only push the sufferer farther away from you and the rest of the world. OCD sufferers, you have to take action. You have to commit yourself to stopping your brain from ruling your life and forcing misery upon your every waking moment. In this day and time, there is no reason to continue living in despair for a single day longer.

Often I have thought about how close I came to killing myself. I am very happy that I never succeeded.

In the months after beginning my therapy, I remember thinking about the darkness in which I had lived when I actually felt my father's presence for the very first time, as if he were saying, "I was always there, Steven." It was a wonderful feeling. I finally understand so many things that my mind wasn't able to grasp before. There was and is so much life in me now. I have so much left to accomplish. In reality, I feel like I am only beginning when I used to feel so strongly that I was at the very end of my life.

It saddens me greatly that one in fifty people have OCD and do not know it. Think about that for a second. I am sure that you know more than fifty people. Who among your circle of friends and family is living among horrible secrets, thinking they would rather die than live another day? OCD sufferers live among us. Yet, you have no clue as to what is actually going on inside of them.

One in fifty is feeling alone while being completely surrounded by people who care. One in fifty is feeling horribly guilty and blaming herself or himself for things they are not fully responsible for. One in fifty cries every day of his or her life and has no idea why. One in fifty will suffer a lifetime of thinking he or she is going insane and has to be stopped before he or she hurts someone or themselves. One in fifty is living a secret life of loneliness, hate, anger, and deep depression while smiling and looking great the whole day through. All the while these people feel that they are the only ones. One in fifty might actually commit suicide when they could have ended the craziness instead of ending a precious life. Someday all of those one-in-fifties will hopefully find the way to professional help. No one on this earth is better qualified to tell you all of this than someone who's been there, someone who was in a really bad way. I used to be a one-in-fifty and I survived. So can you.

Brother Charlie once told me that people in this world have a higher purpose if they wish to find it. I now know that all of my magic training and performing career was a stepping stone for what I was really meant to do in this world. I believe strongly that my higher purpose is to seek out those who are suffering from OCD, spread the word of hope and encourage those in need to take that first big step of actually getting help for the first time. Magic has allowed me to touch the hearts of many smiling faces over the years in more then thirty countries around the world, but my story might touch the lives of millions and encourage them to seek help and provide hope to them, so that they can live a new life and enjoy every second. That is my real purpose in life. What's yours?

I challenge you to find out. Share your life if you don't have OCD and help those you can that do. After all, when you think about it, so many have shared their lives with you. Now it's your turn to give back. I promise that good things will come. If OCD sufferers take only one thing from this book, I want it to be that help is there, if you desire it. Once that knowledge is yours, I have done my job. The rest is up to you. There is an old saying that I love: "You can lead a man to congress, but you can not make him think." Truer words have never been spoken. If you doubt this, look at the fools on Capital Hill that we elect and pay to be there. Some of them are so closed-minded and old that it takes more time for them to recover than it does to tire them out! I better not get started on politics. My point is that I can help you find the right help and find some answers to your questions, but I can't make you take physical action. You are ultimately the one who has to muster the courage to take that first step.

The Osmonds' Magical Christmas show closed on December 15, 2001. It was not only the final performance of the Christmas show; it was the final performance for the Osmond Brothers in that theater. It was their theater, and it was time to move on. Everyone involved was shocked. It became front-page news when they announced that the great decade of live performances in their Branson theater had come to an end. The theater had been secretly sold. I thought it a befitting finale to one of the most difficult times of my life.

I was so ashamed to see Jimmy's face again. I was embarrassed at the way I had treated him, his employees and everyone in the cast. I had not been a very friendly guy to deal with. I now have a brand-new respect for women going through their time of the month.

I spent many weeks on the Internet and in every bookstore I could find from Branson to California in search of books on OCD that could help me gain more insight to this disorder the doctors tell me I have. Amazingly, they were very hard to find. The books I did find either read like a medical journal or were so above my head that I never really finished reading them or they were written by some doctor who had never had OCD. I couldn't find anything that spoke to me on an everyday level. I searched and searched to no avail. Most of the books I read told the same story. I feel I had lived and suffered more and in a completely different way from what these books had described.

The Internet became my most valuable source of information. There were many great web sites that helped to answer some of my most urgent questions, and I had quite a few. Sometimes I was having trouble asking the doctors. Some things were too personal and very difficult to talk about at the time.

In Branson as the final curtain went down and the house lights came up and the audience left for the last time, I was very relieved. The Osmonds decided not to take the new show to China in the end. They didn't want to be that far from their mother, Olive, who was still in the hospital recovering. I certainly didn't blame them one bit.

I returned to Las Vegas to begin my therapy and to start my new life. I knew that the magic would still be there whenever I got better. There are plenty of gigs out there. Agents continued to call everyday. For a while, I was advised by my doctors to take some time off to heal and figure out my next step in life. That didn't last very long. What happens during the process of healing? What exactly is OCD? What are the typical symptoms? What is the best treatment? There are many questions to be answered along the way. For me, I got the answers to my questions by going through the process and finding out the long, hard way. I decided to answer all of the most popular questions you are going to have from day one. I realize that some of this information is being repeated. However, I felt it was important to include the information in an easy-to-read Q&A format. Each one of these questions was an actual question I asked at some point throughout my treatment. So here we go!

CHAPTER SEVENTEEN

The Answers

What is OCD?

OCD, Obsessive Compulsive Disorder is basically an anxiety disorder that research has linked to a chemical imbalance in the brain. One of the weirdest things about OCD is that you realize and are clearly aware that your behaviors are totally irrational, yet you find yourself powerless to stop them. Your worries, doubts, fears, anxiety, depressions and even self-made superstitious beliefs simply became a way of life for you.

The problem is they become so excessive, such as hours and hours of hand washing or intrusive thoughts that won't go away driving you to the point of exhaustion. How about driving around and around the block just to check that an accident didn't occur because of your last trip around the block? These are only a few examples of the million and one ways that OCD can manifest itself in your life. OCD gets you stuck on a particular thought or ritual or gives you an uncontrollable urge and forces you to stick with it. Believe me when I tell you that it's NOT your fault or the result of a "weak" or unstable personality. It's not your family's fault or the fault of your upbringing. Those things can help the progress of your level of OCD such as in my case, but the blame should be put squarely no where. OCD is a medical brain disorder that you would have no matter what family tree you blamed. It causes serious problems in the processing of information in your brain. Long before the arrival of modern medications and cognitive behavior therapy that I mentioned earlier, OCD was in large part thought to be untreatable. But we live in truly amazing times. Today, treatment can help nearly everyone out there without even a hiccup! Most people treated today, who do as they are taught and continue taking the medications as they are instructed, achieve meaningful and long-term symptom relief, which was the case for me.

What is an Obsession?

There are two components to OCD. The first being the obsessions. By obsessions I mean any thoughts, images, or impulses that occur over and over again, making the sufferer feel totally out of control. If you don't want these ideas, find them disturbing and intrusive in nature and you realize that they don't really make any sense at all, you may have OCD. Another side to OCD is that it often fills you with fear, disgust, doubts, or a sensation that things have to be done in a "special" or "exact" way.

What is compulsion?

The second component is, of course, the actual compulsion itself. People with OCD typically try to make their obsessions go away by performing compulsive actions. Compulsions are defined as any act the person must perform over and over for a reason that only makes sense to the OCD sufferer and him alone. The sufferer often has certain rules that go along with the ritual. He feels that he must follow these certain rules exactly or he must start all over and do it again. One of my biggest compulsions was my obsession about contamination. I was what we survivors generally refer to as a germ freak.

Just ask anyone who knows me and they will tell you what I used to be like. I couldn't drink from public water fountains, I couldn't drink from another person's glass, or eat from another person's plate, not even my mother's or father's. I couldn't touch animals without having to wash my hands for fifteen minutes afterwards. I had serious problems kissing anyone at all. Especially on the lips. I had to wash my hands after shaking someone's hand. To this day, I carry a bottle of antibacterial hand gel. The hand gel has certainly helped me because I often shake hundreds of hands a day. Some people with contamination compulsions will wash constantly to the point that their hands become raw and inflamed or infected.

Some people have to repeatedly check that they have turned off the stove or iron because of an obsessive fear of burning the house down. Others have to count everything they see over and over because of an obsessive fear of losing them. These compulsions are not like drinking or gambling compulsions. With drinking or gambling, the sufferer derives some sort of pleasure, which is what I call a payoff, at the end. OCD sufferers do not get pleasure out of what they do over and over. The stupid rituals they know are silly are performed in order to obtain some sort of relief from the discomfort caused by the obsessions. OCD produces a great deal of distress, takes up vast amounts of time every day, or significantly interferes with the person's work, social life or relationships. I think that most people with OCD clearly realize at some point that their obsessions are coming from within their own minds and are both excessive and unreasonable. Sometimes, a person's battle with OCD may wax or wane over time. Some OCD symptoms may be little more than background noise. In others like me, OCD produces extremely severe distress.

Here are some common obsessions:
1. Contamination. fears of germs, dirt and other unclean things, which usually leads to excessive washing. Yup! That's me!

2. Imagining having harmed self or others. This would be a repeating compulsion. Yup! Me too.

3. Imagining losing control of aggressive urges. This would be a checking compulsion.

4. Intrusive sexual thoughts or urges. This would be a touching compulsion. I was guilty of this one as well.

5. Excessive religious or moral doubt. This falls under the counting compulsion which my own mother suffers from.

6. Forbidden thoughts. This would be an ordering/arranging compulsion. Also me.

7. A need to have things just so or what is sometimes referred to me as being a clean freak. This is a case of hoarding

or saving usually objects with no value. Yup! That's me all the way, too!

8.   A need to tell, ask or confess. This one also applies to my mother and is a praying compulsion.

What are some of the symptoms of OCD?

The most common symptoms are unwanted behaviors and/or thoughts that occur at least several times each day. They can include, but are not limited to, the following:

1.   Checking switches, doors, locks, stoves and other things repeatedly every day.

2.   Counting throughout the day, silently or out loud, while performing normal, everyday tasks.

3.   Feeling compelled to do certain things a specific number of times.

4.   Arranging things in an extremely orderly way with a set of rules for how they must be done. Usually it makes no sense to anyone except the OCD sufferer.

5.   Being haunted by pictures, words, or phrases (sometimes disturbing, sometimes nonsensical) that refuse to go away.

6.   Hoarding of objects with (usually) no apparent value.

Fearing contamination; obsession with germs and cleanness.

Only a small number of those with OCD will have the full collection and additional personality traits called Obsessive Compulsive Personality Disorder or (OCPC) like me. See how lucky I was? Despite the fact it has a similar name, OCPC does not involve obsessions and compulsions, but rather is a personality pattern that involves a preoccupation with rules, schedules and lists, perfectionism, and excessive devotion to work, with rigidity and inflexibility also in the mix. Not to say that I didn't have compulsions and daily rituals, because I did. However, OCPC was clearly alive and well in my workaholic world and most visible in my obsession with being a perfectionist. I was doomed from the start because perfection is not humanly possible. It is perfectly possible to have both disorders as I well learned.

When can OCD begin?

OCD can begin at any time from preschool to adulthood, usually before a person turns forty. About one-third to one-half of adults with OCD report that it started for them during childhood as mine did. Unfortunately, OCD is most often misdiagnosed as ADD or ADHD or whatever else they can find to blame the symptoms on. Which is why I suggest going to a doctor known for treating OCD patients. OCD can also remain undiagnosed for reasons such as the patient being secretive about symptoms or having a lack of insight about the illness, or ignorance of the fact that the illness exists, which was the case with me. Many health care providers are not familiar with the true symptoms or are not trained in providing the right treatments.

Lack of funds prevents some people from receiving any treatment whatsoever, a fact I myself am hoping to change. Being broke or on a limited income should not be a reason to keep from getting treatment. It's wrong, and I am going after the drug companies on this one as we speak!

Is OCD inherited?

The jury is still out on this one since no specific genes for OCD have been identified, yet. Believe me, science is working hard on it. I am confident that a gene or genes will indeed be found soon, finally leading us to the answer that OCD is inherited. Most researchers suggest that genes do play a role of some sort in the early development of the disorder. However, they fall short of making that claim officially as yet. It appears to most researchers that the onset of childhood OCD does run in families, which is the case in mine.

As you would imagine, when a parent has OCD, it slightly increases the risk that a child will develop the disorder, although the risk is low. There is no doubt in my mind that I have a mother with OCD. Since she refuses to be tested or take medications, I will never officially know. There is no single answer as to where my OCD came from either, because I take after my mom, personality and all. Physically I took after my father, bald head and all. (Thanks, Dad! You always told me that I would come out on top one day!) I have my mother's brain and personality for sure.

If the chance exists that OCD doesn't come from your parents, then what causes OCD?

We really don't know for sure. There's no single scientifically proven cause of OCD as of yet. We do know that OCD involves problems with the communication between the front part of the brain called the orbital cortex and much deeper structures in the back, called the basal ganglia. These brain parts use a special chemical messenger service called serotonin. Without getting much more technical than that, all a person needs to know is that this fluid called serotonin is very important. People with OCD are likely not producing enough of this fluid to get the messages across from one part of the brain to the other, effectively rewiring the brain. Doctors wrote all of the books I have read on OCD. The way they explain this is like reading a medical journal. Serotonin is involved in sleep, depression, memory, and other neurological processes. It is a very important part of the way we work.

What about treatment?

The first step in treating OCD is education. First, educating the sufferer and then the family. Both need to be carefully informed about the possibility of treatment of OCD as a medical illness. Over the last twenty years or so, two effective treatments for OCD have been developed. One called Cognitive Behavioral Psychotherapy or (CBT) we have already covered.

The other is treatment using medications with a Serotonin Re-uptake Inhibitor or SRIs.

There are basically two stages of Treatment.

Acute Phase: This is treatment aimed at ending the

current episode of OCD.

   Maintenance Phase: This is treatment aimed at preventing future episodes of OCD.

 Treatment is comprised of three distinct Components:
   Education: This is crucial in helping patients and families learn how best to manage OCD and prevents its complications.

   Psychotherapy: Don't let this word scare you. It basically means CBT is the key element of treatment for most patients of OCD. It's completely painless. I have found that this word frightens many people and conjures up images you wouldn't believe, like electroshock. It simply won't happen. CBT helps the patient internalize a strategy for resisting OCD that will be of lifelong benefit.

   Medication: Medication with a serotonin re-uptake inhibitor is very helpful for many sufferers.

 If I have any of these symptoms, does it mean that I have OCD?

 No, it does not. The level to which the symptoms manifest themselves makes all the difference in the world.

 When your symptoms begin to interfere with your ability to reason or think clearly, to function on a normal level or if symptoms are affecting your relationship with your family, friends, or at work these may be an indicator that treatment might be appropriate.

 Does everyone with OCD have obsessions and compulsions?

More then eighty percent of people with OCD do.

How common is OCD?

More than five million Americans, or roughly one in fifty, have OCD, and those are statistics from only one country. OCD afflicts everyone across the board. This includes men, women and children of every nation in the world. No matter the race, no matter the age, no matter the socioeconomic background, if your heart beats, you can get OCD.

I have been asked many times if OCD was the latest fad diagnosis. The truth is that OCD has been documented throughout the centuries. It's nothing new. However, the secretive and sometimes hidden inner nature of OCD has kept many sufferers away from doctors, treatment, or any type of help at all. This has now begun to change a little.

I remember seeing the TV commercials for Paxil and thought to myself, that sounds like me. I wonder if it's for people with Alzheimer's? Well, it is not, but those commercials have really opened up a lot of people to the idea of getting help. I have heard from many people who never realized they might have an illness that could be treated until they saw those ads on TV. They thought as I did, that it was just the way they were.

OCD is not just the way you are. OCD is a serious illness that can be successfully treated.

I am afraid of taking medication. What medications are used and how can they help me?

Don't be afraid of the medications. Research clearly

shows that the serotonin re-uptake inhibitors (SRI's) are uniquely effective and safe forms of treatment for OCD. These medications increase the concentration of serotonin, a chemical messenger in the brain. Six SRI's are currently the most frequently used.

>Paxil or Paroxetine, Manufactured by Smith-Kline Beecham.
>Anafranil or Clomipramine. Manufactured by Ciba-Geigy.
>Prozac Fluoxetine. Manufactured by Lilly.
>Luvox or Fluvoxamine. Manufactured by Solvay.
>Zoloft or Sertraline. Manufactured by Pfizer.
>Celexa or Citalopram. Marketed by Forest Laboratories, Inc.

How well do these medications really work?

Pretty darn well! When people ask me about how well the meds really work, I tell them that the vast majority of people treated report a marked improvement after only eight to ten weeks on a serotonin re-uptake inhibitors. Unfortunately, medications alone usually do not work. Research shows that fewer then twenty percent of those using only medications end up free of OCD symptoms. About twenty percent don't experience much improvement at all with the first SRI and need to try a different SRI. Everybody is different and a little shuffling around might take place until the doctors are able to find the right dosage and/or correct medications.

What are the side effects of these medications?

Most people with OCD are able to tolerate the medications with few or no side effects. Some of the side effects can include nervousness, insomnia, restlessness, nausea, diarrhea, dry mouth, sedation, dizziness and weight gain. Don't allow that to scare you. It doesn't mean you will necessarily have them. I think the most often asked question I get about the medications comes from men. The only side effects most males worry about are the sexual ones. Guys, stop worrying. Some of the medications can cause a weaker or slightly abnormal ejaculation, but for the most part, your Willy will continue to work fine.

About the only side effect I have had long term is dry mouth. From time to time, especially in the summertime, I find myself drinking more water. In the beginning I did have a little restlessness, diarrhea and some weight gain. However, everything went away within a few weeks except for the occasional dry mouth. If that's as bad as it gets, I consider it a very small price to pay in exchange for getting my life back.

What if I can't afford the medications?

This is the most important part of the book in my opinion. Because there are so many people out there suffering with OCD who can't afford the high cost of these medications, the drug companies that make these drugs for the most part have some sort of program for the financially unable. The Pharmaceutical Research and Manufacturers Association publishes a directory of programs for those who cannot afford medications, which your doctor or health care worker can request. The phone number can be found on my web site. Also, there is a list of drug manufacturers and their phone numbers that you can call to get on the support programs yourself. Calling them directly is usually the faster method.

If you need these drugs and your doctors say that you do, they cannot deny you the medications because you can't afford them.

Use these programs only if you really need them. They are for the needy and not the greedy.

One of the greatest resources for medical attention for those unable to pay is the local health clinic. Every town in the United States has one at least. It's a great place to get very low-cost or free medical care from professionals who truly do care. They certainly don't do it for the money, believe me. I was a frequent patient of my public health clinic when I was on the street. Without them I am sure that I would not have survived. They provide both medical and mental services. Do not be ashamed to use a public health clinic. They provide great care for those in need. I, personally, owe a lot to the people who work there. They saved my life.

Most clinics have a sliding fee scale, which only means that you pay whatever you can afford to pay. Did you know that pharmaceutical company representatives often leave free samples? Ask your doctor about free samples to get you going. If they have them, most doctors will be more than happy to give them to you. My foundation is being funded by the sales of this book and from the donations of private individuals who truly care and need the tax write-off. We are using those funds to help even more OCD sufferers who really need it and to make the public more aware about OCD and the treatments that are available. Education is the key. I know what it's like to need the medications and be unable to afford them. I am working hard to make the medications available for anyone who truly needs them by helping those in need to get into the right programs through my foundation. Visit my website for more information on how you can help.

I donate a portion of every live performance I do towards helping someone in need. I also do benefit shows to raise money for the foundation's cause.

It's an important cause and one I feel very serious about. I'm going to do whatever I can to make a difference in the lives of those who have suffered as I did. OCD is no way to exist. In the modern times we live in, no one at all should have to live in misery.

Are there any support groups I can attend?

You had better believe there are! Those support groups are an invaluable part of treatment. They provide a forum for mutual acceptance, understanding and self-discovery. Most people develop a sense of camaraderie with other attendees because they have all lived with and survived OCD. Most of the time, it's the first time a sufferer has ever met another person with OCD. You can find a listing on my web site for more information about finding a support group in your area.

After year of therapy, I couldn't wait any longer. The wait was killing me! I had to get back on a stage somewhere, somehow. I missed performing and I felt as if I had so much more to offer this time. I felt better then I had felt before in my whole life. I was ready to return and had produced yet another version of the show I had originally created. I picked up the phone one day and called my trusty agent and told him to take the very next offer that came in. Thanks to a few calls from the Osmonds on my behalf, a couple of weeks later I was back on stage. This time the stage was moving. It was aboard a cruise ship traveling the world with some of the most wonderful people I ever met in my life. It was perfect. I had lots of down time, which meant that I could relax more, but I still got my performing fix along the way.

I was living the good life, eating the finest food and sailing the world while visiting some of the most beautiful locales I had ever seen. It was exactly what I needed. It gave me time away from everything I knew along with the room I needed to think.

I came to realize on that trip that it was as if I had been living my entire life in black and white. Now, for the first time, I could see life in true, vivid, spectacular colors. The audience loved my new show. I felt more alive than I ever had before. I was so excited to hear that applause once again. It was the greatest reward I could have been given. I told the audience so that night on stage. I told them that the time they had chosen to spend with me that night was a great gift that I would never take for granted again. I have kept my promise.

What a journey! What a long and twisted road I have traveled in my short life. I have only hit upon the highlights as they related to my OCD. As I got to know a lot of the passengers on each and every cruise, I was able to spot OCD everywhere I went. I was shocked at how easy it was for me to spot and how many people in this world have it. Now, it's like second nature to me. I can usually see it rather quickly. I wanted something to help point people in the right direction. I was wishing for a document that clearly explained, from a survivor's point of view, what OCD was like and how to find the help that's out there.

I wanted to hand this document to each and every one of them I met. More than a few had lengthy conversations with me about the disorder. Some knew they had it and others did not. I felt good to be helping these people. So I began to think about being the one to write it all down. I never intended for it to be autobiographical at all. I couldn't find a way to explain it otherwise. It was all that I knew. I certainly had no desire whatsoever to air my dirty laundry. Who does?

When I first mentioned to my family that I was thinking of writing a book, my mother, Shirley, went crazy. She threatened to disown me and move far away, changing her name so that she couldn't be found. Her true fear lies in how this book is going to make her look and how it will affect her reputation at church. No one at her church would believe that my mother could utter such words. They think she is the sweetest woman in town. Like all the other sufferers I have ever met, denial and secrecy are paramount. My mother is a very sad case these days. Now in her golden years she continues to refuse any treatment, or acknowledge that she needs help. My sisters and I have done everything we know to try and help her. The last time I saw my mother she asked me if I was going to write the book anyway. When I told her that the book was nearly finished, she looked me in the eye and calmly said, "Well then, have a nice life." I was devastated. Hurt beyond imagination.

I understand her and her mental illness. I love her with all my heart. We didn't speak for a very long time. Some tell me that it's cruel, and that I shouldn't give up on my mother. That is not what I have done at all. Tough Love is what I had to do. Until she is ready to be helped, my hands are tied. I felt that I had done all I could and that at this point in my life, I couldn't afford to allow such negativity to re-enter. Remember what I said about negative people, If you are not careful, they can drag you down with them. Every year around Mother's Day I become emotionally upset. Try as I may, I realize that there are some people in this world who are happy being miserable and Shirley is one of them. I still send her a card from time to time.

I thought long and hard about this book and if I should release it. Then a passenger said to me one day, "You need to write a book. People need to hear your story. It might change some lives." I felt as if I had won the lottery. Suddenly I got it. As Reverend Don, Brother Charlie and Burton Brown had all tried to tell me, this is the right thing to do. Writing a book and sharing my life with others might inspire someone out there to find the help they need although that meant ending my relationship with Shirley. I love her dearly. I have forgiven her and care for her more than ever, but I can't continue to fight with her anymore. At some point you have to forgive, let go and move on. I have suffered enough in my life and refuse to suffer one day longer.

It was another done deal. That was it.

I had one problem. I had never written a book before and I didn't know how, not to mention that I am the world's worst speller.

The passenger I spoke of earlier went on to say, "You know how you write a book?"

"Not really!" I replied.

Then she said, "One page at a time, my friend. One page

at a time. The same way we live our lives."

Wow! Another home run! Lenny could have hit me over the head with a baseball bat and I wouldn't have felt it. So simple, yet it made perfect sense to me. I was letting the image in my mind of what writing a book must entail overwhelm me, because that is what OCD does. So I remembered the Four R's and got myself back on track.

I wrote the first chapter that very night, alone in my cabin with my duck and a Dell laptop that barely worked. Finally, I was truly doing what I was born to do and loving every minute of it. I was climbing my way to the top. This time, I was going to stay.

I decided to move out of the Las Vegas scene for a while where there were too many distractions for me to begin to relax. I ended up on the beautiful island of Oahu in Hawaii. Waikiki Beach, to be exact. The people, the ocean and the life in Waikiki are all very relaxing to me. I stopped living my life at the speed of light. I slowed down and have learned to enjoy whatever comes my way. One page at a time.

The daily rituals have almost completely gone away. Through therapy I have learned how to relax and let life flow as it is meant to be. Today, I continue to perform all over the world when I can, and I now give "Creative Lectures" on OCD and Anxiety / Stress management to whomever wants to listen. I still can be found on the occasional cruise ship, and I enjoy performing on them, too. I've traveled a long hard road when life was a daily struggle to survive. I felt that I had earned a little peace. Today, I can often be found somewhere along the beach sitting there, watching the sun and ocean play, and spending a little quiet time with Mother Nature. She heals open wounds so well.

LIFE TODAY - 2007

You might be wondering about Matthew, Jim and Javier or even Brother Charlie. So here is the latest. Matthew Green has a very successful consulting production company in Branson Mo. He is currently working for another magician who thinks he's a star. Matt and I rarely have the pleasure of speaking these days. Jim Meadows is also living and working in Branson Mo. doing what he does best - production work. I still keep in close contact with him on a regular basis. Tato Farfan works in Vegas and produces live shows and acts around the world on the side. He continues the family's show business tradition and also consults for some of the largest production shows on the planet.

Our great government, under the less than great leadership of George W. Bush who I enjoy calling "President Shrub" deported Javier. Despite the fact we had spent tens of thousands of dollars going through the stupid and insane immigration process the United States currently employees, he was ordered out. He now lives in Spain and has moved on with his life.

Brother Charlie and I have yet to meet in person, but continue to keep in touch over the Internet and by phone from time to time. He still has not wavered one bit and is the very same as the day I first opened his email. I have kept every email as they are among my most treasured items and may someday share the wisdom contained within. Only recently have I learned what he actually looks like when I found a website with a picture of him standing next to their Royal Majesties, King Harald V and Queen

Sonja of Norway. When we first met, he was a simple monk. Today he is the director of a monastic community in the hills of northern Greece, near the town of Ormylia, Chalkidike.

AS FOR ME...

For the first time, my life is wonderful and worth living. Today I live to teach. I developed a very popular and critically acclaimed audio course called "When Anxiety Attacks". It teaches you scientifically proven skills that will end your daily struggle with anxiety and stress. It's a new approach and in the hands of the willing is powerful stuff. It really works and has helped thousands end the suffering in their lives. That fact alone has made my journey worth the trip. It wasn't easy. Problems never go completely away. Neither does OCD. But I have learned to manage it and control it without the use of medication. I have learned so much in life. I have learned that more money only exchanges the little problems we sometimes perceive as overwhelming, for bigger more expensive ones that truly are. I no longer worry about how much I have in the bank because I have finally learned that wealth is not what makes me who I am. I no longer care what brand of clothes I wear or what kind of car I drive. I find that now that I have stopped focusing on money, I actually have more of it. Strange as that may sound, it's true. I didn't believe that I would make it this far. I feel that despite it all, I didn't turn out all that badly. I have learned a great deal as I endured the life I lived. Now I want to share what I know with others. Isn't that what life is truly about? Sharing, Loving, Caring and Educating future generations. We all bleed RED. So why don't we love each other as one?

I find that its an amazing thing to know in your heart at

last why you are here, why you suffered all you did and what you have been born to do. It's a humbling feeling that I am unable to describe in words. More importantly, having survived and lived to tell the tale is something that thrills me and makes me excited to get out of bed each day.

For everyone like me in this world, and there are millions out there living with what nearly ended my life, OCD, Anxiety and Stress - I am going to ensure that one way or another the world knows that help is out there and where to find it. It's my life's mission. I consider myself a very lucky guy to be alive today. I guess what I am most thankful for are the beautiful people who stood by me when I was at my worst. They know who they are.

With such loving friends and so many who cared for me, what more could I possibly ask for? The nightmare is finally over and I now have the skills I need to cope, manage, and survive. My path is clearly defined, "get out there and teach" my heart tells me everyday. Life's greatest lesson is hidden in our hearts. When we listen to our hearts and just accept what it tells us, resistance in life simply melts away and things seem so much easier. Simple isn't it?

Try it and you will see your true purpose revealed before you in the blink of an eye. Everything we need is right within us, and creating silence in your life, mind, body and spirit will produce the key that will unlock the many secrets to be told. Spread the word.

That's my story so far. I still have a lot of life yet to live. I want to thank you for having the guts to stick with me to the end of my babble and for having the courage to help, either yourself or someone you love. Always remember that OCD victims are NOT crazy or alone. Many people out there really care and want to help. They believe in you, and so do I. Keep whatever faith you find wherever you may go and remember to listen to your heart. It will always be your best guide, if you allow it to be.

Until we meet again, I wish you peace, joy and laughter.
Steven Diamond
Survivor

Be sure to visit my website at: www.attackanxiety.com

OTHER OCD RESOURCES

I highly recommend that you continue your research and investigate as far and as deep as you possibly can. Knowledge is the single most important key in learning to control this disorder. I also recommend to you seek professional help. All through out the United States and in many other countries around the world there are many avenues in which you can find answers.

Here are a few of the great organizations that can help.

Obsessive Compulsive Information Center
Madison Institute of Medicine
7617 Mineral Point Road, Suite 300
Madison, WI 53717
(608) 827-2470

Anxiety Disorders Association of America (ADAA)
6000 Executive Boulevard, Suite 513
Rockville, MD 20852
(301) 231-9350
Association for Advancement of Behavior Therapy
305 Seventh Avenue, Suite 1601
New York, NY 10001 (212) 647-1890

Freedom from Fear
308 Seaview Avenue
Staten Island, NY 10305
(718)-351-1717

National Alliance for the Mentally Ill
200 North Glove Road, Suite 1015
Arlington, Virginia 22203
(800) 950-6264

National Mental Health Association
1021 Prince Street
Alexandria, Virginia 22314-2971
(703) 684-7722

Obsessive Compulsive Foundation (OCF)
P.O. Box #70
Milford, CT 06460
(203) 878-5669
(203) 874-3483 Information line with national referral list.

National Institute of Mental Health
C/o OCD Outpatient Research
Building 10, Room 3D41
10 Center Drive, MSC 1264
Bethesda, MD 20892
(301) 496-3421
Public Inquiries Contact:
Room 7C-02, MSC 8030
5600 Fishers Lane
Rockville, MD 20892-8030
(301) 443-4513

There aren't enough pages in all the world to list those I would like to thank. So many never believed in me, but here's a list of a few who did. I love you all and thank you for the great gift of sharing your life and knowledge with me.

<u>My Family</u>

My Sister Robin – My role model. I love you so much.

Pete – Your kindness has touched me. Thank you.

Jill – You know I love you so much. eep those emails coming.

Jennifer – I pray for you every night. Mostly that you don't change your screen name yet again. Love you!

Maggie You are my one true love. The sexiest girl I know. Your beautiful dark hair and eyes are pure magic. Your warm kisses when I least expect them fill my heart with joy. Breath mints would be nice. (Wink) You are, and always will be, the only girl for me. I love you dearly. Especially when we roll on the floor while watching the food channel! Kisses.

My sister Shelia – Better known at work as "Weeza". Not a role model, but I love you dearly anyway and you have always been there for me. Thank you for loving me so much.

Brandi and Pete – Keep your chins up. And stop making babies.

Michala – Don't forget your uncle who's always gone.

Logan – Keep working on your magic. Love Uncle Stevie.

Meagan – Just marry Chris and get it over with.

Tommy – Tommy, I feel for you, man. However, you were warned about this family. Be strong. Be very strong.

Michael – Learn from your father's mistakes.

Jim Meadows – My eternal brother, Thank you for everything. I'll always be there for you. And I am sorry for all the pain I have caused.

Larry (Hot Chocolate) Edwards – eternal brother #2. We are pushing 20 years of friendship and I hope it never ends. Thanks for putting up with me. Please Visit: www.larryedwardslive.com

Bill Robinson – You know you are family! My closest friend. I love you so much. After all these years you still put up with me. Thank you.

Uncle Ronnie and Pat – You are in my heart always.

Uncle Burchel and Laura – I love you.

Aunt Joyce & Uncle Don – I will always love you. Thanks Don, for showing me the French drop.

Jimmy and Dawn Grosso – For driving Shirley crazy when I am not there.

Fina Castillo – For understanding, your love and kindness. Thank you. I only wish things could have been different. We were both very young.

<u>My Friends</u> (In no particular order)

Matthew Green – My little brother and great friend. I wish great things to come. Thank you for helping me and caring when no one else did.

Bob Turk and Mr. Jim – For wisdom, guidance, truth and so much love.

Javier C - It's the good times I'll always remember.

Armando (Tato) Farfan Jr. – I have learned so much from

you. I love you dearly and always will. Thank you for teaching me what's right.

The Osmond Family – You saved my life. I will always hold you in my heart and I will strive to share the love you showed me with all whom I meet. Special thanks to Jimmy for your understanding and true friendship. You have hearts of gold.

Don Wayne – For your never-ending support and faith in me.

Marty Allen and Karen – You both inspire me everyday. I love you.

Sue Watts – You never stopped believing. Thank You.

Billy Sadler – I have always held you in my heart. I will not forget.

Bob and Shelly North – Thank you, for your faith and trust in me. Please visit: www.Splashescreative.Com

Liberace – I will never forget you.

Wayne Newton – For keeping on keeping on and for teaching me through your live performances what being a showman is all about.

Jonathan Clark – Captain Family promises to be good. Thanks for being a real friend and telling me the truth.

Colleen Austin – For everything you are! I adore you!

Jan North – For your help with my emergency wardrobe needs. You are great!

Roy Shank – Stop being so damn moody. I still think you are very good at what you do. Keep it up, I need more illusions built.

George Pecoraro – I screwed up but that's life and how

you get better at what you do. Thanks for all of your help, George.

Julie Godin – My biggest fan in England and soon to be fan club president.

Chalet Magic – For helping me out of jams. (No pun intended)

Sandy Dobritch – I haven't forgotten you either.

Alex Esqueda – For giving me my first chance.

David Copperfield – For inspiring me in so many ways to keep going.

Betty and Harold – For helping me when ever you could. Thank You.

Jon Orlando – Thanks for reminding me just what show business can really do to you! (Wink) And for all the advise.

Thom and Vinny – I wish things had worked out differently. But thanks anyway . Tell Russ to bite me! Hate and anger will never get you anywhere Russ except exactly where you are right now.

Walter Rodgers – For having the faith to fight for what you know is right!

Oprah Winfrey – For teaching me so much and for giving me someone to look up to. I have finally found my spirit. Thank you.

Bill Sage – For guiding me in the right direction. You are a true genesis.

Enrique Gonzales – For booking me on every TV show in the universe.

Tony Orlando – For not listening to Quasimodo and giving me a chance.

Willy Kennedy – For all of the sleepless nights while trying to make my shipping deadlines. Thank you.

Momma Yvonne – For your love and endless support. I could never thank you enough and I miss my girls from the corn fields everyday.

Kevin A. – I am torn about what to say. I can't imagine what you could have achieved had you used your awesome talents for the good of all. None the less, you taught me a lot, both good and bad and for that I am grateful.

Wild Bill Melton – For laughing at me when I was at my worst and taking the pictures to prove it. Without question, the most talented photographer I know. Visit: www.wildbillstudios.com

David Saxe – For providing me a job when I REALLY needed it.

Pete and Kim DeSantis – For giving me a job when no one else would dare think of hiring someone in my situation and for helping me off the street. I love you both dearly!

Barry Ball – For working so hard to keep me working on the ships. Andre and Thomas too!

Ken Stevens – For putting up with my craziness and allowing me to do what's best for me. Thank you.

The Boys at the Hard Rock Hotel – You know who you are and for what!

The Boys at Caesars Place, The Paris, The Rio, The Old Desert Inn, The Old Sands, The Old Aladdin, The Old

Dunes, The Riv, The Golden Nugget, Binnions, The Plaza, Vegas World, The Tropicana, The Sahara, The old Crazy Horse. Thanks for the contacts, info, cash and free tickets and buffets. They really helped me, when I needed it most.

Momma Heath – For just being you. You have taught me more than most.

Mary and Gent – I will love you forever and always.

The Turners – Freddie, Jan, Scott and Penny. My second family. Thank you for everything. Especially the P&J sandwiches.

Piggy and Amy Bryant – What every neighbor should be to their neighbors.

To every schoolteacher I ever had – I'm so sorry to have put you through that. I hated school, not you.

Adrian N. – I owe you big time. Thank you for being there.

Veronica D. – I wish I could find you. I love you and always will. Contact me. You know how.

Bobby McLamb – Thank You for being there always. I stand strong in your corner! I will always be there for you as you have always been there for me. No one ever believed in me more. For that I love you dearly.

Roberto A. – What more could a friend ask for? I love you, my little brother.

Rudolpho P. – I miss eating those dinners with the inner circle, but I miss you the most. Your wisdom inspires me to this day. Thank you.

Leon W. – Every person in this world should be so lucky

as to have a friend like you. Wherever you are. Contact me.

Carol and Rick – Thank you 8,250 times. Thank you for all the packages, for all the love, for all the letters with mad money. Thank you. Your kindness for someone you have never met inspires me more then you know.

Jane Pauley - For having the courage to tell the world. Thank you for all you did for me and my cause. I am truly grateful.

Jaki Baskow - Thank you for everything.

David Adams - For all the hard work in the studio.

Bobby Katz - For listening to Tony Orlando and giving me a chance.

Bill H & Jack L - For all the laughs and eye candy around the pool. Great times! Thank you.

Jason Warren - For the pits and a million and one laughs.

Grant & Allen - For some really great times at the bar!

Matt Falber - Don't give up. You'll make it. Never let them tell you no.

The Venetian Concierge - What a wonderful, loving group of people who are THE best at what they do. No finer department on the strip exists.

SPECIAL THANKS -

      George and Dena Leviton - It's not often I am left without words. Yet, I do not know how to express my love and gratefulness for what you have given and shared with me. You saved me in so many ways when I was ready to just end it all. You teach me, love me, guide me, and listen to my past. You help me up when I feel down and you have made me a better human being. Who ever knew how life would change the day our paths crossed in the video store. Who knew the millions of laughs we would share? Who knew the crazy adventures that would unfold? Who knew? Who knows what lies ahead still yet to be revealed? Thank you just doesn't seem enough. Yet it's all I have. Love you both so much.

Web Sites You Should Know About

www.AttackAnxiety.Com

www.StevenDiamond.com
www.ocdonline.com
www.ocfoundation.org
www.nimh.nih.gov/publicat/ocd.cfm
www.hopkinsmedicine.org/ocd

www.adaa.org
www.freedomfromfear.com
www.pparx.org
http://www.ormyliacenter.gr/

Notes

Notes

www.ingramcontent.com/pod-product-compliance
Lightning Source LLC
Chambersburg PA
CBHW022000160426
43197CB00007B/200